Invitation to Systemic Functional Linguistics through the Cardiff Grammar

Equinox Textbooks and Surveys in Linguistics
Series Editor: Robin P. Fawcett, Cardiff University

Already published:

Analysing Casual Conversation by Suzanne Eggins and Diana Slade
Multimodal Transcription and Text Analysis: A Multimodal Toolkit and Coursebook with Associated On-line Course by Anthony Baldry and Paul J. Thibault
Meaning-Centered Grammar: An Introductory Text by Craig Hancock
Genre Relations: Mapping Culture by J.R. Martin and David Rose
Language in Psychiatry: A Handbook of Clinical Practice by Jonathan Fine
The Power of Language: How Discourse Influences Society by Lynne Young and Brigid Fitzgerald
An Introduction to English Sentence Structure: Clauses, Markers, Missing Elements by Jon Jonz
The Western Classical Tradition in Linguistics by Keith Allan
Intonation in the Grammar of English by M.A.K. Halliday and William S. Greaves
Writing Readable Research: A Guide for Students of Social Science by Beverly Lewin

Forthcoming titles in the series:

The Functional Syntax Handbook: Analyzing English at the level of Form by Robin P. Fawcett
Text Linguistics: The How and Why of Meaning by M.A.K. Halliday and Jonathan Webster
Teaching Multimodal Literacy in English as a Foreign Language by Len Unsworth, Viviane Heberle and Robyn Louise Bush
Learning to Write/Reading to Learn: Scaffolding Democracy in Literacy Classrooms by J. R. Martin and David Rose
Multimodal Corpus-Based Approaches to Website Analysis by Anthony Baldry and Kay O'Halloran
Corpora and Meaning by Steven Jones and Howard Jackson

Invitation to Systemic Functional Linguistics through the Cardiff Grammar

An extension and simplification of Halliday's Systemic Functional Grammar

Third Edition

Robin P. Fawcett

Emeritus Professor, Cardiff University

LONDON OAKVILLE

Published by Equinox Publishing Ltd

UK: 1 Chelsea Manor Studios,
Flood Street,
London SW3 5SR

US: DBBC,
28 Main Street,
Oakville, CT 06779

www.equinoxpub.com

First edition published 1997 in the journal *Helicon 22*, Nara, Japan. Second edition published 2005 by the Centre for Language and Communication, Cardiff University. Third edition published 2008.

British Library Cataloguing-in-Publication Data
A catalogue record for this book is available from the British Library.

Library of Congress Cataloging-in-Publication Data
Fawcett, Robin P.
Invitation to systemic functional linguistics through the Cardiff grammar : an extension and simplification of Halliday's systemic functional grammar / Robin P. Fawcett. -- 3rd ed.
p. cm. -- (Equinox textbooks and surveys in linguistics)
Includes bibliographical references and index.
ISBN-13: 978-1-84553-395-3 (hb)
ISBN-13: 978-1-84553-396-0 (pb)
1. Systemic grammar. I. Title.
P149.F35 2008
415--dc22

2008001737

ISBN-13 978 1 84553 395 3 (hardback)
978 1 84553 396 0 (paperback)

Typeset by Chris Allen and Robin P. Fawcett
Printed and bound in Great Britain by Lightning Source UK Ltd., Milton Keynes and Lightning Source Inc., La Vergne, TN

Contents

Preface to the Third Edition

The unusual origin of this book is explained in the Preface to the Second Edition, which follows over the page. Here I wish to make just two additional points.[1]

The Second Edition, which was a hurriedly tidied-up version of the 1997 version, was published within Cardiff University in 2005, primarily for the use of Cardiff students. Soon after this, however, I received a request for permission to translate it into Chinese, and then, a little later, a similar request for Spanish - to both of which I was naturally happy to say 'Yes'. But then a new idea emerged. If there was interest in this book from speakers of those two major world languages, we reasoned, perhaps it should also be published in English? And so the idea for the present edition was born.

At first I intended to make only a few minor revisions, but as I began to work on these I realized that the book would benefit from both a more through revision and certain additions. After all, it was ten years since the first edition. So in this Third Edition (i) the description of English reflects a number of improvements in

---

1 Much of the research that led to the development of the model of language presented here was carried out as part of the COMMUNAL Project. COMMUNAL was supported by grants from the Speech Research Unit at DRA Malvern for over ten years, as part of Assignment No. ASO4BP44, on Spoken Language Understanding and Dialogue (SLUD); by ICL (in Phase 1); and by Cardiff University.

However, I would also like to express my personal thanks to the two friends and colleagues to whom I feel most indebted. The first is Michael Halliday, the 'father' of Systemic Functional Linguistics and the linguist to whom I, like very many others, owe the basic principles of my current model of language. However, this has not prevented me from developing a different position from his on a number of matters - always, I hope, on good scientific grounds. The second major debt has been to Gordon Tucker, who has been the main co-developer with me of the version of Systemic Functional Grammar that has come to be known as the Cardiff Grammar, and without whom the COMMUNAL Project could not have achieved all it has. There will be references to these gifted linguists throughout the book.

the Cardiff Grammar since the mid-1990s; (ii) some of the material has been re-arranged in a more logical order; (iii) certain gaps have been filled in; (iv) the references have been updated, especially those that are part of the growing literature on the Cardiff Grammar; and (v) the 'book within a book' that gives the reasons why the version of SFG presented here differs from the Sydney Grammar (as presented in Halliday's *Introduction to Functional Grammar*) has been revised and extended.

At the same time I have tried to retain the characteristics that made the original book attractive to its readers: (i) its relatively short length; (ii) its straightforward way of presenting the key concepts that one must grasp in order to understand the English clause, (iii) its emphasis on 'learning through doing', (iv) its detailed *Guidelines* (including many simple tests) to enable you to analyze clause-length texts with confidence; and (v) its clear explanations of why the analyses given here are as they are.

I am delighted to be able to say that versions of this book are being published almost concurrently in English, Chinese and Spanish. (For details, see the References.)

Robin P. Fawcett — Cardiff, October 2007

Preface to the Second Edition (updated)

This short book began its life as the annual Open Lecture given at Tezukayama College in Nara, Japan, in the Autumn of 1996, and a lightly edited version of that lecture that was published in Japan in the journal *Helicon* as Fawcett 1997. The purpose of the original lecture was to present the basic concepts of the version of **Systemic Functional Grammar** (SFG) that has come to be known, for reasons that I shall explain in Chapter 1, as 'the Cardiff Grammar'. This second edition aims to meet essentially the same need - though rather more adequately than was possible in a single lecture and extended article.

One of the strengths of the Cardiff Grammar's approach to text analysis is that it provides clear criteria at every point. This means that, whenever you find a problem in analyzing a sentence - whether in a natural text or isolated as an example - there are always tests that you can apply to ensure that your analysis is on the right lines (the 'right lines', that is, in terms of the theory of language that underlies this description of English). So you will find, from Chapter 4 onwards, that there is a strong emphasis on establishing and applying reliable criteria for identifying the elements of the clause, whenever you are engaged on the task of analyzing the sentences of a text.

Any framework that provides a **description** of all or a part of a language must, if it is to be insightful and reliable, be based in a sound **theory**. The theory of language on which this book is based is Systemic Functional Linguistics, and the theory of syntax that I suggest is required for this theory is set out in full in Fawcett 2000a. That book also provides, as an illustration of the concepts, an overview of the use of the theory to describe the syntax of English from a functional viewpoint - so providing the theoretical background to both the present book and the very much fuller description of the functional syntax of English that you will find in my *Functional Syntax Handbook (*Fawcett forthcoming 2011a). The short description of the simple clause in English presented here is derived directly from that much fuller work.

However, a great deal of that description has already appeared in other publications and, since the present book covers only the syntax of the simple clause (though with summaries of the other units in Appendix 1), the experienced linguist may wish to complement the present book by consulting those other works for descriptions of the other units.

There are summaries of all the main units in Fawcett 2000a, but you should read Tucker 1998 for the most complete study ever made (in any theory of language) of 'qualities' in English (roughly, 'adjectives and 'manner adverbs'), and their realization in the 'quality group'. And you should consult Huang 1996 and 2002 for an equally thorough description of the 'experiential enhanced theme construction'. Fawcett 1996 describes in detail the Cardiff Grammar's position on the main types of dependent clauses, and Ball and Tucker 2004 lists the many functionally distinct 'experiential' Adjuncts that are recognized in the Cardiff Grammar. Tench 1996 provides the functional description of English intonation that is needed to complement the Cardiff Grammar's descriptions of functional syntax and lexis. Fawcett 1999 sets out the argument for the Cardiff Grammar's position on the concept of the 'Subject' in English, and Fawcett 2000b and 2000c demonstrate the advantages of a model of syntax in which there is no 'verbal group' - and on both of these matters our position is rather different from that of Halliday.

Surprisingly, perhaps, one of the clearest and most readily available published accounts of the aspects of functional syntax that are not covered here are to be found in the relevant parts of Butler 2003a and 2003b - even though Butler is not a systemic functional linguist. See, for example, pages 309-17 of Butler 2003a for insightful summaries of the nominal and quality groups in the Cardiff Grammar, which complement those given in Appendix 1 of the present book (though Butler omits the more recently introduced unit of the quantity group).

Butler's descriptions of the Cardiff Grammar are part of his impressively thorough survey of the three current 'structural-functional' theories of language that he considers most valuable.[2] In his 'final assessment', he states:

> There can be no doubt that SFG has lived up to its claim to be a text-oriented theory of language; ... it has achieved a much wider coverage of English grammar than other approaches, this being especially true of the Cardiff grammar' (Butler 2003b: 471).

And on the same page he also writes:

> In my view the Cardiff model represents a substantial improvement on the Sydney account (Butler 2003b: 471).

Perhaps Butler's comments will encourage you to tackle the task of reading this little book, and then in turn the other books and papers to which it provides an introductory invitation.

Robin P. Fawcett Cardiff, September 2005

---

2 The two theories of language that Butler describes, as well as Systemic Functional Linguistics, are Simon Dik's Functional Grammar (e.g. 1997a and 1997b) and Robert van Valin's Role and Reference Grammar (e.g. 1993).

Chapter 1
Who this book is for, where it comes from and how to read it

1.1 A book for two sorts of reader

The slim book that you are now holding is in fact not one book but two - and each is designed for a different type of reader.

If you leaf through its pages, you may get the impression that it is an introductory book that could be suitable for first or second year university students - and so it is. But at the same time it is also a scholarly monograph that presents the arguments for and against two alternative functional approaches to the major unit in the most studied language in the world: the clause in English.

So the two sorts of reader for whom this book is intended are:

1 those who are just beginning their study of language, and
2 experienced linguists who are interested in a study which
   (i) compares the two main versions of Systemic Functional Grammar with respect to the syntax of the English clause, and
   (ii) gives reasons at every point of difference for preferring one analysis to the other.

Indeed, readers of the second sort might well include those who teach readers of the first sort.

The rest of this chapter - except the last section - is for readers who are experienced linguists. So, if you are a beginner in Linguistics, I suggest that you go straight to Section 1.11. But you might want to return to this chapter later on, to learn more about how the ideas presented in this book fit into the field of Linguistics as a whole.

The footnotes are intended for 'experienced linguists'.

1.2 A note to the 'experienced linguist': three ways to read this book

The scholarly aspects of this book are manifested in two ways. The first and most obvious is in the many detailed and sometimes extended footnotes. But it is the main text that provides the overall structure of the argument within which these footnotes find their place. Indeed, writing the main text has required as much careful scholarship as writing the footnotes. So the 'second book' for the 'experienced linguist' that this volume contains is not, as you might at first think, located solely in the part of the text that appears below the line that marks the boundary between the main text and the footnotes. It is the whole book.[3]

Let me explain how I hope the 'footnotes' will be used. There are two sorts, but both are designed for the experienced linguist rather than the beginner. Some of them serve the usual range of purposes that footnotes serve, but a large proportion consist of a series of notes - some amounting to short essays - that explicitly compare the description of the English clause given here with that found in the three editions of Halliday's *Introduction to Functional Gram-mar* (Halliday 1985 and 1994, and Halliday and Matthiessen 2004), which is also known as *IFG*. In recent years the version of Systemic Functional Grammar presented here has come to be known as 'the Cardiff Grammar', and by extension of that concept the *IFG* grammar has come to be known as 'the Sydney Grammar'. (See Sections 1.4 onwards for the similarities and differences.) So the second type of 'footnote' is headed **Comparison with the Sydney Grammar**.

These footnotes are therefore best thought of as a series of amplifications of the sections of the main text in which they appear. Quite often they present, in summary form, longer and more fully documented arguments that have been presented elsewhere (e.g. in Fawcett 1996, 1999, 2000a, 2000b, 2000c, 2003, 2004b, 2007a).

---

3 Indeed, I consider this short book to be as 'scholarly' as any of my publications over the last thirty years. It is certainly the one which has been re-worked the most often!

While a few of the footnotes refer to relevant works by other authors, there is no systematic attempt to draw comparisons with descriptions of the English clause proposed in theories of language other than Systemic Functional Linguistics. Nor, I think, is there any need to provide these for the 'experienced linguist', because you will be able to make such comparisons for yourself. A detailed comparison between two significantly different descriptions is probably sufficient for one book!

So what is the best way for the 'experienced linguist' to read this book? As always with footnotes, there is a danger that reading them will interrupt the flow of the main presentation. But I have tried to reduce this problem to the minimum by ensuring that they really do consist of (i) explanations of the different approach taken in *IFG* (and occasionally in traditional grammar) and (ii) reasons for taking the position presented in the main text - rather than side-excursions. But if you find the footnotes annoying you might wish to consider reading the book twice - first quickly reading the main text, and then reading the 'second book', i.e. the main text plus the footnotes. A third approach, of course, would be to focus predominantly on the main text, and to consult the footnotes only when you find yourself wondering why a particular clause has been analyzed as it has, rather than as it would be in Halliday's *IFG* - or indeed in traditional grammar.

1.3 A controversial question

The goal of this section and the next few is to place the approach to understanding the grammar of English that is taken here in the context of other current approaches. Let me begin by asking this challenging question: Who is the world's greatest living linguist?

No doubt many would give this honour to Noam Chomsky, and it is certainly true that his influence has been very great - especially as it is reflected in those university departments, books, journals, websites and conferences etc where the focus is on linguistic theory in its own right. This is in contrast with the many other university departments, books, journals, websites and conferences that treat a theory of language as part of a wider theory of human communication. And such theories also tend to treat the development of linguistic theory as a process that proceeds hand in hand with the use of linguistic theory in the demanding tasks of (i) describing languages and (ii) analyzing real life texts - and so as something that is USABLE (a term that is preferable to 'applicable') in various fields of human endeavour.

My considered view is that the fifty years of work in the Chomskyan paradigm by many good scholars has not in fact greatly benefited either (i) our understanding of the nature of human language or (ii) the status of Linguistics as an evidence-based science. Many versions of Chomsky's own theory have come and gone, and counter-theories that nonetheless accept broadly the same goals, research methods and assumptions about language as Chomsky have similarly come and - generally - gone. The picture of language that has emerged from all this work has been seriously misleading in a number of respects, and the relatively few insights to have emerged from it which have validity outside the theoretical frameworks in which they originated have been quite limited. This is because Chomsky and his followers have focussed too much on THEORY at the expense of DESCRIBING REAL LANGUAGE IN USE, and too much on the FORMAL SYNTAX of language at the expense of its MEANINGS and its FUNCTIONS.[4]

---

4 We have to recognize, however, the ferment of intellectual activity that Chomsky's ideas created in America in the 1960s and early 1970s - and so, given the socio-political climate of the time, in the rest of the 'Western' world too. I observed at first hand the way in which many good scholars allowed themselves to be diverted away from addressing the major challenges that we face in the scientific study of language and its use, and into working in the framework of this narrow, syntax-oriented view of language - an approach which creates its own norms in terms of goals, methods, assumptions and potential uses in other fields and that even today continues to exert a powerful influence.

Chomsky's 'revolution', as it was perceived to be by many, was certainly 'revolutionary' in the goals that his theory set for Linguistics, in the sources of evidence that it sanctioned and that it scorned, and even in the enormous reliance that it placed on the already old idea of the syntactic transformation (which can be found, for example, in Jesperson 1928/65). But in its assumptions about 'the autonomy of syntax' - and so the centrality that this component was accorded in his overall model of language - the 'new' theory echoed the structuralist preoccupations of Linguistics at the time, and his formal proposals about the nature of syntactic rules owe a major debt to his teacher, Zellig Harris.

In my view, then, the world's greatest living linguist is not Noam Chomsky. It is Michael Halliday - the 'father' and the major architect of the very differently grounded theoretical approach to language known as **Systemic Functional Linguistics**. In other words, I believe that Halliday has given us more insights into the nature of language and its use than any other linguist since Saussure - and probably even more than him.

Before Halliday's writings in the late 1960s and early 1970s, Linguistics was very largely preoccupied with a narrowly structuralist view of language, in which a language's syntax was seen as constituting its essential core - a limitation that Chomsky's so-called 'revolution' notably failed to challenge. Then, in a series of genuinely revolutionary proposals in the half dozen years beginning in 1966, Halliday fundamentally changed the view of the nature of language - and so Linguistics - for those of us who were working in SFL at the time. It is hard for those who came into Linguistics after this time to understand how revolutionary these proposals were - and how revolutionary they still are, I suggest.

Here is a very brief summary of the five great innovations that Halliday introduced in that short period of time:

1 He proposed a change in the 'balance of power' in linguistic theory and language description by giving a central role to the concept of 'system', so raising 'system' above 'structure' - i.e. treating **paradigmatic** relations as more fundamental than **syntagmatic** relations.
2 He then proposed that the system networks for TRANSITIVITY, MOOD, THEME and the like should be seen as presenting choices between **meanings** rather than between **forms** - most famously in Halliday 1970a.
3 He suggested that a clause is the simultaneous realization of **several different strands of meaning** (or 'metafunctions').
4 He suggested the possibility that system networks might one day be extended beyond the modelling of **grammatical** structures and words to the task of modelling the whole of a language's **lexis** - so creating a unified 'lexicogrammar'.
5 And he demonstrated, by providing us with a remarkably full description of it, that **intonation** too can and should be brought within the central 'lexicogrammar' of a language.

Taken together, these five innovations have immeasurably broadened and revolutionized our view of both the nature of language and how we should model it, in a way that those who came into Linguistics after the 1970s will find it hard to appreciate.[5]

In a historical perspective, then, I believe that we are currently still in the middle of the long process of:

1 revising and extending the descriptions of languages made prior to the emergence of this new view of language,
2 testing and evaluating our revised descriptions in various ways (see Section 1.9 for two major ways),
3 revising again (and sometimes rejecting) large and small parts of them,
4 revising some early theoretical assumptions on this evidence,
5 re-testing, re-evaluating and revising our descriptions ....

and so on, as we develop the new descriptions implied by these challenging new concepts, and then implement, test and evaluate them - while also integrating with them other new concepts that need to be incorporated into the model (such as probabilities).

1.4 The current scene in SFL: The Sydney Grammar and the Cardiff Grammar

To say, as I just have, that Michael Halliday is the greatest linguist of the twentieth century doesn't mean that I think that he is

---

5 See Section 3.2 of Chapter 3 of Fawcett forthcoming 2010 for a fuller explanation of Halliday's five key innovations, and for their impact on the relatively small band of linguists who were working in SFL at the time.

Other SFL scholars might protest that I haven't mentioned (i) Halliday's strongly social orientation and (ii) the various aspects of his view of the overall architecture of language and its use that follows from that - or they might wish to suggest that other innovations that Halliday has made are even more significant than these five. But it was these five innovations that specifically affected our descriptions of language itself - or that should have affected them, in my view; see further below. And it is the effect of those innovations on the descriptions of English that we make that is the topic of this book.

For an account of the various overall architectures for language and its use proposed in SFL - and for a detailed proposal for a comprehensive framework that includes Halliday's social concerns, see Fawcett forthcoming 2010.

always 'right' about every aspect of the grammar of English! And nor do I think he is 'right' about absolutely every aspect of the overall theory of language and its use that is the ultimate goal of Linguistics. No human could be - nor should we expect one to be.

Like many others, I have good reason to be grateful to Halliday for being willing to go into print about his currently developing ideas. Indeed, it was this that made the 1970s such an exciting era in Linguistics. And many of us, while recognizing that he was the outstanding source of insights into the nature of language of the last century, have been implementing his ideas in new ways.

One of the many good things about Systemic Functional Linguistics is that we who work in its framework are able to accept that there can be differences between our versions of the theory. Michael Halliday has suggested a useful metaphor for this, i.e. that our different versions of SFL are like different 'dialects' of the 'language' of Systemic Functional Linguistics, so that we should expect to find the Sydney dialect, the Cardiff dialect, the Nottingham dialect, the Madrid dialect and so on. What is more, we who 'speak' these different dialects remain friends - something that does not always happen when linguists disagree![6]

---

6 Halliday originally suggested this metaphor in a comment on a plenary talk that I gave at the 1995 International Systemic Functional Congress in Beijing. Other SFL scholars have suggested that a more appropriate metaphor than 'dialects' would be 'registers' (e.g. Hasan et al 2007: 710). Their grounds are that what is different in the two approaches is the equivalent of the differences of 'meaning' between two registers of a common language. (In a simplified version of the SFL model of 'varieties of language', different **registers** are seen as varying by presenting different probabilities between choices in **meaning** in different contexts of situation, whereas different **dialects** are seen as varieties that vary with social group (by geography, social class, age, etc), so providing different **forms**, Halliday suggests, for essentially the same set of meanings.)

But both the Sydney Grammar and the Cardiff Grammar are ultimately trying to model the same thing: language and its use (as I have demonstrated in Fawcett forthcoming 2010), so the 'meaning' is essentially the same in each case. The 'register' metaphor implies a 'horses for courses' distinction; in such an approach one might use one version of a description of English for one purpose and another version for another purpose. In my view this runs the danger of being an 'ad hoc' approach. It is not, I suggest, a scientific view. My view is that we need one GENERAL model of language and its use that is as comprehensive as possible - difficult though it undoubtedly is to keep all the

The version of Systemic Functional Grammar (SFG) to which this short book introduces you has in recent years come to be called the 'Cardiff Grammar' - e.g. by Butler (2003a and 2003b) in his comprehensive and masterly comparison of what he considers to be the three leading 'structural-functional' theories of language: Systemic Functional Grammar, Functional Grammar (as developed by Simon Dik and colleagues) and Role and Reference Grammar (as developed by Robert van Valin and colleagues). Within the SFG 'strand' however, Butler describes and compares the main two versions: the **Sydney Grammar** and the **Cardiff Grammar**. (You will find Butler's 'final assessment' of the two versions of the theory at the end of the 'Preface to the Second Edition'.)

These two grammars have the same historical roots and they still share (in my view) essentially the same basic concepts. These roots are in (i) Halliday's work on the grammar of English in the 1960s and 1970s, and (ii) the five great innovative concepts identified in the last section. Chapter 2 will illustrate this viewpoint by describing the way in which a systemic functional grammar works that is equally relevant to the Sydney Grammar and the Cardiff Grammar. But the description of English given here has many

---

necessary aspects in mind at the same time. (This is where modelling language in the computer helps us.)

Note that taking this view doesn't rule out the possibility that to work on specific tasks we often need to select DIFFERENT PARTS OF THE OVERALL MODEL for our different purposes. For example, the version of the grammar of English that we use for analyzing texts doesn't need to have the fully explicit realization rules that are required for the full generative grammar that is used in text generation in the computer. Indeed, it must not have them all; if it wasn't simplified it would be unusable. Furthermore, for the insightful analysis of a speech about foreign policy by a right-wing American politician, we might need to bring into the picture certain ideological aspects of his culture (part of his 'belief system'). But if our task was to analyze the spoken text of an autistic child, it would be important to foreground the cognitive-interactive aspects of the model, including the child's model of the Addressee.

Ideally, however, the text analyst should be alert to ALL aspects of the production of ALL text types, because the fact is that one never knows in advance what may or may not turn out to be significant.

In my view, then, Halliday's original suggestion of the metaphor of differences of dialect is in fact the more insightful one, for the reasons set out above. And in addition it recognizes the cohesive influence of physical proximity in a group who are working together.

differences from the description of English presented in Halliday's *Introduction to Functional Grammar.* Some are relatively minor, as we shall see, but many are significantly different and have far-reaching implications for the overall model of language.

One of the advantages of the present approach is that many of the aspects of *IFG* that readers find most difficult to understand and use are avoided.[7] But there are also a few aspects of English clause structure that are not covered adequately in *IFG* but which are covered here - and many others that are covered in my *Functional Syntax Handbook.* It is in these ways, then, that the Cardiff Grammar is - to cite the subtitle of this book - both an EXTENSION of the Sydney Grammar in various ways that are necessary to provide a full and consistent coverage of English, and also a SIMPLIFICATION of it.[8]

1.5 The common ground between the Sydney Grammar and the Cardiff Grammar

Where there are alternative versions of a theory, it is natural for scholars to focus on what distinguishes them rather than on what they have in common. In much of the rest of this book - and specifically in most of the footnotes - we shall be concerned with the differences between the Sydney and Cardiff versions of SFL, so it is essential to begin by emphasizing that the two versions of the theory have far more in common - in terms of both theory and description - than they differ over. And it is these important common assumptions that differentiate them from all other theories of language. So what are they?

Firstly, the general approach to understanding language that is taken in both versions of the theory is **functional** rather than

---

7 However, some of the difficulties in analyzing language texts are inherent in language itself, and these cannot be avoided. They can, however, be left to a later stage, and that strategy has been followed here.

8 Butler's view (Butler 2003b: 471), which I noted in the 'Preface to the Second Edition', supports the first half of this claim, i.e. he states that 'SFG ... has achieved a much wider coverage of English grammar than other [structural-functional] approaches, this being especially true of the Cardiff grammar.'

formal. Notice, however, that this emphasis should not be taken - as it too often is - as sanctioning the linguist to pay less attention to the problems of realizing meaning, systematically and explicitly, at the level of form. A good functional theory of language should be strong at the levels of BOTH function AND form, for the simple reason that every functional description must, if it is to be sufficiently explicit to be testable, also attend carefully to the level of form, since this is the level that is directly observable.[9]

However, there are many theories of language that claim to be 'functional'. Within the broad family of functional approaches to language, **Systemic Functional Linguistics (SFL)** is unique in the emphasis that it places on **paradigmatic** relations in language - and the part of the name of the theory that represents the concept of paradigmatic relations is the word 'systemic'. The key concepts of a SFL model of language - including the concept of a 'system' - will be introduced in Chapter 2, and they will be illustrated in a very small **systemic functional grammar** in Chapter 7. In SFL, the model of language itself is referred to as a 'systemic functional grammar' (hence as a **SFG** for short). What is its key concept? The key concept in 'formal' (or 'generative') grammars in the Chomskyan tradition is the set of 're-write rules' that have the form S → NP VP (plus the concept of the 'syntactic transformation'). But such rules have no place at all in a SFG, which is built around a very different idea. This is the concept that a language should be modelled as a giant network of 'meanings', i.e. semantic features (in a very broad sense of both 'meaning' and 'semantic'), such that these 'meanings' are related to each other by 'or' and 'and' relationships of several different types. (See Chapter 7 for a simple example of such a network.) In principle, the producer of a text chooses between these features as she or he generates a spoken or written text.[10] It is therefore a theory of language as **choice between meanings.**

---

9 Indeed, one of the claims made for the Cardiff Grammar is that it fulfils this obligation significantly more thoroughly than does the Sydney Grammar.

10 Note the words 'in principle'; in practice the choices may become so strongly 'habituated' over time that they come to be used as formulaic - or semi-formulaic - 'chunks' of language. Some examples of this phenomenon are

The common ground between the Cardiff Grammar and the Sydney Grammar can be expressed most simply by saying that both originate from Halliday's theory of language and his description of English (insofar as this was available) AS THESE WERE IN THE EARLY 1970S. The picture of the components of a SFG that I shall give in Chapters 2 and 8 is modelled on his description at that time. However, there have been many changes - though always within this basic framework - in the approach to understanding language that has developed, as a result of the factors to be described in the next section, into 'the Cardiff Grammar'. The relationship between Halliday's current model and the one that he gave us in the early 1970s is in some ways less clear, and we shall consider it in Section 1.7.

1.6 Eight factors that led to developments in the Cardiff Grammar 1970-2007

I shall now list eight developments in describing language since the 1970s that have led directly to improvements in the descriptions of English and other languages made by my colleagues and myself at Cardiff University - and so in turn, we believe, to advances in both SFL theory and our understanding of language and its use. These eight developments are as follows:

1 The growing emphasis in Linguistics in general on providing descriptions of languages in terms of MEANING and FUNCTION (in a broad sense of both terms) AS WELL AS FORM - but not replacing form.[11]

given in Section 11.3 of Chapter 11. See Tucker 1996 and 2006 for the ways in which the Cardiff Grammar handles these important phenomena.

11 A functional model of language that is not fully explicit about (i) the forms through which the meanings are realized and (ii) the way in which meanings are changed into forms (realization rules, in a SFG) is not a model of language, in the scientific sense of the term 'model', but merely a sketch of what a model of language might be. Such sketches have their place - and Halliday excels in producing potentially valuable ones. But it must be recognized that any such innovative proposal requires a rigorous and extended process of (i) implementing it in a detailed description, (ii) testing it, evaluating it and probably (iii) revising, retesting and re-evaluating it, before it can be accepted as

It was this factor, to which Halliday himself made the most telling contribution of all (through the revolutionary innovations listed in Section 1.3), that was the biggest inspiration to us to set ourselves the goal of developing a version of SFL in which semanticized versions of the system networks of TRANSITIVITY, MOOD, THEME, TIME, etc constitute the semantics of the language.

2 The enormous amount of work in applying SFG descriptions of English (and to a lesser extent other languages) to THE DETAILED ANALYSIS OF VERY LARGE QUANTITIES OF TEXT (by university teachers, researchers and their students) - and so in turn the enormous amount of work in EXTENDING and REFINING those descriptions.
In developing the version of SFG that became the Cardiff Grammar, the two main influences of this type have been: (i) the very large research project carried out by myself and Michael Perkins at the Polytechnic of Wales (now the University of Glamorgan) in the late 1970s, in which a team of 15 syntax analysts analyzed the functional syntax of the speech of 120 children, so creating a parsed corpus of nearly 70,000 words (Fawcett and Perkins 1980); and (ii) three decades of project work with undergraduate and postgraduate students involving the detailed analysis of texts. This informal way of testing a description often leads to the discovery of inadequacies in the description (and in some cases the theory), and in our case it led to many changes in the model. There has been similar work elsewhere that has led scholars to suggest changes in Halliday's 1970s model (e.g. Downing 1991).

3 The great amount of TRADITIONAL DESCRIPTIVE WORK BY OTHER FUNCTIONALLY-ORIENTED SCHOLARS working in linguistics and pragmatics (some drawing implicitly or even explicitly on SFL ideas).
I have particularly valued what I have learned from (i) Geoffrey Leech's meticulous descriptions of various aspects of English, (ii) the great description of English of Quirk et al 1985 and its

---

part of the 'standard' model. The initial sketch is simply the first step on a long, often tortuous, but potentially rewarding road.

probability-oriented successor Biber et al 1999 (in both of which Leech was a co-author) and (iii) Sinclair's COBUILD Dictionary (all of which, like Halliday's work, grew out of the Firthian tradition, i.e. the London School of Linguistics) - but also work by West Coast functionalists such as Chafe and Prince, and others too numerous to name here.

4 The enormous amount of WORK BY FORMALLY-ORIENTED LINGUISTS FOCUSSED PRIMARILY ON SYNTAX (e.g. those working in the Chomskyan paradigm), much of which is too theory-dependent to be relevant outside their own theoretical frameworks, but some of which has been valuable in identifying the data of syntactic structures whose relationship to meaning requires careful modelling.
Specifically, their focus on complex constructions whose names reflect a 'transformational' approach (such as 'raising', 'cleft', 'pseudo-cleft', 'extraposition' and 'left-dislocation') challenged us to develop new syntactic and semantic analyses within a systemic functional model, such as the definitive study of what is now increasingly referred to as the 'experiential enhanced theme' construction (aka 'it-cleft') by Huang (1996, 2002). See Fawcett 2007a and 2009 for SFG accounts of most of the rest.

5 The enormous quantities of new evidence now available to linguists through our ability to study patterns of language in VERY LARGE CORPORA (stored in and accessed through computers).
As well as being influenced by the data of our own parsed corpus (as mentioned in 2 above), the Cardiff Grammar has benefited enormously, in countless ways, from evidence derived from the great corpora of the British National Corpus and the Bank of English. Huang Guowen, Gordon Tucker, Fiona Barker (née Ball), Amy Neale, Michael Day and I have all made innovative contributions to the development of the Cardiff Grammar as a direct result of work with these corpora.

6 The growing appreciation of THE ROLE OF PROBABILITIES IN MODELLING LANGUAGE (in contrast with the crude 'grammatical' v. 'ungrammatical' distinction still found in most formal

grammars), the probabilities typically being derived from computer corpora.
Using corpora wherever possible as a source, the Cardiff Grammar has accepted the general principle that 'probability' is a more significant concept than 'grammaticality' (and indeed that it comprehends it). For one application of this principle, see the system networks in Figures 11-1 and 11-2, and for another see the diagrams in Appendix 1 - and for a demanding use of corpus-based structural data, see Day's probabilistic parser (Day 2007).

7 The important lessons to be learnt from developing and formalizing VERY LARGE SFGS IN A COMPUTER MODEL OF LANGUAGE, so that they can be tested by running them, both in the **production** of text (in the sub-field of Computational Linguistics known as Natural Language Generation) and in the **understanding** of text (in the sub-field of Natural Language Understanding, which includes parsing).
This has been a major influence on the development of the Cardiff Grammar. In the years from 1987 to the present, we *have been constantly influenced by the challenge of how to transfer any innovation that we made in the* DESCRIPTIVE FRAMEWORK FOR ANALYZING TEXTS *to the* LARGE-SCALE COMPUTER IMPLEMENTATION OF A COMPREHENSIVE, GENERATIVE SFG *that we were developing concurrently - and we have constantly reaped the benefits of responding to that challenge. The interplay between the two modes of developing the model has led to the continual development of both versions of the Cardiff Grammar. And there has been a similar benefit in the 2000s from working on the probabilistic parser (Day 2007).*

8 The steadily growing recognition that no account of language and its use can be complete without being set within the framework of A COGNITIVE-INTERACTIVE MODEL OF COMMUNICATION - such that the model does not ignore either (i) the role of society and culture in understanding language and its use or (ii) the need for the detailed modelling of how we plan and execute texts (e.g. for understanding the meaning and use of concepts such as 'Theme' and 'New').

The Cardiff Grammar has had a cognitive-interactive orientation from its origins in my early work (e.g. as found in Fawcett 1973/81 and above all in Fawcett 1980). It has been disappointing to find what one might term 'a wary disapproval' of what was perceived as an excessively 'cognitivist' approach by some socially-oriented SFL scholars (though never by Halliday himself). And it has been a source of encouragement that increasing numbers of scholars working in other functionally-oriented approaches to language (including some of those mentioned in 3 above) have independently adopted a fairly similar approach. This has led in turn to a series of major studies of WHAT GUIDES US WHEN WE CHOOSE BETWEEN THE FEATURES IN A SYSTEM NETWORK, *and so of the* OVERALL ARCHITECTURE OF LANGUAGE AND ITS USE *in which the lexicogrammar is set. Fawcett forthcoming 2010 surveys the various 'architectures' that have been suggested in SFL, and then makes a detailed pro-posal, based on the work mentioned above, for a framework that is sufficiently comprehensive to include both the 'socio-cultural' and the 'cognitive-interactive' aspects of language and its use.*

As the italicized paragraphs below the description of each of the eight factors indicate, today's Cardiff Grammar is both a far more comprehensive and a far more adequately tested model of language than the relatively tentative and partial descriptions given in Fawcett 1973/81, 1974-6/81 and 1980.[12] This is not the place to list

12 Indeed, there are other fields, such as Psycholinguistics, that some scholars would consider equally or more important. Research in Psycholinguistics played a major role in first building up and then demolishing the idea that the concept of the syntactic transformation had some sort of 'psychological reality', and in so doing it demonstrated the dangers of relying on laboratory experiments as a method of testing the validity of models of language. However, Psycholinguistics has produced some interesting findings (e.g. on the strategies used in interpreting syntax, such as the question of where to attach a prepositional group), and 'broad-brush' works on the psychology of language such as Clark and Clark 1977 (which draws on work outside Psycholinguistics and which, interestingly, is structured on Hallidayan lines) provide a useful check for work in the computer modelling of language.

Perhaps the most significant work in Psycholinguistics, from the viewpoint of our topic in this book, was the indirect support for the approach to functional

all the improvements in the lexicogrammar, but some will be illustrated in this book, and a great many more in my *Functional Syntax Handbook* and my *Functional Semantics Handbook.* The result, we believe, is that the systemic functional description of English Grammar that these works provide is a significant advance on those that were available forty years ago, in the 1970s. And these improved **descriptions** have led to a more complete and more insightful **theory** of language and its use (as described in Fawcett, Tucker and Lin 1993, Tucker 1996, Fawcett 2000a, and Huang 2002 - among other works).[13]

These factors have of course been recognized in the Sydney Grammar (see Matthiessen 2007), but they have not led to the significant changes in theory and description that they have in the Cardiff Grammar.

---

syntax taken in the Cardiff Grammar that comes from the work of George Miller. His well-known characterization of the limits of human short term memory as being 'the magical number seven plus or minus two' elements (Miller 1956) can be interpreted as a prediction about (i) the maximum NUMBER OF ELEMENTS and (ii) the maximum DEPTH OF UNITS that we are likely to find in a clause. In a study of the clause structure of children aged 6, 8, 10 and 12 (in a corpus of almost 70,000 words) we found that, for the highest five clauses per child on each of these two dimensions, the average - FOR BOTH VARIABLES - was a little under seven. Moreover, there were only minimal increases over this six-year age span.

The results would have been totally different, of course, if we have been using a Chomsky-style 'phrase structure' grammar. My guess is that an analysis in terms of the Sydney Grammar would reduce 'clause length' by roughly one element, and it would almost certainly recognize much less depth in structure. (However, there are serious problems in calculating the depth of a unit in the Sydney Grammar, because Halliday's diagrams ignore the fact - which is stated clearly in his theoretical writings - that 'unit complexes' count as units. See Fawcett 2000a: 317-33 for a discussion of this issue in relation to 'hypotaxis'.)

13 There have also been major developments at Cardiff - and in related work by Victor Castel and his colleagues at Mendoza, Argentina - on **the architecture of language and its use** (of which the lexicogrammar itself is a central component). But since our focus here is on lexicogrammar (and within that on the structure of the English clause) I shall have very little to say about this in the present book. See Fawcett forthcoming 2010 for a full account of this much broader aspect of modelling language and its use.

1.7 Developments in the Sydney Grammar since the 1970s compared with those in the Cardiff Grammar

Over the past two decades, the research of those working on lexicogrammar in the framework of the Cardiff Grammar and those working on it in the framework of the Sydney Grammar have been interestingly different. As we have seen, the major effort in the Cardiff Grammar has been to develop a very large, fully integrated description of English based on the principles implied by Halliday's five innovations of the 1970s. While there has also been work on building generative SFGs of both Chinese and Japanese, the basic strategy has been to develop a very full description of English, taking account of the factors described in Section 1.6, before applying our experience of describing English to other languages. And there has also been a major research programme that seeks to provide explicit answers to the important question of how we choose between the options in system networks - a question that is addressed in Fawcett forthcoming 2010.

But work in the framework of the Sydney Grammar in the period since the 1970s has focussed on very different areas. Let us look at developments in the core area of 'lexicogrammar', as seen by one its leading scholars.

By good fortune, 2007 saw the publication of a very full summary by Christian Matthiessen of 'descriptive and theoretical developments in the "IFG" tradition since the 1970s' (Matthiessen 2007b). I shall therefore draw on that summary here. [14]

The chapter gives a positive overview of a great deal of scholarly work in the Sydney Grammar tradition, much of it having been done by - or inspired by - Matthiessen himself. There has been (i) the development of a plethora of new theoretical concepts; (ii) a substantial quantity of work on languages other than English (e.g. as presented in Cafferel et al 2004); and (iii) the publication of the three editions of *IFG* in 1985, 1994 and 2004 - these being

---

14 The same volume also contains a second extensive survey by Matthiessen of developments since the 1970s in 'the architecture of language' from a Sydney Grammar viewpoint (Matthiessen 2007a). Here the term 'architecture' is interpreted in a far more general way than it is in Fawcett forthcoming 2010 of proposals for the architecture of language and its use in ALL variants of SFL.

followed in turn by a series of excellent textbook introductions to *IFG*. As Matthiessen says, '*IFG* has served as the foundation for a growing number of descriptions of English [i.e. the introductions to *IFG*] and as a model for descriptions of languages other than English' (2007b: 739). In terms of innovative descriptive work, then, the greatest achievement of the last few decades by Sydney grammarians has undoubtedly been the impressive range of papers and books that describe languages other than English.

In terms of the description of English, Matthiessen's overview shows that much of the work in lexicogrammar in the period since the 1970s (other than the introductory textbooks) is that of (i) Halliday, largely as published in *IFG*, and (ii) Matthiessen himself - much deriving from his years as 'resident grammarian' on the Penman Project in Computational Linguistics, where his role was to implement Halliday's grammar as the 'Nigel' component of the Penman project.[15] Two areas in which he cites the publications of quite a wide range of scholars are (i) Theme in English (where there are references to most - though not all - of the many papers that have suggested modifications to the description in *IFG*), and (ii) 'grammatical metaphor', which has been in an exploratory phase during much of this time. Another important topic - and one to which Matthiessen himself has made a significant contribution - is the quantitative study of texts, and so the relationship of, for example, 'transitivity types' to 'text types'. All this work, then, takes *IFG* as its starting point - a matter to which we shall return shortly.

In the period under review, Halliday's major contribution in the area of lexicogrammar was the preparation of the first edition of *IFG* for publication in 1985, and the revisions for the second edition and then, with Matthiessen taking the lead, the third.

Let me now explain how an understanding of the work being undertaken in the framework of the Sydney Grammar helps to understand how the Cardiff Grammar came into being as a separate 'dialect' of the theory.

---

15 However, see my comment below on the extent to which the description of English in *IFG* can rightly be counted among the 'developments since the 1970s'.

The beginning of the 1970s was, you will recall, the period in which Halliday's five revolutionary innovations (described in Section 1.3) were published. But the 1970s was also the period when he was developing and publishing a further series of innovatory concepts that extended, broadened, and in one case challenged the new model described in Halliday 1970a and embodied in the first three of his five great innovations. This 'second wave' of innovations included, among others, three new ideas, each of which would provide a sufficient challenge to most scholars to motivate a lifetime of research! These were:

(i) his new, functionally based theory of child language development (Halliday 1975),
(ii) his 'explorations' of the concept of 'language as social semiotic' (Halliday 1973 and 1978), which developed into
(iii) a third concept which was then - and remains today - a problematical one for many scholars, including myself.[16]

I shall now explain this problem, because it played a major - though indirect - role in the birth of the Cardiff Grammar.

In Section 1.3 I emphasized the importance of Halliday's introduction in the early 1970s of the concept that the system networks of TRANSITIVITY, MOOD, THEME etc should be regarded as choices between meanings. Yet the fact is that Halliday was simultaneously exploring a SECOND hypothesis about the level of language to which these system networks might belong. This was the hypothesis that they should NOT, after all, be regarded as the semantics of a language, and that they are essentially SYSTEMS AT THE LEVEL OF FORM - so leaving the way open for the development of an additional layer of system networks that would themselves constitute 'the semantics'.

For the next decade or so his writings sometimes seemed to support what we might term the 'one system network for choices between meanings' model (e.g. Halliday 1970a and many parts of

---

16 Other major ideas were to follow, including (i) a sketch of the developments in the language of science and (ii) arising out of this, an overall theory of the stages of development of a language in relation to stages in the development of human society.

Halliday 1973), while at other times his writings assumed a 'two system networks of meaning' model. His writings in this period are simply EXPLORATIONS of one or other of the two positions - and sometimes both - as is suggested in the title of his *Explorations in the Functions of Language* (1973) - rather than being the presentation of ARGUMENTS for and against the two positions.

It seems that, since he himself was not certain about the level at which his existing system networks were, he and those working most closely with him accepted his existing description of English (which was later to appear in *IFG*) as being 'right' in all essential matters, and so a 'good enough' basis to build on for uses such as computer modelling, describing other languages, and so on.

Hence the emphasis of the work by SFL linguists associated with Sydney on using *IFG* as a basis for describing other languages, and hence their broad acceptance of its description of English (except for minor aspects of Theme) - just as described in Matthiessen's 2007 survey.

This position is reflected in a comparison of the three editions of *IFG*. There are certainly differences between the three volumes - including, significantly, the replacement of the term 'semantics' to refer to the level at which TRANSITIVITY belongs on p. 102 of the 1985 edition of *IFG* by the term 'grammar' on p. 108 of the 1994 edition. But if you compare the core areas of the description of English in the three editions, you will find that they are almost exactly the same - usually with identical wording for page after page. And if you then extract from the description of English in *IFG* the principles of the theory that underlies the description, you will find that these too are virtually as they were in the foundation statements in Halliday 1961 (as I show in Fawcett 2000a: 102).[17]

---

17 The one major exception is the use throughout *IFG* of a type of diagram (first introduced much earlier, e.g. in Halliday 1970/76b: 24), which represents the three (or four) 'strands of meaning' (or 'metafunctions') that Halliday recognizes - each shown by a line of boxes labelled as elements of that type of structure. However, these structures in fact raise serious problems for the explicit version of the Halliday's theory. See Chapter 7 of Fawcett 2000a for a fuller account of these problems, and also for an alternative approach to showing the multifunctional nature of language, i.e. as illustrated here in Figure 17-2 of Chapter 17.

However, we can trace Halliday's description of English back to twenty years before *IFG*, i.e. to his 1964 description (published in Halliday 1976: 101). A study of his earlier systems confirms that, while his system network for TRANSITIVITY shows change and development, the description of most of the rest of the grammar in *IFG* is essentially the same as it was in his grammar of the late 1960s and early 1970s.[18]

The fact is that, in the crucial period between the revolutionary innovations of the early 1970s and the publication of *IFG* in 1985 Halliday published relatively little that was a direct contribution to the description of the lexicogrammar of English (or of any other language). The result was that we who were working in the framework of SFL in the 1970s and early 1980s simply did not know what changes to the description of English (and other languages) Halliday might be envisaging as the result of his proposal that the system networks of TRANSITIVITY, MOOD, THEME etc should now be regarded as being the semantics of a language. I cannot speak for the others who were around at the time, but I for one assumed that he would accept that his changes to the **theory** would demand changes to the **descriptions** of languages.

The consequence was that WE BEGAN TO DEVELOP OUR OWN DESCRIPTIONS, on the basis of the new principles. That was the birth of the Cardiff Grammar - though I didn't know it at the time. Those of us who were working in lexicogrammar in the 1970s believed that we were making contributions, following Halliday's proposals, to the development of a new SFG - a SFG in which the system networks would no longer be choices between **forms** and would instead be choices between **meanings**.[19]

---

18 In the footnotes in Chapter 3 and the following chapters, we shall note a number of problems that appear to derive directly from fact that Halliday did not make the changes in his description of English that follow from his apparent changes to the theory.

19 As one example, consider the similarity of the descriptions of MOOD network in Halliday 1976 and in Halliday and Matthiessen 2004, and contrast the latter with the semantic system networks for MOOD in the Cardiff Grammar, as illustrated in Figures 11-1 and 11-2 in Chapter 11.

What does Halliday himself say about this relative lack of development in his description of the lexicogrammar of English? He writes:

> Systemic work .... has tended to expand by moving into new spheres of activity, rather than by re-working earlier positions (Halliday 1993: 4507).

In other words, he now interprets his major innovations of the 1970s that set 'choice between meanings' at the centre of his theory as being simply ADDITIONS to the theory rather than revolutionary CHANGES that should involve re-assessing the existing concepts.

The difference between expanding a theory and changing it is an important one. The term 'expand' typically implies additions rather than alterations, so that THE 'EXPANSION' OF A THEORY DOES NOT NECESSARILY REQUIRE ONE TO 'RE-WORK' THE CONCEPTS OF THE EARLIER VERSION. In contrast, any CHANGE to the existing set of concepts in a theory needs to be followed by a thorough check to discover whether or not these changes involve further changes in other parts of the overall language system. In a theory of language, as in language itself, *tout se tient* (Meillet 1937).

It is certainly true that 'systemic work' has expanded greatly, as Halliday says - in the senses (i) that it now covers many additional aspects of language and many additional languages, and (ii) that is has been used in many additional areas of application - just as Matthiessen describes it in his 2007 survey.

In my view, many of Halliday's innovations - including those summarized in Section 1.3 - have been nothing less than revolutionary in their implications. And such changes do indeed demand the 're-working [of] earlier positions', in order to develop new descriptions. That is precisely the research programme that the Cardiff Grammar is following.

To conclude this section, let me now attempt a 'broad brush' summary of the differences between the two versions of the theory in the area of lexicogrammar.

The broad assumption among those working in the framework of the Sydney Grammar is this: (i) the description of the grammar of English, whose outputs are described in *IFG*, has not been in need of improvements (and so changes) for the period since the

1970s (other than minor tinkering here and there), but (ii) it needs to be supplemented by the addition of a higher level of system networks. The consequence is that the Sydney group have felt that the *IFG* description of English provided a sound framework for use in describing other languages (while omitting their semantics).

In contrast, the view of those working in the framework of the Cardiff Grammar is that, if (i) the system networks of the 1970s for TRANSITIVITY, MOOD, THEME and the like are converted into explicitly semantic system networks, and (ii) more sophisticated realization rules are used that can generate structures directly from those networks, there is no need for an additional layer of semantic system networks - SO RETAINING THE SIMPLER OVERALL MODEL OF LANGUAGE. The consequence has been than we have concentrated on developing ever more comprehensive descriptive and generative grammars (using English as the main test language for the new version of the theory), based on Halliday's five great innovations of the 1970s. In other words, we believe that we are carrying out a programme of research that implements - and so tests - Halliday's proposals of the 1970s. And the success of our work suggests that Halliday's revolutionary proposals were 'right' - even though he now appears to hold a different view. (There has also been important research on other languages at Cardiff, as will be mentioned in Section 1.9, though less than that carried out in the Sydney Grammar.)[20]

1.8 A note on works that describe the Sydney Grammar and the Cardiff Grammar

Where do we find the definitive descriptions of these two grammars of English and the theories that underlie them?

The authoritative version of the Sydney Grammar's description of the functional structure of English is undoubtedly that set out in Halliday's *Introduction to Functional Grammar* (Halliday 1985,

---

20 There are still some unresolved problems in the description - as in all descriptions. These include some that led Halliday to develop the concept of 'grammatical metaphor'. But there are alternative ways for modelling these - one for MOOD meanings being described in Chapter 11, and several others in Fawcett forthcoming 2010.

1994 and, with revisions by Matthiessen, 2004). But *IFG* has many shortcomings if we are looking to it for a statement of Halliday's theory of language (as I show in Chapter 7 of Fawcett 2000a) - starting with the basic fact that virtually the whole of the book is focussed on the task of describing the OUTPUTS from the grammar, rather than the grammar itself. As Halliday says:

> what is presented here .... is not the systemic portion of a description of English, with the grammar represented as a network of choices, but the structural portion which shows how the options are realized. (Halliday 1994: xv)

Halliday's main theoretical statement is his short paper 'Systemic theory' (1993), and there is useful supplementary material (including system networks) in Matthiessen 1995. Halliday and Matthiessen 1999, however, is an exploration of one aspect of their theory rather than a statement of it. So, for a major theory of language, there is, surprisingly, no single, complete account of the theory.

The nearest equivalent to *IFG* in the literature of the Cardiff Grammar is the description of the functional syntax of English in my *Functional Syntax Handbook,* to which the present book functions as an introduction. But there is also a more theoretical book on the functional syntax of the Cardiff Grammar, for which there is no equivalent in the literature of the Sydney Grammar (except, perhaps, for my summary of the Sydney Grammar's theory of syntax in the first part of that book). This is *A Theory of Syntax for Systemic Functional Linguistics* (Fawcett 2000a). This work includes at least as much about the theory of language as a whole - so not just the theory of syntax - as Halliday 1993. Two other recent books that include good overall descriptions of the Cardiff Grammar are Tucker 1998 and Huang 2004, and the work that gives the fullest description of the grammar 'at work' is Fawcett, Tucker and Lin 1993.

1.9 Research methods and research personnel in the Cardiff Grammar

Some readers may be interested to know who has worked on the Cardiff Grammar, and what our research methods have been.

I should begin by making explicit that the reason why the model of language presented here is called the 'Cardiff Grammar' is simply that it has been developed by a number of linguists working at (or otherwise associated with) Cardiff University.

Throughout the period since 1987, I have been the Director of the Computational Linguistics Unit at Cardiff University, which is located within the Centre for Language and Communication Research. Almost all of the work carried out by members of the unit was on sub-projects of the COMMUNAL Project. This is a major project in building a computer model of the generation of language texts - to which we later added work on parsing (the first stage in understanding language texts). And since we view the lexicogrammar itself as the central component in the process of generation, much of the work was also a contribution to the SFL description of English, i.e. the Cardiff Grammar.[21]

But throughout all this time (and indeed from long before) my colleagues and I have also taught Linguistics to undergraduate and MA students - largely through teaching them how to analyze texts. And using a description of the functional syntax of a language to analyze very large quantities of text is as demanding a test of a model of language as can be devised - informal though it may be as a scientific testing procedure. It is important to emphasize,

---

21 COMMUNAL stands for COnvivial Man-Machine Understanding through NAtural Language. This project is a long-term project whose goal is to contribute to building the various components that are required for a fully integrated model of the generation and understanding of language-texts, using unrestricted natural language. It draws on Systemic Functional Linguistics (supplemented by concepts developed in other frameworks when they are found useful). At its heart lies the GENESYS sentence generator, so called because it GENErates SYStemically, i.e. using a systemic functional grammar (SFG). For a detailed description of how a SFG generates a sentence, see Fawcett, Tucker and Lin 1993 - with special reference to how it works in a computer. Surprisingly, this is still the only complete SFL account of the generation of a clause to have been published. Other descriptions, such as those in Halliday 1969/72/81 and Matthiessen and Bateman 1991, only generate clauses, and not the units that fill their elements. For an overview of the architecture of language and its use in which the SFG plays a central role, see Fawcett 1993 and, for a fuller picture, see Fawcett forthcoming 2010.

therefore, that there are two inter-related sides to our research interests and our research methods. These are:

1 modelling language through the metaphor of the computer, and
2 developing a framework for describing English sentences at the levels of both form and meaning (syntax and semantics) that can be used for describing (i) languages (English, Chinese, Japanese and others) and (ii) the texts that are produced when those languages are used.

Here at Cardiff my fellow researchers and I have developed, over the last twenty years, a series of increasingly complex computer models for generating English sentences, as part of a wider program for modelling the generation and understanding of texts. The generative grammar for English developed in this project has been recognized by Halliday as being, with the 'Nigel Grammar' in the Penman Project that implements his version of SFG, 'among the largest grammars existing anywhere in computational form' (Halliday 1994: xii). Butler goes even further, describing it as 'the largest computer-based systemic grammar in the world' (Butler 1993: 4503). We believe that this is still the case today. Thus one important side of our work at Cardiff is concerned with building a COMPUTER SYSTEM FOR GENERATING TEXTS in English. This is a highly demanding way to carry out research on language, but the rigour that it requires brings with it many new insights.

However, Cardiff grammarians are equally interested in developing a genuinely adequate FRAMEWORK FOR DESCRIBING TEXTS, e.g. for the purposes of language teaching, literary stylistics, and the many other areas where there is a crying need for a comprehensive, functionally motivated and genuinely applicable description of English and other languages. This book is just one product of that research, others being *The Functional Syntax Handbook* (Fawcett forthcoming 2011a) and *The Functional Semantics Handbook* (Fawcett forthcoming 2011b). The present book draws directly on the first of the two handbooks, and can be regarded as an introduction to it.

As Section 1.6 has indicated, we have made increasing use of Corpus Linguistics as the 1990s progressed, with Gordon Tucker taking the lead in this work, and this has led to many improvements in our description of English. See especially Tucker 1996 and 2006 and Neale 2006. Fawcett 2006 describes the use of a series of different types of research method, including the use of corpora, in the exploration of a particular problem in the structure of the nominal group (the realization of 'typicity').

We turn finally to the researchers who have undertaken all this work, so that the last part of this section will constitute a selective 'Who's Who' in the development of the Cardiff Grammar.

My principle co-developer of the theory has been my colleague Dr Gordon Tucker, the Deputy Director of the Computational Linguistics Unit. But Dr Paul Tench, also a member of the Centre for Language and Communication Research, has also made a major contribution, and his description of English intonation (1996) is an integral part of the Cardiff Grammar.

There have also been important inputs from many other scholars: in the 1970s from Professor Erich Steiner, now of the University of the Saarland, on grammatical tests (e.g. for Participant Roles) and on 'mental' Processes; in the late 1980s from David Young (largely on the morphology for generation) and from other members of the research team, especially Joan Wright of the Cardiff Computing Centre and, for six fruitful years, Professor Francis Lin, now of Beijing Normal University; from a series of gifted MSc and PhD students who have worked with us over the years, especially Dr Fiona Barker (née Ball), Dr Bethan Davis, Dr Michael Day, Dr Amy Neale and Dr Ruvan Weerasinghe; and from a number of distinguished scholars who it has been our good fortune to have as visitors to Cardiff - including Professor Huang Guowen, now of Sun Yat-sen University, Guangzhou, China; Professor Masa-aki Tatsuki of Doshisha University, Kyoto, Japan; Dr Hiroshi Funamoto of Hokuriku University, Kanazawa, Japan; Dr Zhou Xiaokang from the University of Melbourne, Australia; Dr Yang Guowen of the Chinese Academy of Social Sciences, Beijing, China; Professor Victor Castel from the University of Cuyo, Mendoza, Argentina, and many others. Contributors to the 'Cardiff Grammar', then, are not confined to members of Cardiff University!

Using the same theoretical framework - but with carefully adapted or newly created descriptive categories - members of the unit, working with visiting scholars, have developed descriptions for some central portions of two major languages other than English, i.e. Chinese and Japanese. Indeed, we have built small but significant computer implementations of a generative SFG for both of these languages, with associated publications (Zhou 1995 and 1997 for Chinese, and Tatsuki 1998 and Tatsuki and Fawcett 2008 for Japanese). Moreover, the full-time members of the Cardiff team are familiar with various other languages, including French, German, Italian and Swahili, and, like other linguists, we make a practice of cross-referencing our work on English with our knowledge of these other languages, to ensure the general validity of the theory's concepts.

It is this team of researchers, then, using the methods described here, that has developed this 'extension and simplification of Halliday's Systemic Functional Grammar' (to cite this book's sub-title).

1.10 How to use this book as an introductory text

However, this book is not simply an introduction to Systemic Functional Grammar. Because it follows the principle of 'learning through doing', it works well as a first textbook in SFG.

Appendix 1 provides an important supplement to this book, and in so doing plays a key role in enabling this book to be used as an introductory textbook. Although it consists of only three pages (plus a key), THESE THREE PAGES SUMMARIZE MOST OF THE SYNTAX OF ENGLISH. More specifically, they summarize much of what can be taught satisfactorily in a 10-12 week course (assuming two hours of lectures a week plus a weekly or fortnightly seminar of text analysis practice).

The main body of the book focuses on the simple clause, which would normally occupy 70 to 80 per cent of a 10-12 week course, so the question is: How would you teach (i) the structures of the other units, and (ii) relations between clauses and groups?

All these matters are covered in *The Functional Syntax Handbook* (Fawcett forthcoming 2011a). However, because the structures of the other units are much simpler than those of the clause, it is quite possible to teach an introductory text analysis course based on the present book, by using Appendix A intelligently and, if you wish, by borrowing materials from other recent publications. These are the introductory descriptions of the **nominal group** - and also incidentally the **prepositional group** - in Fawcett 2007b (pp. 171-6), and there is a full description of the **quality group** in Tucker 1998 (pp 65-89). Brief descriptions of ALL the units can also be found in Fawcett 2000a (pp 201-13), and of all but the quantity group in Butler 2003a. Secondly, practically all - and I mean 'all' - of the **filling** relations between the units (in which a unit fills an element of a higher unit in the structure) are spelled out (including their probabilities) in Appendix 1. And for many further examples of clauses and groups within clauses and groups, see Fawcett 1996 and Tucker 1998.

Finally, I should point out that, if your goal is for your students to learn analysis skills for all the main units of English in a 10-12 week course (rather than mere 'facts' about this model of language), you would need to present some parts of this book only very briefly or not at all (e.g. Chapters 1, 2 and 7, and the more advanced sections of Chapters 8 to 14).

1.11 How to read this book

This section, like the first, is addressed to both 'experienced linguists' and 'beginners'.

In order to introduce the basic concepts of the English clause to you, I am going use a method that is a little unusual. It is in fact unusual in three ways.

The first is that, for each bit of the language that we examine, the general pattern will be to work from the relatively observable phenomena at the level of **form** to the less directly observable phenomena at the level of **meaning**. In other words, we shall be working from **syntax** to **semantics**. And the order in which we examine the elements will be dictated by the sequence in which it makes sense to learn about them, as we learn the skill of analyzing text-sentences.[22]

---

22 While the general approach of working from syntax to semantics is not unusual in introductory books in Linguistics as a whole - nor, arguably, in Systemic Functional Linguistics (SFL) - most introductions to SFL are organized on a different principle. Taking their cue from Halliday's *IFG*, they use the **strands of meaning** (or 'metafunctions') found in the clause as the main

The second feature of the book is the generous use of diagrams. In the past, diagrams were used quite sparingly in such books - largely because it has until recently been expensive to reproduce them. But in the age of electronic publishing, where authors themselves can prepare their diagrams to a high standard, expense is less of a problem. The problem of space remains, but it is rightly said that a good diagram is worth a thousand words. So I have used diagrams throughout this book as an integral part of the explanation, in the belief that they have a vital role in communicating ideas about the structure of both languages and texts.

The third feature of this book is that, following the principle of 'learning through doing', I shall be regularly inviting you to make your own analyses of sentences. So I am going to work your diagram-reading and diagram-drawing skills almost as hard as your text-reading skills!

But before we start analyzing clauses I shall give you a quick sketch of the relationship between the main topic of this book - the syntax of the English clause - and the rest of a full model of English. I shall do this by introducing three pairs of concepts that were suggested by Saussure at the start of the last century as relationships that are vital for understanding the nature of language, but which are only now being fully implemented in describing languages. But from Chapter 3 onwards we shall be working in a very practical way on (i) understanding the functional syntax of English, (ii) learning how to analyze clauses, and (iii) learning to recognize the eight major strands of meaning that a clause expresses.

---

organizing principle (with a different chapter for each strand of meaning). Here we shall follow the rather different strategy described above. The reason is that the basic assumption in the present theory of language is that when the different strands of meaning are expressed at the level of form, they are all mapped into a single, integrated structure. So it is with the central elements of that 'integrated structure' that we shall start.

Chapter 2
The place of syntax in an overall model of language

2.1 Saussure and Systemic Functional Grammar

Saussure is widely recognized as the 'father' of modern linguistics. His ideas have provided the overall framework for most of the theories of language developed in the 20th century, and for some quite specific aspects of several of those theories. The influence of Saussure's ideas on the version of Systemic Functional Grammar (SFG) presented here will quickly become clear in what follows.[23]

2.2 Form and meaning

Saussure's most basic concept was that of the 'linguistic sign'. For Saussure, any 'sign' consists of a 'signifier' and a 'signified' - i.e. a **form** and a **meaning**. It was he who led the way to the growing appreciation by functional linguists in the later half of the twentieth century that forms and meanings are mutually defining.

However, what we need is not simply an insightful model of a single 'sign', such as the sentence *I'm hungry*, but a model of the full set of signs that make up a whole 'sign system', such as the English language. In other words, just as a single SIGN has both a form and a meaning, a SIGN SYSTEM such as a natural human language has, in the simplest way of looking at it, the two levels

---

23 **Comparison with the Sydney Grammar** The main influences on Halliday - and so in turn on other Sydney grammarians such as Matthiessen - were the Chinese linguist Wang Li, and J.R. Firth, the leading figure of the London School of Linguistics. The main influences on myself are Saussure and Halliday - and so, indirectly, J.R. Firth and Wang Li - and British descriptive linguists such as Randolph Quirk and Geoffrey Leech.

shown in Figure 2-1. Figure 2-1 can therefore be seen as a very simple model of A LANGUAGE AS A WHOLE.

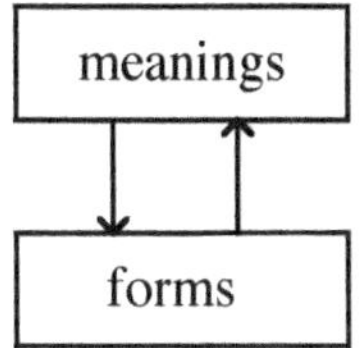

Figure 2-1: A simple model of any sign system

Because a sign system is something to be used, Figure 2-1 includes two arrows. These indicate that the function of a sign system is to turn meanings into forms, and forms into meanings. For example, a simple traffic control system has just two FORMS - a red disk and a green disk - and two MEANINGS - which we can express as 'stop' and 'go'. A human language, however, is rather more complex than this, as we shall soon see. Nonetheless, it is often useful to recall this very simple model when we are working within some sub-component of the overall model of language, as we shall be for most of this book. In other words, we cannot expect to understand the FORMS of language without considering the MEANINGS of language - and vice versa.

2.3 Language and text

In adding the concept of a 'sign system' to the concept of a 'sign', we have already made use of a second vital distinction made by Saussure - i.e. the distinction between a sign system and an instance of it, i.e. a single sign. Essentially, this is the distinction between a **language** considered as a whole - i.e. as a resource for communicating meanings to our fellow human beings - and an output from it, i.e. a **text**. So a text is defined in the theory presented here AS AN INSTANCE OF LANGUAGE IN USE. And for the linguist a text may be either spoken or written - though in everyday usage a 'text' is assumed to be written.

This distinction between a 'language' and a 'text' can be expressed in more general terms as the distinction between a **potential** and an **instance**. So, since this model of language has the two levels of **meaning** and **form**, it is logical to expect that it will have, at each of these two levels, ways of specifying both (i) the potential and (ii) the instances that are the output of a use of that potential.

These two pairs of concepts give us a model of a semiotic system - and so a model of language - that is much more satisfactory than that in Figure 2-1. We can represent this enriched model of the two **components** and their **outputs** as in Figure 2-2. (We shall come to the question of where the further arrows between the boxes should go in Figure 2-3, and there will be a demonstration of how the model works in Chapter 7.)

The pair of boxes on the left represent the **components** of any semiotic system, and the pair on the right the **outputs** from those components. Above the boxes I give in brackets the terms that would be used when the semiotic system is language.

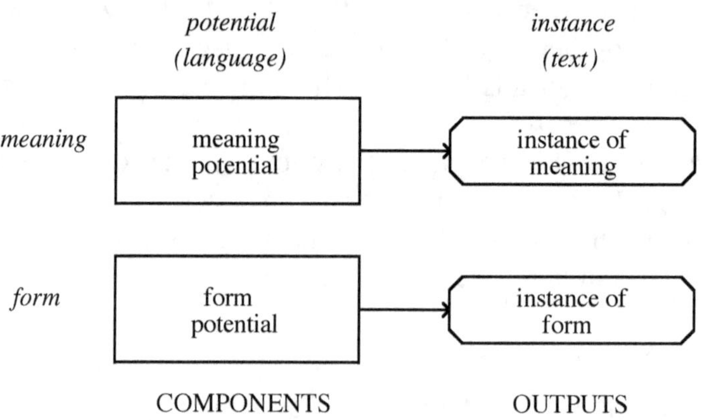

Figure 2-2:
The components and their outputs in any semiotic system

Let me now say a word or two about each of the boxes in Figure 2-2 - starting with the top left box. This is the component that specifies what Halliday has aptly termed the **meaning potential** of a language. In a Systemic Functional Grammar (a SFG), this takes the form of a vast **system network** of choices between **semantic features**. We shall return to this topic in the next section, and there will be an example of a system network for a very small SFG in Chapter 7.

Then, given the concepts of 'potential' and 'instance', we would logically expect the model to **generate** (i.e. to 'produce') **instances** of the 'meanings' in the 'meaning potential'. And indeed it does. So in Chapter 7 we shall also see simple examples of **selection expressions** of semantic features from the system networks.

However, since it is the level of **form** that is the focus of attention in this book, I shall have very little more to say about either the **meaning potential** or the **instances of meaning** - except in Chapter 7.

What about the level of **form**? Here too we should expect to find (i) a component that specifies what we might term the **form potential** of a language, and (ii) - as at the level of meaning - the **instances** of text-sentences that are its outputs. And here too a SFG has both.

The 'form potential' consists of **realization rules**, and Chapter 7 gives simple examples of realizations in **syntax** and **words**.

However, it is **instances** at the level of form that are the focus of this book. This concept is in fact already familiar to us all, since this is exactly what **sentences** are. And a sentence is frequently a single clause, such as the one that we shall take as our example in Chapter 3.

In this book I shall occasionally refer to a 'sentence' as a **text-sentence**, in order to remind us that the natural environment of a sentence is not standing alone as a numbered example (as you may find in a book such as this), but as AN ELEMENT IN THE DISCOURSE STRUCTURE OF A LONGER TEXT.

2.4 Paradigmatic and syntagmatic relations

However, Saussure made a third crucial distinction between two pairs of concepts: that between **paradigmatic** and **syntagmatic** relations in language. This distinction is particularly important for SFL, because it introduces the concept that is the most central of all in understanding how a Systemic Functional Grammar differs from other functional approaches to language, such as those of Dik (e.g. 1997a and 1997b) and van Valin (e.g. 1993).

Paradigmatic relations are relations of contrast, e.g. between the features 'near' and 'un-near' (to the Performer) at the level of meaning, and between *this* and *that* at the level of form. There are two key points to make. Firstly, paradigmatic relations exist only in the **language** that is used to generate a text-sentence, and not in the sentence itself. For example, a 'thing' may have the meaning of 'near' or 'un-near', but not both. And at the level of form we may refer to something by saying *this* or *that* - but not both.

The second key point is that, while it is clear that there are relations of contrast at the levels of both **form** and **meaning** (as we have just seen), in a modern SFG the system network models **choices between meanings**. And it is these system networks of choices between semantic features - i.e. 'meanings' - that are the generative base of a systemic functional grammar. The result is that the purely formal contrasts in a language play no role in how the grammar operates in the generation of a sentence.

Although the system networks of English are NOT the main topic of this book, they are so central to the way a SFG works that we shall devote Chapter 7 to (i) explaining the concept of a system network, (ii) presenting an example of a little SFG, and then (iii) demonstrating how it generates the various types of clause structure that we will have met by that point in the book. (Chapter 11 provides a more sophisticated example of a system network.)

We turn finally to **syntagmatic relations**. All we need to say about these at this point is that there are two major types of syntagmatic relations in language: **part-whole relations** and **sequential relations**. However, while both are required at each of the two levels of language, those at the level of form are more complex.

Using the three pairs of concepts introduced here, we can say that this book is about **syntagmatic relations** within the **instances** of language that are the grammar's outputs at the level of **form**.

2.5 From Saussure to Systemic Functional Grammar

Figure 2-3 brings these three pairs of concepts from Saussure together in an outline model of a systemic functional grammar (SFG). As you can see, its overall shape is like the introductory model of 'any semiotic system' summarized in Figure 2-2. But in the present case (i) the labels on the boxes describe the contents explicitly in terms of a systemic functional model of LANGUAGE, and (ii) there are more ARROWS to indicate the way in which it generates sentences. As you can see, this involves a 'Z-shaped' line through the four boxes (with two ways forward from the realization rules, one being a **re-entry** to the system network to create lower units in the structure).

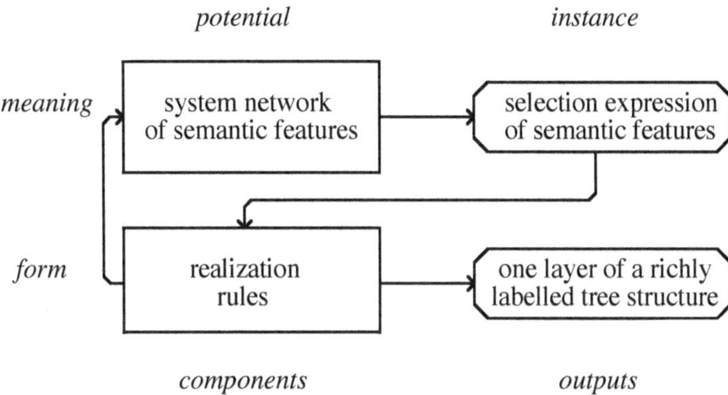

Figure 2-3: The components and their outputs in a systemic functional grammar

At this point we shall suspend this overview of language as a whole, even though it may still seem rather abstract. To take the explanation further requires a demonstration of a small SFG that illustrates these concepts - and this you will find in Chapter 7. And Chapter 7 will make much more sense after we have covered Chapters 3, 4, 5 and 6.

Figure 2-3 therefore summarizes the model of language within which the contents of this book are to be understood. As you can see, the relationship between (i) the **system networks** of 'choices between meanings' and (ii) the **clause structures** of English that we shall be studying throughout this book is made via a **selection expression** of semantic features from the system network and the **realization rules**.

2.6 The answers to two questions about SFL

This is a good point to answer two questions that often arise in the minds of those who are used to working with other types of grammar, including traditional grammar. These are:

1 Why do systemic functional linguists give priority to **paradigmatic** relations over **syntagmatic** relations? and
2 Why do they give priority to paradigmatic relations between **meanings** over paradigmatic relations between **forms**?

These are both good questions. And because they are interrelated my reply will answer both questions at the same time. The answer that I shall give may appear to some systemicists to reflect a **cognitive-interactive** viewpoint rather than a **socio-cultural** one, but it is in practice the reason that underlies the work of ALL versions of Systemic Functional Linguistics.

The reason why the core concept of SFL is **paradigmatic** relations at the level of **meaning** - i.e. 'choice between meanings' - is that **generating** (i.e. 'producing') a **text-sentence** involves the 'producer' of the text - whether a human or a computer program - in making planning decisions, i.e. choices. And it is the contrasts between alternative **meanings** between which we have to choose - rather than the contrasts between alternative **forms** - because IT IS THE MEANINGS THAT MATTER IN OUR PLANNING, NOT THE FORMS. The contrasts between forms are merely the **realizations** of contrasts between meanings (though often not in a one-to-one relationship).

For example, if two outputs from the same grammar display a contrast in form, e.g. between *this woman* and *these women*, the importance of the contrast is that the forms express a contrast in meaning which the Performer wishes to communicate to the Addressee. In other words, the difference between 'singular' and 'plural' is ultimately a difference of meaning rather than form.

Yet it is equally true that meaning depends on form - in the sense that we cannot communicate a meaning without using a form. Meaning and form in language are mutually defining.[24]

---

24 **Comparison with the Sydney Grammar** Halliday (1994: xix) describes his functional grammar as 'one that is pushed in the direction of the semantics', and he goes on to state that the Sydney Grammar has been 'pushed fairly far' in that direction. The general picture that emerges from *IFG* is this. Although the system networks of TRANSITIVITY, MOOD and THEME, etc are presented as capturing what Halliday has termed the 'meaning potential' of language, he thinks that they would need to be pushed a little further if they were to constitute the system networks at the level of semantics. In the Cardiff

Grammar we consider that we have done just that - i.e. that we have pushed our system networks of 'meaning potential' the further distance towards the semantics that is needed to reach the point where they ARE the semantics.

In the light of Halliday's own description of his networks (as cited above), you might think that this would result in relatively little difference between the two models. However, at other points in his writings (e.g. Halliday 1994: xx), Halliday clearly states that his system networks for TRANSITIVITY, MOOD and THEME have NOT been pushed as far as the semantics, and that they constitute a layer of 'meaning potential' that lies, in some sense, WITHIN the same 'level' as the output from the lexicogrammar - and so, in terms of Figure 2-3, at the level of form. On the other hand, his networks are clearly well above the level of form itself - if only because, as we have just noted, Halliday himself says that his grammar has been 'pushed fairly far' towards the semantics.

So the picture that he gives us of the level of these system networks is not as clear as many of his readers would wish. Indeed, his writings on this topic have long been open to this criticism. For example, Butler (1985: 79) points out that, on the question of 'the relationship between syntax and semantics', ... 'we find a confusing juxtaposition of statements' in Halliday's *Explorations in the Functions of Language* (1973) - and he then goes on to provide a page and a half of examples that illustrate the point.

In more recent years, however, Halliday's publications have increasingly explicitly adopted the position that there is a need for a higher layer of system networks - i.e. ANOTHER level of 'meaning potential' above the 'meaning potential' of the networks for TRANSITIVITY, MOOD, THEME etc - and that it is this network that constitutes the 'true' semantics. However, he considers that 'at the present state of our knowledge we cannot yet describe the semantic system of a language' (Halliday 1994: xx). It is an interesting fact that (i) the fragments of 'semantic' system networks drawn by those who use the Sydney Grammar (e.g. Hasan 1992) generate essentially the same range of forms as does the semantic system network for MOOD in the Cardiff Grammar, and (ii) they generate forms by FIRST 'preselecting' features in the MOOD network in the lexicogrammar and THEN applying realization rules. Yet the features in the Cardiff networks are realized DIRECTLY in the forms, via explicit realization rules - so showing that the intermediate stratum is not required. What this suggests is that when the system networks are 'pushed' all the way to the semantics, as in the Cardiff Grammar, THERE IS NO NEED TO HAVE TWO STRATA OF SYSTEM NETWORKS OF 'MEANING POTENTIAL', as proposed by Halliday. The Cardiff Grammar therefore has ONLY ONE such layer of meaning potential, while the Sydney Grammar has two (or, more accurately, it will have two, when the full sets of system networks for the new 'semantics' are produced).

This difference in the number of strata of system networks is therefore a fundamental difference between the two models.

Chapter 3
The syntax of TRANSITIVITY and MOOD: a simple example

3.1 The clause in its context

Sentences occur naturally in texts so, as I said in the last chapter, I shall occasionally use the term **text-sentence** rather than 'sentence' as a reminder that sentences really belong in texts - rather than as numbered examples such as the one below.

And texts - whether spoken or written - occur in specific 'contexts of situation', i.e. socially defined contexts. For our first example, we shall consider a text-sentence that occurs in the following context of situation. Paula is teaching her eight-year-old nephew Adam how to cook a particularly delicious vegetable dish. It is carrots and leeks, cooked in a little water and butter. They have just sliced the vegetables and put them in the saucepan, and now Paula says to Adam: 'And what do you think we are going to do next?' Then she answers her question herself: 'We shall simmer them gently. For about ten minutes.'

We shall take just one of Paula's sentences as our first example to be analyzed. Our sentence consists of a single **clause**, and it is:

(1) We shall simmer them gently.

3.2 Halliday's multifunctional principle

Before we begin work on the analysis itself, I must introduce one of the most important concepts in modern Linguistics. It was introduced by Halliday in the late 1960s as one of the founding principles of Systemic Functional Grammar. We shall call it **the multifunctional principle**, and it states that:

Each clause serves several different functions at the same time.

But how does a single line of words - which is all you see of a clause when it is written down on a piece of paper - do this? There is no simple answer, but by the end of this short book you will have an answer that is both full and - I hope - clear.

We sometimes refer to a line of words on a page as a 'string' of words - perhaps thinking that the words are like beads. But this is emphatically NOT a helpful metaphor. However, there are three metaphors that ARE helpful - and here are the first two.

A clause and the many functions that it serves is like a beam of white light which, when it travels through a prism, emerges as a beautiful display of all the colours of the spectrum - as on the cover of this book. So the function of someone who is analyzing a text is like the function of the prism - it is to analyze the various 'strands of meaning' that are hidden within the 'white light' of a single line of spoken or written text.[25]

It is also helpful to think of a clause as being like a strong hemp or nylon rope. Imagine a rope of this sort that consists of several strands that are twisted round each other, the result being that you can see only some of the strands in any one point in the rope.

Let us now combine these two metaphors, and so create an even better one. Now we see each strand of the rope as a different colour from every other strand - but at every point some strands are invisible - just like the strands of meaning in language. And each strand contains within itself finer meanings and structures, just as each strand of a rope contains finer strands. (I shall save the third helpful metaphor for the end of Chapter 17.)

While these different types of meaning are represented SEPARATELY FROM EACH OTHER in the **semantics** - i.e. as different areas of the system networks of meanings - their 'realizations' in the clause at the level of **form** are so closely interwoven with each other that they make up what we perceive as A SINGLE LINE OF WORDS. In other words, the different strands of meaning have

---

25 The inspiration for this metaphor comes from J.R. Firth's suggestion that 'the procedure for dealing with meaning is its dispersion into modes, rather like the dispersion of light of mixed wave-lengths into a spectrum' (1951/57: 192). However, it must be pointed out that, for Firth, the 'modes of meaning' do not correspond to the notion of 'strands of meaning', as used in Systemic Functional Linguistics. Instead, they correspond, roughly, to different levels and components of language (which were, for Firth, 'context of situation', 'syntax', 'vocabulary', 'phonology' and 'phonetics').

come to function as a single 'rope' of words, many of which express simultaneously several different meanings.

The fact is that every clause of every text that is ever produced is, in this special sense, 'multifunctional'. Three of the main strands of meaning are termed in SFG **experiential**, **interpersonal** and **thematic** meaning (though there are several others that we shall meet in due course). We shall come to the first two of these in a moment. Then, as the book unfolds, we shall steadily meet the rest of the strands of meaning that the Cardiff Grammar recognizes, and by the end of Chapter 12 the set will be complete. As we meet each new strand of meaning, I shall say a little about the sort of 'meaning' that it is - i.e. the sort of 'function' that it serves.

This 'multifunctional principle' does not apply just to English, but to all natural human languages. (However, it does not necessarily apply to artificial 'languages', such as some types of logic, which typically omit several types of meaning.)

I fully realize that the last few paragraphs are expressed in terms that are too general to mean much to you - unless you have met these concepts before - and that there is a serious risk that they may leave you wondering what on earth I am talking about. But by the end of this book you will, I promise, be as familiar with these concepts as any systemic functional linguist! It is when you see such abstract concepts at work that it is easiest to grasp them fully.

Throughout this book, then, we shall steadily build up the full picture of (i) the various strands of meaning that get expressed in English syntax, and (ii) the way in which the structures and words that express them combine in the clause. But in this chapter we shall focus on just TWO of the eight strands of meaning that we shall encounter: **experiential** meaning and **interpersonal** meaning. And the system networks that tell us the main choices in each of these are called TRANSITIVITY and MOOD. By the end of the next three sections you will know what these four terms mean.

3.3 The syntax of TRANSITIVITY in our example

I have said that the main way in which the **experiential** strand of meaning is expressed in the clause is through TRANSITIVITY. The experiential meaning of a clause is a representation of WHAT

THE CLAUSE IS ABOUT. So the question is: What specific types of experiential meaning does TRANSITIVITY cover?

First, notice that it is written in capital letters. This is because, in Systemic Functional Linguistics (SFL), we signify important areas in the **system network** of meanings in this way. (We shall meet a very small TRANSITIVITY network in Chapter 7.)

TRANSITIVITY is the backbone, as it were, of experiential meaning, and it is found in all human languages. TRANSITIVITY defines (i) the range of types of **process** that it is possible to express through the language concerned (English, in our case) and (ii) the **participants** in each of those types of process. All of the meanings in TRANSITIVITY are experiential - but there are other types of experiential meaning besides TRANSITIVITY - as we shall see, in due course.

That description of TRANSITIVITY is rather too abstract to mean much on its own - so let's use Example (1) to make it clearer. We shall begin with some key points about the **process**.

In Example (1) the process is 'simmering'. In SFL the term 'process' is used in a broad sense. A 'process' may be an 'action' such as 'simmering' or 'kissing', or a 'mental' state such as 'knowing' or 'loving', or merely a 'relationship', such as 'being' or 'having'. The second point is that the term 'process' belongs at the level of MEANING rather than at the level of FORM. And, since the word 'semantics' is simply a more technical name for 'the level of meaning', we can use the derived adjective 'semantic' to say that the term 'process' is part of the **semantic description** of a clause.

Every process functions as the pivotal element of a **situation** - the name for the unit at the level of meaning that is equivalent to the clause at the level of form.[26] So we can say that, in Example

---

26 **Comparison with the Sydney Grammar** In the Cardiff Grammar the term 'situation' is the equivalent, at the level of semantics, of (i) the 'event' in the mind of the Performer and (ii) the clause in which it is realized. (It is therefore NOT used here to refer to the 'situation in which the interaction occurs', which is here termed, following Firth and Halliday, the 'context of situation'.) Halliday, however, has no equivalent term to ours for the 'situation' as a semantic unit. (His term 'figure', as used in Halliday and Matthiessen 1999, seems to be closer to our term 'event' - though it is not fully equivalent to it, since it is a term for

(1), the **situation** of 'Paula and Adam simmering the vegetables gently' has 'simmering' as its **Process**. And, similarly, we can say that the **clause** with the words *We shall simmer them gently* has *simmer* as its **Main Verb**.

We have just made statements about each of the two levels of MEANING (or SEMANTICS) and FORM. So, to summarize so far, we can say:

(i) At the level of MEANING:
the semantic unit of the **situation** has, as a pivotal element, a **Process**.

(ii) At the level of FORM:
the syntactic unit of the **clause** has, as a pivotal element, a **Main Verb**.

(iii) And the **Process** is typically expressed in the **Main Verb** (90% valid).

You may have noticed that I have switched to writing 'Process' and 'Main Verb' with initial capital letters. This is because it is the practice in SFL to write the names of ALL the elements of a situation and a clause in this way. This helps such words to stand out from the rest of the text, and in this way to remind the reader that they are being used as technical terms in the task of modelling the grammar of English.

We come now to THE MOST VALUABLE SINGLE PRINCIPLE OF SYNTAX ANALYSIS. This is:

There is one Main Verb per clause.

---

the OUTPUT from a system network at that higher level.) Halliday in fact uses the term 'clause' for both (i) the feature that is the entry condition to the system network whose meanings are realized in the clause and (ii) the syntactic unit that is the output from the grammar. It seems likely that the use of 'clause' as the entry condition to the system network became established in the period BEFORE Halliday proposed the concept that syntax should be viewed as the realization of choices in meaning in the system networks, and that he simply never made the change that the revolutionary new proposals suggested. And, since he no longer treats the meanings that are expressed in the clause as being at the level of semantics (as we saw in Footnote 25), there is now less reason for him to consider changing the entry condition to the network from 'clause'.

For our present purposes, we can say that this simple principle is 100% valid - and you will find that it provides the basis for all of our work on the analysis of clauses.[27]

---

27 **Comparison with the Sydney Grammar** This one simple statement involves two major departures from the view of language given in *IFG*. Let us take first the claim that the Main Verb functions as an element of the clause. In the Sydney Grammar the Main Verb functions as an element of a different unit: the 'verbal group'. The existence of this class of group is a central requirement for Halliday's concept of the 'rank scale', which is one of the organizing principles of his model. The 'rank scale' model of syntax claims that every element of every unit is filled, in principle, by an instance of THE UNIT NEXT BELOW IT ON THE RANK SCALE - though Halliday acknowledges that there are a few exceptions, such as the Linker *and* and the 'conjunctive' Adjunct *however*.

In contrast, those who use the Cardiff Grammar find the concept of the 'verbal group' a hindrance to understanding the nature of English syntax rather than an aid - and we therefore operate with a greatly modified concept of 'rank scale' that it based on probabilities. (See Chapter 5 and Appendix 1.)

Let me now summarize some of the major reasons for treating the Main Verb as an element of the clause, rather than as an element of a 'verbal group' that fills the Predicator of the clause. I shall draw mainly on Fawcett 2000b and 2000c, but also on the summary of that two-part paper in Fawcett 2000a.

Firstly, the Main Verb has a direct relationship with many aspects of the meanings and forms of the clause. The most important is that it expresses the Process which 'predicts' the Participant Roles of the clause. It makes sense, in both generating and understanding text-sentences, to be able to relate the Participant Roles of the clause directly to the element that expresses the Process AS SISTER ELEMENTS OF THE SAME UNIT (i.e. the clause).

Secondly, Halliday has since the 1960s (Halliday 1967:218) recognized that one element of the 'verbal group' (which he calls the 'Finite operator' (or 'Finite' for short), is best regarded as an element of the clause. (The nearest equivalent term in the Cardiff Grammar is the **Operator**, which we shall meet in Section 3.4.) However, it frequently happens that the Operator is conflated with the Main Verb (as we shall see in Chapter 6) - and the grammar can only conflate two elements WHEN THEY ARE IN THE SAME UNIT. Moreover, the Operator is also frequently conflated with other elements of the supposed 'verbal group', such as the three Auxiliary Verbs that we shall meet in Chapter 8. It would therefore be logical for the Sydney Grammar to follow the Cardiff Grammar in 'promoting' the other elements of the 'verbal group' to function as clause elements, in the same way that the Finite has already been 'promoted'.

Thirdly, The Process is often expressed in another element as well as the Main Verb, i.e. *off* in both *George Fox wouldn't take off his hat before the judge* and *George Fox wouldn't take his hat off before the judge.* This is the **Main Verb Extension**, an element that we shall meet in Chapter 13 - and, as the

We can summarize the ideas presented so far in the diagram in Figure 3-1:

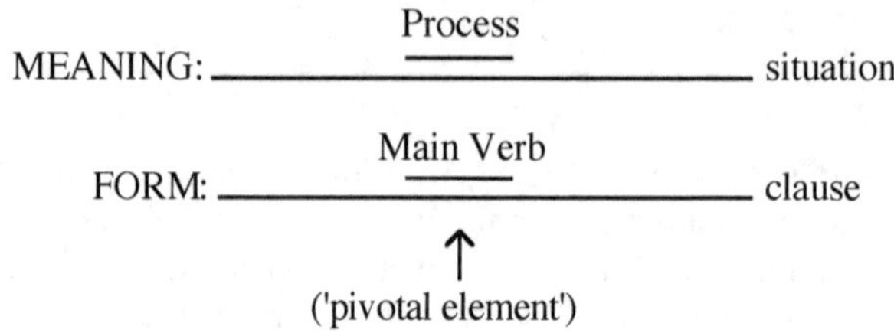

Figure 3-1: The relations of a Process and a simple Main Verb

---

underlined portions of the two examples show, it doesn't necessarily occur next to the Main Verb. So it too is therefore best treated as an element of the clause.

Even if Halliday's 'verbal group' did not raise structural problems such as these, it is unlike other classes of group in several ways: (i) every one of its elements expresses a meaning that is an aspect of the 'situation' (the semantic equivalent of the clause); (ii) the elements of the 'verbal group' are very frequently interrupted by elements of the clause (e.g. various types of Adjunct and, most frequently of all, the Subject); and (iii) it cannot stand on its own as a referring expression - e.g. as a reply to a question - as all other groups can (e.g. in *The boys have been eating ice-cream in the garden,* each of *the boys, ice-cream* and *in the garden* is a referring expression, but *have been eating* is not).

There are many other reasons why it is more elegant to treat the elements that in the Sydney Grammar are presented as elements of the 'verbal group' as direct elements of the clause. All these reasons are spelled out in full in Fawcett 2000b and 2000c. And at the time of writing (late 2007) no advocate of the Sydney Grammar has yet published a reply that explains why these reasons should be disregarded.

The second major difference from the Sydney Grammar is that Halliday allows a clause to contain more than one Main Verb. See Fawcett 1996: 340-42 for the explicit justification of the following three principles: '(1a) Each clause expresses one and only one process', and therefore that '(1b) Each clause can have only one Main Verb'; '(2) The Main Verb is a direct element of the clause in which it occurs'; and '(3) A clause that is "dependent" on a verb in another clause is modelled as **filling** a **Participant Role** in the situation expressed in the higher clause, and so as **embedded** in it'. So in (i) *Ivy wants Ike to go to Paris, Ike to go to Paris* is a clause that fills the Complement/Phenomenon in the 'emotion' Process of 'wanting', and so too is *to go to Paris* in (ii) *Ivy wants to go to Paris.* See Fawcett 1996 for a comprehensive description of a generative grammar of 'complementation' in English (so including Complements that follow the Main Verb *want*).

In Figure 3-2 the aspect of **form** that is relevant is **syntax**, but we should note for future reference that in this grammar 'form' also includes **items** (words and morphemes) and, depending on whether the medium is speech or writing, **intonation** or **punctuation**.

We come now to another key point. Because Systemic Functional Grammar takes a **functional** approach to language, the units and elements of SYNTAX are matched as closely as possible to the units and elements of SEMANTICS. The effect of this is that, as we learn about syntax, we shall regularly need to bring into the picture the **functions** that syntax serves - i.e. the **meanings** that syntax expresses. And we shall find that this is a great help in analyzing the syntax.

We come now to the **Participants** in the Process. All we need to say at this point is:

Just as:
the PROCESS is typically expressed in the Main Verb,
so too:
the PARTICIPANTS are typically expressed in the Subject and the Complement.

There is more on the Subject and Complement in Chapter 10.

Now we are ready to identify the first strand of meaning in our example. The analysis of the TRANSITIVITY of *We shall simmer them gently* is given in Figure 3-2.

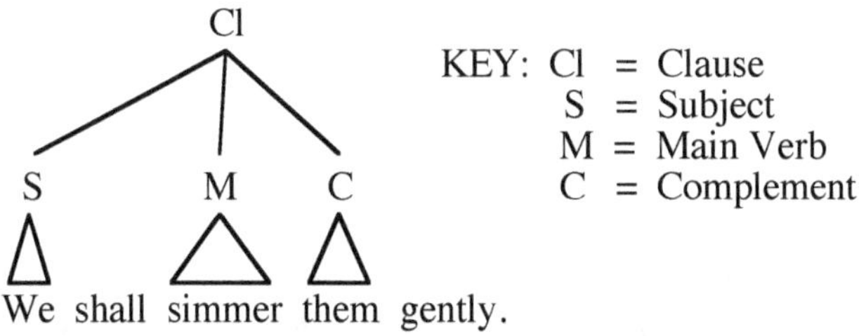

Figure 3-2: The TRANSITIVITY structure of Example (1)

I have not so far explained HOW to recognize that *we* is the Subject and *them* is a Complement. We shall come to those questions very soon, but at this point we are simply illustrating the vital point that the structure of English - like that of all other natural human languages - is **multifunctional**.

The general name for the type of meaning that I have been introducing in this section is **experiential** meaning. It is called 'experiential' because it represents the 'experience' that is being referred to. (It is also sometimes referred to as 'referential meaning', but here we shall stick to the traditional SFL term of 'experiential meaning'.) TRANSITIVITY is simply the most important of several types of experiential meaning that are found in the clause.

3.4 The syntax of MOOD in our example

The second major function of language is to express **interpersonal** meaning. And the part of the semantic system network that expresses interpersonal meaning, as this is expressed in the clause, is termed MOOD. It expresses the meaning of WHAT WE ARE DOING THROUGH LANGUAGE.

The meaning expressed in the structures that realize MOOD is meaning in terms of **communication roles**. But before we can describe these we need to introduce two even more basic concepts: the **Performer** and the **Addressee**. These are the interactants in the process of communication. The Performer is the speaker or writer who is performing the act of communication that is being analyzed, and the Addressee is the person (or persons) to whom the Performer is speaking or writing. (Note the use of initial capital letters to signify that the words are being used as technical terms in the linguistic description.) Sometimes we shall abbreviate the word 'Performer' to 'P' and 'Addressee' to 'A' - so that when Paula is speaking to Adam, P and A can also stand for 'Paula' and 'Adam'. And we shall also assume that the Performer is female and that the Addressee is male, because this will save having to use clumsy expressions such as *she or he*, and *herself/himself*. So, in relation to our example, we can say that Paula is the **Performer** of the information-giving act of *We shall simmer them gently*, and that Adam is the **Addressee**.[28]

---

28 **Comparison with the Sydney Grammar** Many linguists, including Halliday in *IFG,* use the terms 'Speaker' and 'Hearer' (or 'Listener' in Halliday's case) instead of 'Performer' and 'Addressee' - perhaps as a reminder that in the history of humankind (i) speaking preceded writing and (ii) there has been

I can now make the key point about the meaning of MOOD - and so of the **interpersonal** strand of meaning. It is that the Performer, through the use of the structure that expresses one of the MOOD meanings that we shall shortly meet, assigns **communication roles** to P and A (which each keeps for the short period of time for which the current text-sentence lasts). So in our example Paula is, through the act of uttering this clause, assigning herself the role of 'giver of information' (i.e. information about what she and Adam are about to do), and she is assigning Adam the role of 'receiver of information'. Other such roles that are assigned through choices in the system network for MOOD include 'seeker of information' and 'proposer of action'.

There is an interesting relationship between the Performer of the communicative act and the act itself. Notice that we can call both of them an **information giver**. Paula, in her role as the Performer, is an 'information giver', but so is her one-clause utterance. The relationship between them is that the clause functions as a sort of temporary 'extension' of P - as an 'abstract tool', we might say - so that P and her utterance are each, in their different ways, an 'information giver'.

The crucial question for us is: How is the meaning 'information giver' signalled at the level of form? The answer is that, in our current example, it is signalled by the sequence of two elements of clause structure: the **Subject** and the **Operator**.[29] (I shall shortly

---

vastly more speaking than writing. Here, however, we shall use 'Performer' and 'Addressee', because they enable us to generalize across speech and writing. (Some linguists use 'Addressor' and 'Addressee', but our terms have the advantage of giving us two roles that can be shorted to 'P' and 'A'.) Moreover, as the computer and the internet begin to overtake print on paper as the major source of written information in the twenty-first century, the overwhelming predominance of speech over writing has begun to shift - if only, so far, for some people in some societies.

29 **Comparison with the Sydney Grammar** In the Sydney Grammar the nearest equivalent to the Operator is the 'Finite' - which Halliday explains (1994: 196) is short for 'Finite Operator'. And in both grammars this element is treated as an element of the clause. But this apparent similarity of name and function hides a major difference. In the Sydney Grammar the 'Finite' is said to be conflated with the Main Verb in an example such as *Ike likes Ivy*, while in the Cardiff Grammar there is simply no Operator in such cases. In some ways, therefore, the term 'Finite', as it is used in the Sydney Grammar, seems to be

explain how to recognize them - and in due course we shall have to supplement this simple statement.)

The syntax of MOOD in Example (1) is shown in Figure 3-3, and this structure is the realization of the meaning 'information giver'. The MOOD structure of a clause, then, is the expression in the clause of its **interpersonal** meaning. And in this way it is the route through which the grammar represents the **discourse act** that is performed through uttering the clause.[30]

---

more like a **semantic feature** of the clause than an **element** of it, since it 'disappears' when it is conflated with a Main Verb. With an irregular verb form such as *ran* and *sang,* there isn't even a suffix that can be identified as the 'Finite' element.

30 **Comparison with the Sydney Grammar** In the analysis of the structure that realizes the meanings of MOOD in *IFG*, the two elements of Subject and Finite are presented as together forming a single element of the 'interpersonal structure' of the clause (e.g. in the diagram in Halliday 1994: 77). The question that arises is: What is the relationship of the elements 'Subject' and 'Finite' to the element 'Mood'? Clearly, it is NOT one in which (i) the Subject and Finite function together as elements of some unit and (ii) this 'unit' fills the element 'Mood', because there is no mention in *IFG* of such a unit. The concept in Halliday's writings that is relevant here is that of 'delicacy' in the description, which, when applied to structure, led him to talk about the 'primary' and 'secondary' - i.e. 'more detailed' structures. Thus his analysis in terms of 'Subject' and 'Finite' is offered as a more 'delicate' analysis than the one in which the clause is merely divided into 'Mood' and 'Residue'. (See Fawcett 2000a: 22-3 for an examination of the place in the theory of the concept of 'delicacy'.)

The question that this raises is as follows: Is there any value in analyzing the clause into the 'primary' elements of 'Mood' and 'Residue' - AS WELL AS into the elements of 'Subject' and 'Finite' (i.e. Subject and Operator or Main Verb, in Cardiff Grammar terms)? After all, the key concept - on which all systemic functional linguists would agree - is that it is the configuration of the 'Subject' and 'Finite' (or 'Operator') that realizes the main meanings of MOOD in English. In my view, then, the concept of 'Mood' as an element of the functional syntax of the clause is unnecessary - and so not illuminating (as it was no doubt intended to be), but a potential source of confusion. Its inclusion as part of the structural analysis of the clause is perhaps best seen as an attempt to express in the structure the fact that it is these TWO ELEMENTS that together realize the SINGLE MEANING of the features in the MOOD network from which these structures are generated. (Note that for present purposes it doesn't matter that in the Sydney Grammar these reflect the traditional labels of 'declarative' and 'interrogative', etc, and in the Cardiff Grammar they are the more explicitly semantic labels of 'information giver' and 'information seeker', etc.)

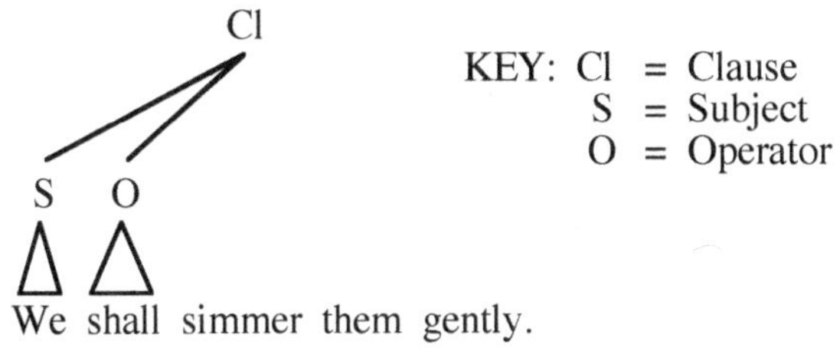

Figure 3-3: The MOOD structure of Example (1)

3.5 Strands of meaning and system networks

Let us now look again at the two pairs of terms of (i) 'experiential' and TRANSITIVITY, and (ii) 'interpersonal' and MOOD. As we have seen, TRANSITIVITY is the name of the **system network** for the part of experiential meaning that covers Processes and Participants, and MOOD is the name for the system network that models the functions that the clause can serve for the Performer. But the words TRANSITIVITY and MOOD can also be used to refer to the expression of these meanings in **structures** at the level of form, so that we can talk of 'TRANSITIVITY structures' and 'MOOD structures'.

The full set of relationships between **strands of meaning** and the **system networks** that are expressed in the clause can be summarized in a single diagram. Figure 17-3 in Chapter 17 will summarize (i) the strands of meaning and (ii) the names of the main system networks within each strand of meaning. But for our present purposes all we need to note is the corner of that diagram shown in Figure 3-4.

strand of meaning or 'function of language'	expressed in the unit of: clause
experiential	TRANSITIVITY (PRs)
interpersonal	MOOD

Figure 3-4: Two major functions of language and two system networks realized in the clause

As Figure 3-4 shows, a 'function of language' is an alternative term for a 'strand of meaning'.[31] In general in this book we shall use the term that most clearly reminds us of the multifunctionality of language, i.e. the metaphor of **strands of meaning**.

It is interesting that both TRANSITIVITY and MOOD are concerned with meanings that are 'roles'. But it is not surprising, in a functional approach to language - since a 'role' IS a **function**. It is in fact quite easy to keep the two types of role separate:

TRANSITIVITY covers
the **Process** and the **Participants** being referred to, and
MOOD covers
the roles of the **interactants** in the act of communication.

3.6 Integrating the structures for TRANSITIVITY and MOOD

If you compare Figure 3-2 and Figure 3-3, you will see that the Subject is involved in the syntax of both TRANSITIVITY and MOOD. This illustrates nicely the principle of 'multifunctionality' that I introduced at the start of this chapter. In Chapter 8 we shall find that the Subject typically (but not always) has a further role - that of expressing the type of THEME which we shall call SUBJECT THEME. So any Subject typically serves THREE different functions at the same time. I shall introduce the concept of SUBJECT THEME in Section 8.5 of Chapter 8, and we shall meet three other types of THEME in Chapters 13 and 14.

---

31 **Comparison with the Sydney Grammar** The term used in Halliday's early writings for what we are here calling 'strands of meaning' was 'functions of language' (e.g. Halliday 1970a) or 'functional components'. Later the term 'metafunction' was introduced to refer to the four broad 'functions of language' that Halliday distinguishes ('experiential', 'logical', 'interpersonal' and 'textual'). And he occasionally uses 'strand of meaning' in the same sense as 'metafunction' (e.g. Halliday 1994: 34). Thus Halliday presents his model of language as having FOUR strands of meaning, whereas in the Cardiff Grammar we find it valuable to distinguish EIGHT ('experiential', 'logical relations', 'interpersonal', 'negativity', validity', 'affective', 'thematic' and 'informational'). When these are introduced in the rest of this book I shall add a brief description of the type of meaning involved.

The multifunctional principle applies to other elements too. For example, the word *shall* in our example has its own internal meaning ('future time'), as well as its function as the Operator in expressing the MOOD meaning of 'information giver'. So the **multifunctional principle** applies to many of the individual elements within the clause - and so by extension to the clause as a whole. You might like to re-read the description of the metaphors introduced in Section 3.2, in the light of our experience so far.[32]

If we now put the TRANSITIVITY analysis and the MOOD analysis together into one unified structure, we get the analysis shown in Figure 3-5:

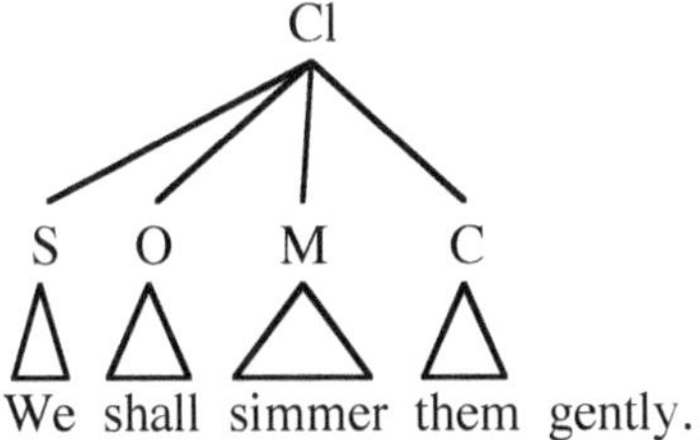

Figure 3-5:
The TRANSITIVITY and MOOD structures of Example (1)

3.7 The Manner of the Process

This leaves only the word *gently*. What kind of meaning is it? Is it experiential, like TRANSITIVITY, or interpersonal, like MOOD? Or is it a new type of meaning?

---

32 **Comparison with the Sydney Grammar** This brings us to one of the most important differences from the Sydney Grammar. The analyses in *IFG* show several lines of analysis, so suggesting that there are several structures. In Chapter 7 of Fawcett 2000a I describe the serious problems that this relatively unchallenged assumption of Halliday's brings with it. I then make the crucial point that, if these multiple simultaneous structures are desirable - and I present reasons why they are not - THEY MUST ULTIMATELY BE MAPPED ONTO EACH OTHER IN A SINGLE STRUCTURE. Indeed, Halliday himself makes the same point. So, if you are one of those who are used to thinking in terms of the structural analyses in *IFG*, you will find it easiest to make sense of the structures proposed here if you think of them as representing the final stage in the process of 'generation' - i.e. the stage when the various rows of elements that you find represented in *IFG*-type diagrams are unified into a single structure.

In a functional approach to understanding language, we should ask: What function does *gently* perform here? The answer is that it describes the way in which the Process of 'simmering' is going to be done. So it seems to be an experiential meaning. But it is not a Participant in the 'simmering' (for reasons that will be spelled out in Chapter 10) and so it is not part of TRANSITIVITY.[33]

The function served by the word *gently* is that of giving Adam valuable information about the **Manner** in which Paula plans to cook the leeks and carrots. (Indeed, Paula may incidentally be teaching her young nephew about the meaning of the word *simmer* by using a word that re-enforces its inherent meaning. After all, to 'simmer something' means to 'cook it gently'.)

So the answer to our question is that 'gently' is part of the **experiential** meaning of the clause - even though it is neither a Participant in the Process nor a part of the Process. The meaning of 'Manner' is one of many types of meaning that are expressed at in syntax as an **Adjunct**; it is termed a 'Circumstance of Manner'.

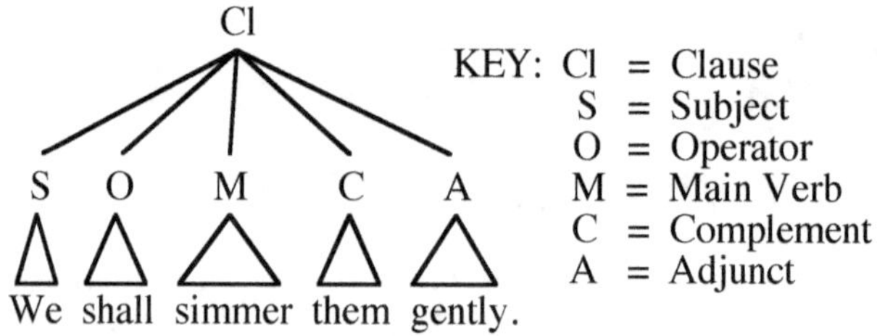

Figure 3-6: The full clause analysis of Example (1)

---

33 **Comparison with the Sydney Grammar** One of Halliday's most valuable contributions to Linguistics has been to extend our view of the concept of 'transitivity' by showing that the terms 'transitive' and 'intransitive' do not only apply to verbs but also to clauses. However, in *IFG* he describes all three of the Process, the Participants and the Circumstances (so 'Manner') as aspects of TRANSITIVITY. In the Cardiff Grammar we limit the scope of the term to just the Processes and their associated Participants. The reason is that, while some Circumstances typically occur with some types of Process, their presence is not PREDICTED by the Process, while the presence of the Participants is. Given that there are around 40 different types of Circumstantial Adjunct in English, there are also practical reasons for treating them separately. Such practical reasons do not always coincide with theoretical reasons, but in this case, luckily, they do.

And, if Paula had wished to specify the POSITION IN TIME at which the event occurs instead, she would have used a different type of Adjunct, such as *now* in *We shall simmer them now.*

The 'Time Position' and the 'Manner' of an event are simply two types of what is termed a 'Circumstance' in SFG - in a very broad sense of this word. Each such **Circumstance** is realized as an Adjunct - and we shall gradually learn more about the range of types of Circ-umstance as we meet more of them in example sentences. Then in Chapter 12 I shall provide an introductory overview of (i) the many functional types of Adjunct; (ii) the places at which they occur in the English clause, and (iii) the meaning of their occurrence at these different 'places'.

3.8 Summary

We have covered a lot of ground in this chapter - even though we have only been examining a single, very simple clause. We have seen that the different elements that make up a clause realize different strands of meaning. The syntax pattern of **S M C** is the expression of choices in the TRANSITIVITY network, which is part of the **experiential** strand of meaning. And, as we have just seen, the Adjunct (**A**) is the expression of a different type of experiential meaning, i.e. a **Circumstance** in the Process of 'someone simmering something' (in an extended sense of the word 'Circumstance'). In contrast, the pattern **S O** expresses the choice of 'information giver' in the system network for MOOD, which is the major network in the **interpersonal** strand meaning.

This is a slightly complex set of concepts, but experience shows that they become clearer through the familiarity of use. Chapter 7 will show them at work in the generation - i.e. the 'production' - of a simple clause, and Chapters 10, 11 and 12 will fill out, respectively, the pictures of (i) TRANSITIVITY (Processes and their inherent Participant Roles), (ii) MOOD (the assignment of communication roles to the Performer and the Addressee), and (iii) Circumstances (and other types of Adjunct).

The goal of the next chapter, however, is to make a start on establishing a reliable set of *Guidelines* for analyzing clauses.

Chapter 4
Developing reliable analysis skills: towards an adequate set of *Guidelines*

4.1 The need for reliable criteria

The time has come to start laying the foundations for efficient clause analysis skills. In Chapter 15 I shall provide a relatively full set of *Guidelines* for analyzing English clauses. By that point we will have established a toolkit of clear criteria for identifying the elements of clauses, each with its associated test. But we need to work our way systematically towards those *Full Guidelines*, and we shall do that in this chapter and the following ones.

4.2 *Preliminary Guidelines 1* (with no tests)

The small set of *Preliminary Guidelines* given below merely gives you the ORDER in which you should look for the elements of clause structure. We shall come to the first of the TESTS shortly - but by a slightly roundabout route.

Note that the order in which to identify elements starts with the Main Verb - and so typically in the MIDDLE of a clause. It is interesting that this is a much better starting point than the starting point that we use when we hear or read a piece of text.

When we are listening to a spoken text we start analyzing it as soon as we have heard the first word - or even the first bit of a word. And when we read a written English sentence we normally start at the left and work through it to the right. However, IN ANALYZING CLAUSES WE DO NOT WORK FROM LEFT TO RIGHT. For a simple clause it pays to START BY LOCATING THE MAIN VERB. (Chapter 10 spells out the reasons why this is the best approach.)

1 Find the Process.	**M**
2 Find the elements that show the MOOD.	**S** and **O** (so far)
3 Find any other Participants.	**C**
4 Find any Adjuncts.	**A**

4.3 A first analysis task

We have come to the time for you to analyze your first couple of clauses in terms of the Cardiff Grammar. This is the first of the 'Analysis Tasks' that you will meet at various points in this book, and the intention is that you should carry out all of them - most being very short - AS AN INTEGRAL PART OF THE PROCESS OF READING THE BOOK. In fact these 'Analysis Tasks' often add important extensions to ideas that have just been introduced - so you will miss some of the key points if you skip them. I suggest that you keep a pencil and paper by you while reading this book, to be ready for these little exercises.

This first 'Analysis Task' is unlike all the rest, in that it asks you to try to analyze two examples with no guidance other than what I have given in the *Preliminary Guidelines* above. But then, immediately afterwards, I shall discuss the vital question of which criteria are the best to use when making such decisions.

So, on the basis of the impressions you have gained so far, I invite you to try to analyze the following two sentences. (You will see shortly why the numbering begins at (2).)

(2) Ivy might visit Fred. (3) Might Ivy visit Fred?

But first read Section 4.4!

4.4 Three tips for drawing syntax diagrams

1 When you write down the clauses to be analyzed, you should LEAVE FOUR OR FIVE LINES OF SPACE ABOVE THE TEXT itself, for the analysis diagram. We would need more for a full analysis, i.e. one that also covered the units that fill the clause elements, and the units that fill their elements - and so on. (For an example of the full analysis of the functional syntax of a complex sentence see Figure 17-1 in Chapter 17.)
2 Save space by writing two or more sentences side by side.
3 It is best to WORK IN PENCIL, with an ERASER ready in case you need to change your analysis.

Now analyze (2) and (3) - and don't turn the page until you have attempted the analysis, or you will see the solutions!

Now please compare your analyses of (2) and (3) with mine, as shown below.

Solutions

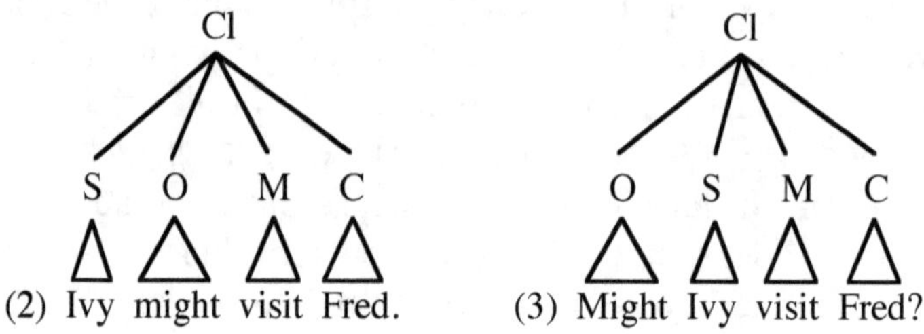

Figure 4-1: The analysis of Examples (2) and (3)

4.5 What were your criteria?

Assuming that your solutions agree with mine, the question is: How did you do it? Let's take (2) first. Since I haven't yet given you any criteria to use, you are quite likely to have analyzed (2) by recognizing its close semantic and syntactic similarities to (1) in the last chapter. I shall assume that you have identified the word *visit* as the **Process**, and so as the **Main Verb (M)**. So the challenge is to identify **S**, **C** and **A** (if any).

It is just possible that you operated purely AT THE LEVEL OF FORM, e.g. reasoning as follows:

> *The first word of (1) in Chapter 1 was **S**, so the first word of (2) is probably **S** too. The second word of (1) was **O**, so the second word of (2) is probably **O** also....* and so on.

But that would not give you any sense of having explained anything. Alternatively, you may have operated AT THE LEVEL OF MEANING, perhaps reasoning along these lines:

> *Although the Process in (2) is different from the Process in (1) in Chapter 1 - i.e. it is 'visiting' rather than 'simmering' - both clauses have two Participants. And in both clauses the FIRST Participant is 'doing the simmering' or 'doing the visiting', while the SECOND Participant is having the 'simmering' or 'visiting' done to it. Therefore the first Participant is **S** and the second is **C**.*

If you analyzed (2) in this way, you will have got the right answer - but by a method that is in fact rather unreliable. Surprising as it may seem, reasoning like this is NOT a good way to identify the Subject. This is because the role of Subject is not part of the clause's **experiential** meaning, but part of its **interpersonal** meaning. (However, as we shall see in Section 4.10, the words that function as the Subject typically also function as a Participant - so they also express an experiential role.)

4.6 Towards a reliable method of analysis

The fact is that the task of identifying the Subject in English is a problem - but it is one that can be solved quite easily, if you apply the principles embodied in the *Mood Test* that we shall shortly meet. It forms the main part - for the moment! - of what will have developed, by Chapter 15, into a full set of *Guidelines* for analyzing simple clauses in English.

4.7 The principles behind the *Mood Test*

The best way to identify the **Subject (S)** in English is by using two of the most frequently used choices in meaning in the system network for MOOD. The two meanings are those of 'information giver' and 'information seeker'. The test in fact identifies the **Operator** as well as the **Subject**, so that it is doubly useful. [34]

---

34 **Comparison with the Sydney Grammar** Most grammar books, including *IFG* and those derived from it, use the terms 'declarative' for our term 'information giver', and 'interrogative' for our term 'information seeker'. Let me give you three reasons for preferring the Cardiff Grammar terms, which are derived directly from the semantic features in the system network for MOOD. (We shall meet the other major types of MOOD in Chapter 11.)

First, for many linguists the terms 'declarative' and 'interrogative' refer to SEQUENCES OF CLAUSE ELEMENTS (e.g. Quirk et al 1985), so that they may describe *So did I* as having 'interrogative syntax'. But since a functional approach should give priority to function over form, we need terms that cannot be interpreted as referring to the level of form. The reason is that there are a number of non-typical but frequent cases of what are clearly, in semantic terms, 'information givers' (e.g. *So can John* and *Seldom have I heard such rubbish,* both of which have the sequence **O S**). Moreover, a very frequent type of 'information seeker' (e.g. *Who would like an ice-cream?*) has the sequence **S O**.

(For this structure see Section 11.2 of Chapter 11.) And the initially attractive idea that there might be a one-to-one relationship between form and meaning in this area of meaning is further clouded when we extend the MOOD network to include meanings such as 'confirmation seeker' and 'request', as we shall in Sections 11.2 and 11.3 of Chapter 11.

The second reason for using the terms 'information seeker' and 'information giver' is that they express in straightforward language the meanings that we wish to convey. Each of these two terms is composed of two of the **semantic features** that occur in the **system network** for MOOD, i.e. the specification of the meanings available in English in this area of the semantics. Yet the terms 'declarative' and 'interrogative', together with 'indicative' and 'imperative', are still regularly found in the system networks shown in most systemic functional grammars. This implies that there has been no change in their status in Halliday's grammar since the early 1960s, i.e. since the period BEFORE Halliday suggested that the system networks should be regarded as choices between meanings. As will be clear, my view is that the MOOD network in the Sydney Grammar needs to be 'semanticized' (as it was long ago in the Cardiff Grammar, in Fawcett 1980 and with substantial extensions in the computer version of the grammar and in later publications) in a manner that is parallel with Halliday's semanticization, initially in Halliday 1967a, 1967b and 1968, of his earlier form-based system networks for TRANSITIVITY.

This brings us to the third reason for using the terms 'information giver' and 'information seeker'. You might ask: Why not use instead the even simpler terms 'statement' and 'question' for the semantic equivalents of 'declarative' and 'interrogative'? The reason why we do not use these terms here is that they are often used as names for the classes of **act** in the structure of **discourse** - and THE ANALYSIS OF A TEXT IN TERMS OF ITS DISCOURSE STRUCTURE IS A DIFFERENT LEVEL OF ANALYSIS FROM THE LEVEL THAT WE ARE CONSIDERING HERE. So the third reason for preferring the terms used here is that they make it clear that we are NOT equating the concept of (i) 'interpersonal meaning of a clause' with either (iia) 'act in discourse' (e.g. in the sense of Sinclair and Coulthard 1975) or (iib) 'speech act' (in the sense of Austin 1962 or Searle 1969) - the latter two being essentially two different viewpoints on the same phenomenon.

In the Cardiff Grammar's approach to this area of the grammar, then, there are THREE relevant levels of representation for a sentence that need to be taken into account: (i) the **discourse act** (which is outside the lexicogrammar), (ii) the **semantics** of MOOD and (iii) the **syntax** of MOOD. The last two, of course, are parts of the two levels of the lexicogrammar, as described in Chapter 2. (Martin 1992, however, treats the concept of a 'discourse act' as part of the semantics, i.e. his 'discourse semantics'. But in my view we need to keep separate the concepts of 'semantics' as a level within the lexicogrammar, and 'discourse structure', which is a different and higher type of structure - as described in Fawcett et al 1988.)

Consider again Examples (2) and (3):

(2) Ivy might visit Fred. with the structure **S O**
(3) Might Ivy visit Fred? with the structure **O S**

These show us that, typically:

S O means 'information giver', and
O S means 'information seeker'.

Note too that:

In any one clause there can be only ONE Subject and only ONE Operator.

In practice, the problems are likely to arise in identifying the Subject. It is nearly always easy to identify the Operator - if there is one. (At this early stage we shall only consider examples that do have an Operator, and we shall deal with the problem of what to do when there isn't one later - in Chapter 9.)

The first step is therefore to identify the **Operator (O)**. It is usually fairly easy to recognize it, since the words that **expound** it can be grouped into a small number of easily remembered pairs of words. We shall meet these in later chapters, but for now we will only use Operators of the type found in the previous examples, i.e. ones like *shall* and *might*. These are called 'modal verbs' and there is a helpful 'starter' list in the following *Guidelines*.

We come now to the first of two 'preliminary' versions of the *Guidelines*; the 'full' *Guidelines* will come in Chapter 15.

4.8 *Preliminary Guidelines 1*

0 **Preparation**: if the clause to be analyzed does NOT have the structure of an **information giver**, first re-express it as one.[35]

35 We shall be meeting other useful tests in the chapters between here and Chapter 15, and almost all of them require you first to re-express the clause that is to be analyzed as an 'information giver' - if it isn't one already. The reason is that this makes the tests easier to apply and more reliable.

Example
Re-express *Will Fiona see him?* as *Fiona will see him.*

(Of course, if the clause to be analyzed already has the structure of an 'information giver', such as *Fiona will see him*, there is no need to re-express it.)

1 Find the **Process** and so the **Main Verb**. (No tests yet.)

2 ***The Mood Test***

2.1 **Find the Operator.** The Operator is either (i) a 'modal verb' (i.e. one of *may, might, shall, should, will, would, can, could* and *must*) or (ii) one of a small number of other verbs which we shall meet shortly.

2.2 Re-express the **information giver** as an **information seeker**. (There are several types of 'information seeker', and the type we need is the one that seeks the answer *Yes* or *No.* There is more about the different types of 'information seeker' in the next section.)

Example
Re-express *Fiona will see him* as *Will Fiona see him?*

2.3 Now you are in a position to identify the **Subject (S)**.

The Subject is the word (or words) which, by occurring before or after the Operator, tells you whether the clause is an 'information giver' or an 'information seeker'.

Example
We know that the word *will* is the Operator, so *Fiona* must be the Subject - because, by occurring after *will*, it shows that the MOOD of the clause is 'information seeker'.

So in *Will Fiona see him?*, *will* is **O** and *Fiona* is **S**.

Note that this test corroborates your analysis of *will* as **O**.

In other words, **in this test** (but NOT in every case):

> **S O** means **'information giver'**, and
> **O S** means **'information seeker'**.

3 **S** is a Participant.
Now find any other Participant, and label it **C**. (No tests yet.)

4 Find any Adjuncts and label them **A**. (No tests yet.)

You will be invited to use these *Guidelines* when analyzing clauses in future chapters, so you might like to put a slip of paper (or a 'post-it') to mark the page, so you can find it quickly - until we replace these *Guidelines* by more complete ones, first in Chapter 9 and then by the *Full Guidelines* in Chapter 15.

4.9 'Information seekers' and 'polarity seekers'

In the introductory version of the test used above, I have used the term 'information seeker', in order to bring out directly the contrast with 'information giver'. But we need to recognize that there are in fact several different types of 'information seeker' - and we must therefore be clear as to which type is needed for the *Mood Test*. The type needed is the **polarity seeker**. This is the type of 'information seeker' that seeks the answer *Yes* or *No*. (We shall meet the other main types in Chapter 11.)

Why does a 'polarity seeker' have this name? The first part of the answer must be to clarify the meanings expressed by *Yes* and *No*. These are:

Yes = 'If I said this clause in full it would be **positive**.'
No = 'If I said this clause in full it would be **negative**.'

In other words, a 'polarity seeker' asks the Addressee to choose between the two 'poles' of 'positive' and 'negative' (rather as a magnetized iron bar has a **positive** pole and a **negative** pole). So, when your purpose is to get the Addressee to answer *Yes* or *No*, you typically use a 'polarity seeker'. This is why an informal name for a 'polarity seeker' is a 'Yes-No question'.

4.10 Summary so far

For a summary of the main concepts introduced so far, please look at Figure 4-2. It shows how the structures for the MOOD and TRANSITIVITY of (3) combine to form one integrated structure.

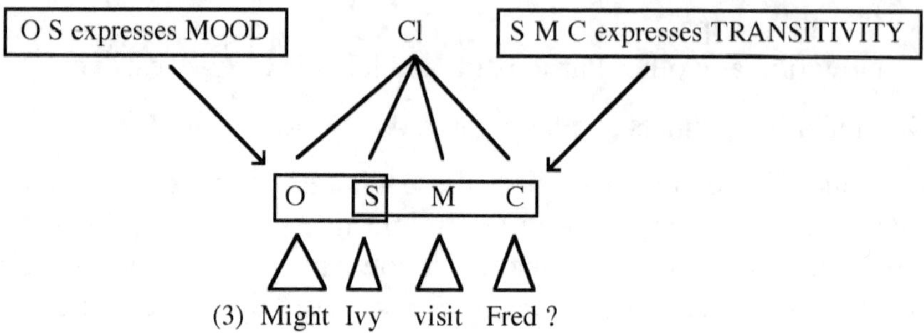

Figure 4-2:
The TRANSITIVITY and MOOD structures of Example (3)

As you can see, the **interpersonal** meaning of 'polarity seeker' is realized through the two elements of **O** and **S** that express the choice of MOOD, and the **experiential** meaning of 'Ivy visiting Fred' is realized through the three elements of **S**, **M** and **C** that express the choices in TRANSITIVITY.

Later, in Section 8.5 of Chapter 8, we shall see that the Subject also typically expresses a third strand of meaning, i.e. a **thematic** meaning.[36]

---

36 **Comparison with the Sydney Grammar** The approach to the concept of the 'Subject' in English that is presented here is essentially the same as that found in Halliday's earlier writings, and so also in the standard introductions to SFG of the 1970s such as Berry (1975: 77). However, two of the innovations that Halliday introduces in *IFG* are to suggest that there is both (i) a different TEST and (ii) a different MEANING for the Subject from the ones he originally used. In other words, I find Halliday's earlier account of the function of the Subject in English more specific and more useful than his later account. Let me explain why. We shall look first at the test for the Subject and then at the problem of characterizing its meaning. As Halliday points out (1994: 73), it is important to distinguish between these two.

On **the test for the Subject in English**, Halliday writes (1994: 73) that 'the Subject ... is that element which is picked up by a pronoun in the tag'. For example, in *Fred will visit Ivy*, the addition of a tag would give us *Fred will visit Ivy, won't he?* In Halliday's test, the acceptability of adding *won't he* shows that Fred is the Subject. (Note that, while it works in Standard English, it wouldn't work in dialects in which a fixed-form tag such as Welsh English *is it* or 'streetwise' young English *innit* is used.) The result of using Halliday's test is the same as ours, as described in the main text - but it has two possible disadvantages (e.g. when being used by those who are not native speakers of Standard English).

The first disadvantage is that the test only identifies the **S** through a secondary connection, i.e. by matching the original **S** with the **S** IN ANOTHER CLAUSE. This is the clause *won't he*, which in the present model is, as Appendix 1 shows, a 'truncated' clause that is embedded at **A** and has only the two elements of **O** and **S**. Thus Halliday's 'tag test' depends on (i) the analyst's ability to use such 'tags' (which is quite an advanced skill for learners of English) - and so in turn (ii) on the ability to recognize intuitively that the referent of the **S** in the tag is the same as the referent of the **S** in the main clause. The test used here is more direct, in that it uses CRITERIA THAT ARE STATED IN TERMS OF THE MAIN CLAUSE ONLY. Thus it has the advantage of using a more central part of the grammar, i.e. the core of the MOOD system.

The second disadvantage of Halliday's test is that there are certain types of clause which do not accept a tag. Examples are (i) 'information seekers' such as *Will you be there?* and *Where do you live?*, and (ii) 'proposals for action' such as *Could you turn the volume down, please?* and *Shall I open the window?* Such examples would therefore need to be turned into 'information givers' before the test can be applied. (Halliday could, of course, provide for such cases by requiring that clauses be turned into 'information givers' before applying his test, but he doesn't specify that this should be done, so his test currently doesn't work in such cases.)

We shall now turn to **the meaning of the Subject in English**. In *IFG* Halliday offers us several attempts to characterize this (possibly in an attempt to find a 'meaning of the Subject' that can be generalized beyond English and the small number of similar languages). However, there are several problems with the descriptions that he provides. One is that he fails to find a wording that would cover all types of MOOD. Another is that none of the various wordings proposed provide for the various types of clause that have an 'experientially empty' Subject. Let us consider Halliday's three attempts to characterize the meaning of the Subject.

Two of these suffer from the failing that they are only applicable to clauses that have 'propositional content', i.e. (i) 'something by reference to which something can be affirmed or denied', and (ii) 'the one on which the validity of the information is made to rest' (Halliday 1994: 76). Interestingly, these two descriptions correspond quite closely to two of the definitions of the Subject in the English grammar books of the 16th and 17th centuries (as recorded in the *Oxford English Dictionary* 1971: 3120), i.e. (i) the 'part of a proposition of which the predicate is affirmed or denied', and, a little less closely, (ii) 'the thing about which a judgement is made'. As we shall see, the fact that his characterizations of the meaning of 'the Subject' are so similar to these early definitions are consistent with the solution to the problem of the meaning of 'the Subject' that I shall suggest shortly.

Halliday's third description of the meaning of the Subject is very different, and seems designed to meet the need to include the Subject (which is covert but recoverable) of a 'proposal for action' such as *Read it!* This third description is 'the one .... who is responsible for the functioning of the clause AS AN INTERACTIVE EVENT [my emphasis]'. (Interestingly, it is this one that is the source of the most commonly used 'reduced definition' of the Subject in many of the writings by systemicists that reflect the influence of *IFG,* where the Subject is referred to as the 'modally responsible' element.) But this description, like the others, uses a metaphor, in that it implies that the referent of the Subject of a clause is 'responsible', when (i) only an animate being can be 'responsible', and (ii) many Subjects are inanimate. So this description of the Subject is like the other two in that it fails to provide us with a characterization of the Subject that applies in all cases.

To generalise across the first two of Halliday's glosses for the 'meaning of the Subject' (since no one has yet found words that can generalize across all three), we may say that his descriptions, like those of the early English grammarians, relate essentially to the ORIGINAL meaning of 'Subject', i.e. 'subject' in its everyday sense of 'what is being talking about'. And the problem that recognizing this creates for Halliday's claim is this: while his intention is to define the meaning of the Subject as an element in terms of the meanings associated with the **interpersonal** strand of meaning, he has ended up with A DESCRIPTION THAT IT IS BROADLY THE SAME AS A DESCRIPTION THAT HE USES FOR AN ELEMENT IN THE **thematic** STRAND OF MEANING (a strand within the **textual** metafunction, in Halliday's terms). This is the meaning of the type of Theme which is 'that with which the clause is concerned' Halliday (1985: 37). This is Halliday's concept of 'topical Theme' - i.e. an element that occurs in the 'theme' strand of the 'textual' metafunction in his model. So the concept of 'that with which the clause is concerned' is said to be a 'textual' meaning, while the very similar concept of 'the one on which the validity of the information is made to rest' is said to be an element in the 'interpersonal' metafunction. The problem for his model, then, is that he is using rather similar descriptions for what he presents as two different clause elements, each of which is supposed to belong to a different metafunction - and so to a different strand of meaning. The fact that they are typically conflated with each other - though not inevitably, as Halliday emphasizes - makes it all the more important that they should be clearly seen as serving a different function in the first place.

The solution to this conundrum is clear. It is to recognize (i) that what Halliday is describing here is not in fact an element of the 'interpersonal structure' of the clause, but one of several types of Theme (the 'Subject Theme', in Cardiff Grammar terms), and (ii) that Halliday's earlier characterization of the interpersonal meaning of the Subject was the more helpful one. This is the concept that, while the Subject does not express an interpersonal meaning ON ITS OWN, it does contribute directly to an interpersonal meaning through its role as a PART of the 'mood block' (**O S** or **S O**, etc), i.e. the part of the clause that tells us the MOOD type of the clause.

A further virtue of this explanation is that it covers Subjects that have no referent, such as (i) *it* in *It's raining*, and (ii) *it* in *It's nice to see you* (where *to see you* is the Carrier and *nice* is the Attribute, so that the analysis is *It* [S] *'s* [O/M] *nice* [C] *to see you* [C].) It also covers (iii) *It's a beer that I need,* and other such constructions, for which see Fawcett 2009). None of Halliday's three descriptions of the Subject makes sense when the Subject has no referent.

To summarize. The reason why Halliday's attempts to characterize the meaning of the Subject in *IFG* are a problem for his position is that, in his model of language, 'interpersonal meaning' is supposed to belong in one metafunction and 'thematic' meaning in another. Yet the conclusion to which the present discussion points is (i) that Halliday's original characterization of the meaning of Subject in English (as retained here) was more insightful than his later one, and (ii) that we need to recognize that there is A TYPE OF THEME THAT IS REALIZED THROUGH PRESENTING A PR AS THE SUBJECT - which is here called the 'Subject Theme'. (For this system, see Section 8.5 of Chapter 8.) It is this functional role, I suggest, that has an equivalent (or near-equivalent) in most of the languages of the world - and NOT the contribution to the meaning of the clause that the Subject makes in English (and just a few other languages).

For the reasons set out above, then, I offer both (i) the characterization of the meaning of 'Subject' in English and (ii) the *Mood Test* for identifying the Subject set out here as clearer, more insightful, and easier to work with than those in *IFG*. (See Fawcett 1999 for a fuller exposition of the argument.)

Chapter 5
A minimal theory of syntax: keeping things simple

5.1 The text analyst's problem

First, cover Figure 5-1 below, so that you can't look at its structure yet!

The main problem for the syntax analyst who is analyzing the sentences of a natural text is usually this: Which words go with which to form a **unit** WITHIN the clause? We have avoided this problem so far, because I have been careful to choose examples in which there is ONLY ONE WORD for each **element** of the clause. If you wanted to analyze an example in which this was not the case, it would take a little more work. Consider the case of (1), and ask yourself: Which words belong with which other words?

(1) That nice lady will cook those delicious vegetables very carefully indeed.

If you are feeling confident, you might like to try analyzing this longer sentence BEFORE *looking at Figure 5-1 below. You should make use of the* ***Guidelines*** *in the last chapter to help you.*

Solution

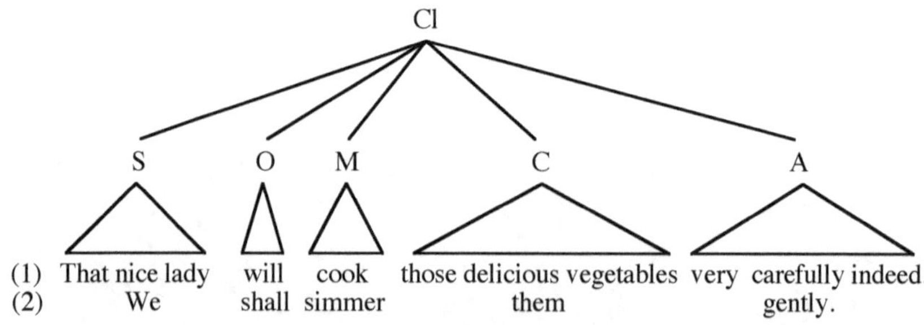

Figure 5-1: An analysis with several words at S, C and A

As Figure 5-1 shows, the clause structures of (1) and (2) - which was (1) in Chapter 3 - are identical. This nicely illustrates the point that, for every example given so far, we could have used SEVERAL WORDS for at least some of the elements that occur in it, and it would still have had exactly the same clause structure.

In order to be able to analyze sentences such as (1) confidently, there is a small set of concepts that we need to be clear about, and these form what the title of this chapter calls - rather grandly - 'a minimal theory of syntax'.[37]

5.2 A minimal theory of syntax: four categories

A theory of syntax must contain, in terms of the model of language shown in Figure 2-3 of Chapter 2, both (i) a theory of 'syntax potential' and (ii) a theory of the 'instances of syntax' that are the output from the lexicogrammar. It is this second part of the theory of syntax that we are concerned with here.[38]

The 'minimal theory of syntax' to be presented here is a framework of eight simple concepts. These are the GENERAL concepts that are essential for building a description of the syntax of a SPECIFIC language, such as English. The eight concepts can be divided into four basic **categories** and four basic **relationships**.

The four categories are **unit**, **place**, **element** and **item**. The best way to explain these concepts is through an example. Consider the tree diagram in Figure 5-2.

Since our topic in this book is the clause and its structure, we shall start at the top of the diagram. (Notice, however, that when you are working on the task of analyzing a string of words from a natural text, you are obliged to start at the bottom - since what you are presented with is a string of words.)

---

37 This 'minimal theory of syntax' is a summary of the most basic concepts in the theory of syntax that is described in my *A Theory of Syntax for Systemic Functional Linguistics* (Fawcett 2000a). It is a modified version of the theory set out in Halliday 1961.

38 The theory of 'syntax potential' is the body of theory that defines the nature of the realization rules of the lexicogrammar in Figure 2-3. See Fawcett, Tucker and Lin 1993 for these, and Chapter 7 for examples of such rules.

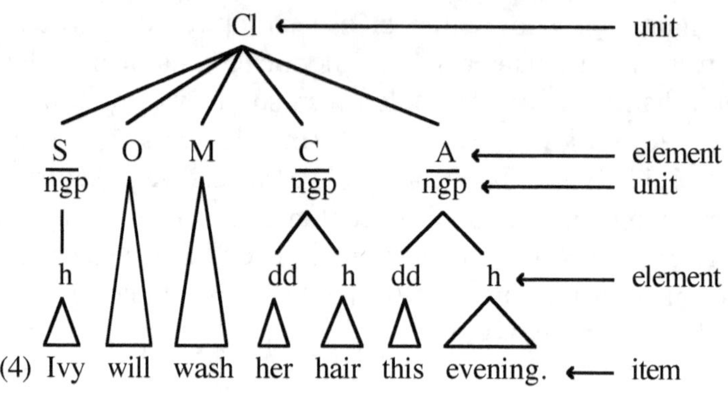

Figure 5-2: The basic categories of syntax

At the top of the tree diagram is the **unit** of the clause, and it has, in this instance, five **elements**. The names of these five elements and their short forms (as used here) will by now be familiar to you. But we should remind ourselves that these specific elements - and also their definitions - are concepts in the **description of English**, and not categories in a **general theory of syntax**. But the concepts of 'unit' and 'element' ARE categories in the general theory.

The third category shown in Figure 5-2 is the **item**. The easiest way to think of an 'item' is as a **word**. In most cases, the items at the foot of a tree diagram - i.e. the 'leaves', in this upside-down picture of a tree - are 'words', in the everyday sense of the term. But sometimes an item may consist of MORE than one written word (e.g. *in spite of*) and sometimes it is LESS than one whole word (e.g. the suffix *n't* or the form *'s*). The identifying characteristic of an item is that IT CAN BE SPOKEN OR WRITTEN. You can't speak or write a clause or a Subject; it is only when you know the 'shape' - as a spoken or written string of items - the clause or Subject takes that you can speak or write it. Compared with **items**, then, the categories of a **unit** and its **elements** are relatively abstract.

Notice that Figure 5-2 shows TWO layers of **units** and so also TWO layers of **elements**. I have kept things simple by showing just one class of unit in the lower layer of units. In each case it is a **nominal group (ngp)** - but this too (like the clause and its elements) is a concept that is part of the description of English rather than a general theory of language. (See Appendix 1 for (i) the full range of units that are available in English; (ii) the range of elements that each class of unit may fill; and (iii) the probability that the unit will fill each element in that range.)

I said at the start of this section that there are four categories, but Figure 5-2 shows only the three mentioned so far. The fourth is the row of numbered **places** in a unit at which the elements are located. We have seen that what makes the crucial difference between an 'information giver' and a 'polarity seeker' is the fact that the Operator is positioned at a **place** before or after the Subject - and the concept of the 'places in a unit' at which its **elements** are located provides a simple way to model this variation in the Operator's position. As this book will show, there is a great deal of variation in the places in the clause at which elements occur (especially the Adjuncts, as described in Chapter 12), and it is the concept of 'place' that enables us to model this. But in the task of ANALYZING text-sentences - in contrast with GENERATING them - it is unnecessary to identify the places as well as the elements, so we simplify our diagrams by leaving them out.

5.3 A minimal theory of syntax: four relationships

Three of the four relationships to be considered here follow directly from the recognition of the three categories in Figure 5-2. Consider Figure 5-3. Here I have expressed these relationships by using verbs, because this is the way of referring to the relationships that we shall use most often in the rest of this book.

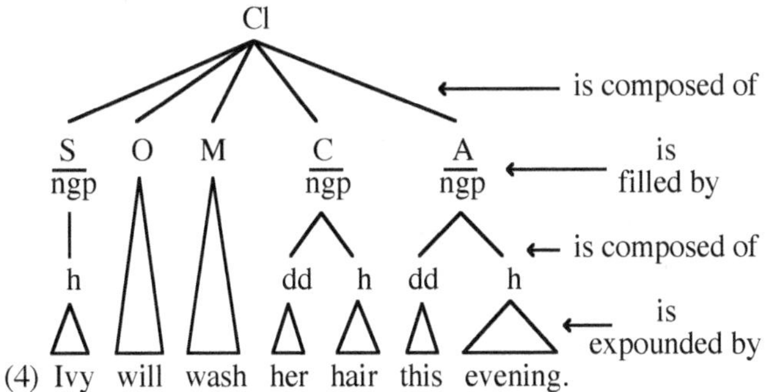

Figure 5-3: The basic relationships of syntax

We can now put these three relationships together with the three categories in Figure 5-2 in the following summarizing statement:

(i) a **unit** is **composed** of one or more **elements**;
(ii) some **elements** are directly **expounded** by **items**;
(iii) other **elements** are **filled** by a **unit** (or co-ordinated **units**);
(iv) any such **unit** is itself **composed** of one or more **elements**;
(v) and so on, up to a maximum depth of around seven units (plus or minus two) until finally -
(vi) the lowest **element** is **expounded** by an **item**.

The fourth type of relationship is between two elements of structure, and the verbal expression for it is '**is conflated with**'. It will be introduced and illustrated in the next chapter.

And that concludes our brief foray into the theory of syntax. Certain other concepts are required in the full picture of a theory of syntax for SFL, as set out in Fawcett 2000a, but those described here are the key concepts for understanding syntax.

These concepts may well seem rather abstract, especially if you are meeting them here for the first time. But they will become familiar through use as the book progresses, and by the end of it they will be old friends. And, if at any point you feel the need, you can come back to this chapter for a quick refresher course![39]

To round off this summary of a 'minimal theory of syntax', let's go back to Figure 5-1 for a moment. As will now be clear, each of *that nice lady*, *those delicious vegetables* and *very carefully indeed* is an example of a **unit** of English syntax - just as the **clause** whose **elements** they **fill** is a unit of English syntax. And each of these lower **units** in the tree has its own **elements**. And the same is true of the units of *Ivy*, *her hair* and *this evening* in Figures 5-2 and 5-3.

In Appendix 1, you will find a full summary of the structures of the two lower units used here - i.e. the nominal groups in Figures 5-1 to 5-3 and the quality group that is used (but left unanalyzed) in *gently* and *very carefully indeed* in Figure 5-1 - and also all the other major units of English syntax.

---

39 The technical names for the four relationships introduced here are **componence**, **filling**, **exponence** and **conflation** - but it is the corresponding verbs that we usually use when talking about these relationships.

5.4 Keeping things simple

In the rest of the present book, however, we shall continue to make the task of analyzing clauses easier in these two ways:

(i) we shall normally use a unit with just one element - and so a single word - as the exponent of the clause elements, and
(ii) on those occasions when a clause element consists of more than one word, we shall include the words under one broad triangle (symbolizing 'this element is **expounded** by the item or items below') - exactly as in Figure 5-1.

However, this still leaves the problem of how to answer the question 'Which words go with which to form a unit within the clause?' For example, how do you decide whether *those* in (1) should (i) stand on its own (as it could in *She will cook those*), (ii) be put together with *delicious*, (iii) be put with *delicious vegetables* - or even (iv) be put with *cook*?

That is precisely what this book is about. It shows you how - and why - to analyze a clause in terms of the words and groups of words of which the clause elements consist. The full answer to these questions lies in discovering THE FUNCTIONS SERVED BY EACH OF THESE WORDS IN THE UNIT OF WHICH THEY ARE ELEMENTS, i.e. a clause or class of group. For this you really need *The Functional Syntax Handbook*, because it shows you how to analyze groups and clusters as well as clauses.[40] In the present book, however, we are focussing on the structure of the clause. So this question arises: Will the *Guidelines* for analyzing clauses that will be introduced at various points in the book work, IF WE DON'T ALSO HAVE *Guidelines* FOR ANALYZING THE GROUPS THAT THE CLAUSE CONTAINS? The answer is that they will - and the full, integrated set of *Guidelines* will be presented in Chapter 15.

We come now to the generalization that is the second most valuable of all to the text analyst - after the basic principle stated at the start of Chapter 3, i.e. that **there is one Main Verb per clause**.

---

40 However, you can get a good idea of what the analysis of the groups (and one cluster) involves by consulting the diagrams in Appendix 1.

5.5 Which elements of the clause can be filled by units?

The extra challenge to the analyst that the eleven words of (1) introduces over the five words of (2) raises an important question. It is this:

How many elements of the clause can be expounded by groups of words in this way?

Before answering, I should point out that most of the next few chapters will introduce elements of the clause other than those introduced so far. You can check Chapter 15 or the 'clause' page of Appendix 1 for the full list; altogether, there are fifteen that are expounded by words. So, if the answer to the question were to be that ALL of them can be expounded by groups of words, this would make the work of analyzing clauses significantly more difficult.

Luckily, the answer is:

Only Subjects, Complements and Adjuncts can be filled by units. (99% reliable)

So the good news for the text analyst is that there is no possibility at all of having more than one word for either the Operator or the Main Verb - and very little possibility indeed for any of the other types of clause element that we shall meet.

There is in fact one other clause element that is regularly filled by a unit (a nominal group). This is the 'fringe' element of the Vocative, which we shall meet in Chapter 14. And in Section 13.2 of Chapter 13 and Section 14.3 of Chapter 14 we will meet two other clause elements that are occasionally filled by a unit, rather than being directly expounded by an item.

However, I must now point out that it is one of the most important facts about English that there is enormous scope for complexity within each of **S**, **C** and **A**. The various diagrams in Appendix 1 summarize the ways by which the English language supplements the structure of a single clause, in order to attain this great complexity, and most of the units described in Appendix 1 can fill most cases of **S**, **C** and **A**.

It may sound as if there is a lot to learn about the structure of English. It is true that there is quite a lot - but it is not too much for the average human mind to grasp quite easily. As Appendix 1 demonstrates, the essential relationships of English syntax can be summarized on JUST THREE PAGES. Surprisingly, perhaps, we shall find that this relatively SMALL SET OF DESCRIPTIVE CATEGORIES enables us to understand almost all of the potentially VERY GREAT COMPLEXITY found in the structure of English sentences.[41]

5.6 Replacing the metaphor of 'words as beads on a string'

In Section 3.2 of Chapter 3 we met the amazing concept that the string of words that make up a clause is **multifunctional** - i.e. that a string of words can simultaneously express several different strands of meaning - sometimes, as we have seen, in one element.

Now we are in a position to refine that statement. I said in Section 3.2 that the metaphor which invites us to view the line of words on the page as being like a string of beads is misleading - but I didn't say why.

Now we can see why. As Figures 5-1, 5-2 and 5-3 clearly show, it is NOT the case that a clause consists of a string of **words**. Instead, a clause consists of a string of **elements** - and, while some of these are directly expounded by an **item**, others such as **S**, **C** and **A** typically contain another **unit**, each with its own elements (and so possibly further units with their elements, and so on).

In other words, the representation of the functional syntax of a clause requires the TWO DIMENSIONS that we have at our disposal on a piece of paper or a computer screen. The metaphor to which this set of relationships leads is that of a tree, so that the diagrams that are used to represent these relationships are called, by general agreement, **tree diagrams**.[42]

---

41 Our experience in teaching Linguistics at Cardiff University is that students can learn to analyze quite complex text-sentences in a ten-week course. See the fuller discussion in Section 1.10 of Chapter 1.

42 It is a little odd that we use the term 'tree diagram' for the diagrams that linguists draw to represent the structure of sentences - because the 'trees' in such diagrams are usually depicted as growing upside down, with their 'root' in the air and their 'leaves' at the bottom of the diagram. But the term is so well-established that it is now far too late to change it. For a further comment on tree diagrams, see Section 11.2 of Chapter 11.

The focus in this book is squarely on the elements of the English clause, so that we shall hardly ever require the ability to show units within units that a tree diagram gives us. That is a set of relationships which is covered fully in *The Functional Syntax Handbook.* But in Figure 17-1 in Chapter 17 you can see an example of the analysis of a complex clause in terms of the description of English syntax given in the Cardiff Grammar, and it includes structural relationships that would be virtually impossible to analyze without the use of a tree diagram.

In Section 3.2 of Chapter 3 I introduced **the multifunctional principle**, which was:

Each clause serves several different functions at the same time.

Now we can supplement this in a way that covers the full syntactic structure of a complex sentence by saying:

a single TWO-DIMENSIONAL tree diagram
can express all the necessary information from
a MULTI-DIMENSIONAL array of types of meaning
- often simultaneously in the same element.

If you want to see an example of this at work, look now at Figure 17-2 in Chapter 17. Alternatively, you could decide to wait till you reach that chapter in the book, because the analysis in terms of semantic features given there will be easier to understand if you have read the intervening chapters.

5.7 Summary: theory and practice in the clause

In this section we have stepped aside from the work of analyzing text-sentences in order to clarify the small set of basic concepts that we are using in this task. And to get the full picture, we have gone for a moment outside the syntax of the clause itself - e.g. in our analyses of (4) in Figures 5-2 and 5-3.

But the essential foundation to building a good understanding of the rich complexity of English syntax is to have a clear picture of the structure of the **clause**. And, because we need to focus our attention on the clause itself rather than the units that may fill its elements, I shall continue the practice of using single words for what may occur at each **S**, **C** and **A** for the rest of this book.

You might think that this would seriously distort the examples, but it will not. This is because around 60 per cent of the units that fill **S**, **C** or **A** (depending on the type of text) consist of JUST ONE ELEMENT. Almost all of these could be expanded to a structure with two or more elements, if we wished to, as was done in Figure 5-1 - but the fact is that we normally operate with a fairly high percentage of one-word groups.[43]

In this section we have been considering the complexity that there may be INSIDE the elements of the clause in English, and the 'minimal theory of syntax' that is required in order to enable us to

---

43 **Comparison with the Sydney Grammar** While the theory of syntax presented here clearly has its origin in the 'theory of grammar' presented in Halliday 1961, there are a number of important differences. I have described these in full in Fawcett 2000a, and here I shall make just three points.

First, Halliday uses the term 'unit' in the sense of 'unit on the rank scale', so that for Halliday a 'nominal group' and a 'verbal group' are two **classes** of the same **unit**. In the Cardiff Grammar the term 'unit' is used in the sense of 'class of unit'. Thus the main units of English are the clause, nominal group, prepositional group, quality group and quantity group - as described in Appendix 1 - with no accompanying statement about their place on the 'rank scale'. (We shall return to this matter in a moment.)

The second major difference is in the criteria for recognizing a unit (or 'class of unit'). For Halliday the criterion is the function of the unit in the structure of the unit above it, so that in *Her boyfriend is very tall* both *her boyfriend* and *very tall* are said to be 'nominal groups', because this is considered to be the class of unit that fills a Subject and Complement. In the Cardiff Grammar (as for many systemicists, it should be said) the criterion for recognizing a unit is the set of meanings that the unit is designed to express, and so the elements of structure that realize those meanings. On these criteria, *her boyfriend* in the above example is a **nominal group**, whereas *very tall* is a **quality group**. The reason is that the types of meaning that get realized in each class of unit are different - one of those associated with 'qualities' (such as 'tall') being the 'tempering' of the quality by *very* or *fairly*.

The third major difference is that the expectation that any given element of a clause will be filled by a specific (class of) unit is treated as a PROBABILISTIC matter. So the unrealistically strict predictions of the 'rank scale' hypothesis are set on one side, and the fact - as I take it to be - that units are embedded within other units at many points in any reasonably complex sentence is embraced as part of the richness of language. So 'filling probabilities' replace the 'rank scale' claim that elements of clauses 'should' be filled by groups and elements of groups by words. For further and fuller sets of reasons for preferring the model of syntax used here, see Fawcett 2000a.

provide a principled description of it. We are now ready to return to THE STRUCTURE OF THE CLAUSE ITSELF.

In the next chapter we shall consider a syntactic phenomenon that is the only case of its kind in English - and yet at the same time it is very frequent indeed.

Chapter 6
The special case of 'being' as a Main Verb - and some related concepts

6.1 A unique type of Main Verb

I suggest that you cover the solution below at this point, so that you don't see it before you attempt the analysis.

In this chapter we shall consider the case of the most frequent verb in English, together with its unique behaviour. This will require us to recognize a new concept in clause structure that is frequently required when a form of the verb *be* - i.e. *am, are, is, was* or *were* - is used as a **Main Verb (M)**. (We shall meet other uses of forms of *be* in Chapters 8, 14 and 16.) Since the verb that occurs most frequently at **M** is a form of *be*, it is important to deal with this special case early on.

Example (1), which occurs as a response to the question *Who are those people?*, shows a typical use of a form of the verb *be*:

(1) They are reporters.

Try to analyze (1), using Preliminary Guidelines 1 (as set out in Section 4.8 of Chapter 4) to help you. You will find that there is a small problem, but it will be a useful discovery.

Solution

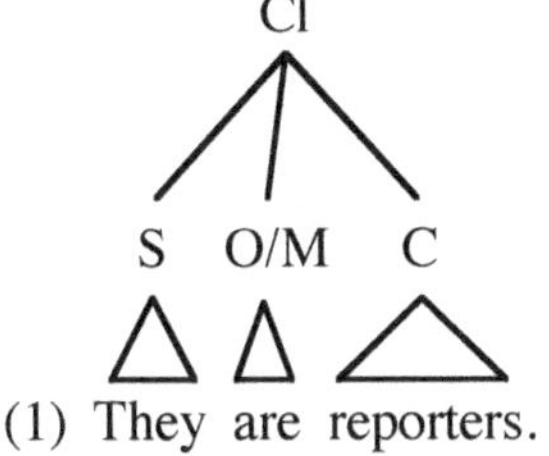

Figure 6-1: The conflation of the Operator and the Main Verb

The 'small problem' arises because the word *are* functions in this clause as both **O** and **M**. It is clearly the Main Verb, and the *Mood Test* shows that it is also the Operator. Specifically, it changes *They are reporters* into *Are they reporters?* - and in doing so it demonstrates that the word *are* is indeed the **O** as well as the **M**. The 'small problem' is that of how to represent the fact that *are* is functioning as both a Main Verb and an Operator - and Figure 6-1 shows you how it is done.

There are three important new points to note:

1 In (1), MOOD is realized by **S O** and TRANSITIVITY is realized by **S M C** - just as it was with *We shall simmer them gently.* But in this case **O** and **M** have been 'fused' together in the word *are*, so that they function as one element. The technical term for this 'fusion' in SFL is to say that the two elements have been **conflated**. We shall find that this concept of 'conflation' is needed at several places in this type of grammar. In the present example - as is often the case - the two elements that are conflated represent meanings from two different strands of meaning. Specifically, the **M** is the pivotal element in the TRANSITIVITY structure of the clause, and the **O** is one of the two key elements in its MOOD structure.

2 In most modern dialects of English, the ONLY verb which (i) occurs at **M** and (ii) can be conflated with **O** is a form of the verb *be*. It is this conflation of **O** and **M** that makes the verb *be* unique.[44] The full set of forms that can function as **O/M** is as follows:

am, are, is, was, were

3 It is important to emphasize that not all cases of *am*, *are*, *is*, *was* and *were* should be analyzed as **O/M**. We shall meet the two most frequent other uses of these forms in Chapter 8, and then a third in Step 7 of the *Guidelines* in Chapter 15.

---

44 Some older people in Britain still say *Have you a pen?* - so for them forms of *have* can still be **O/M**. But most native speakers of English people use one or other of the following two forms: *Have you got a pen?* or, with increasing frequency, *Do you have a pen?*

We shall now turn to the other 'related concepts' of this chapter's title. The first concerns the concept of the **referent** of a Subject or Complement.

6.2 The concepts of 'referent' and 'Participant'

In cases such as *They are reporters*, it is not as easy as it was with earlier examples to answer the question: 'What are the Participants in this Process?' You might be tempted to think like this:

> *'They' and' reporters' refer to the same object (in a broad sense of 'object'), and so they are the same Participant.*

But in fact each **Participant** in (1) has a different **referent**, as I shall now demonstrate. The two referents are:

1 the two or more people who are presumed to have already been identified by the Addressee, and who are referred to by the word *they*, and
2 the general class of 'reporters', which is expressed simply by the word *reporters*.

In effect, the clause says that the first referent ('they') is to be classified as a member of the class of things that is the second referent (the class of 'reporters').

But can 'a class of things' really be a 'referent'? The answer is that it can. Note that we should think of the referent of a Participant as something that is located in the mind of the Performer - rather than in the real world. And in order to understand how language works, our concept of what can count as a 'referent' must be broad enough to include classes of things. For example, in the clause *Reporters sometimes invent stories*, we would not wish to say that *reporters* had no referent. The referent is 'members of the class of reporters' - just as it is in *They are reporters*. So in *They are reporters* we shall say that there are TWO **referents,** and so TWO **Participants**. (Indeed, it is perfectly possible to talk about things that do not exist in the real world, e.g. *Unicorns are beautiful creatures*.)

When you turn the page, cover the solution half way down so that you don't see it before you attempt the analysis!

6.3 Analysis task

Using (i) the *Guidelines* from Chapter 4 and (ii) your new knowledge about analyzing clauses with forms of *be* as the Main Verb, try analyzing (2) and (3).

(2) Is Ivy happy now? (3) Ivy's wealthy.

You will find that these two examples take a stage further the principle about the number of Participants established for (1) - and that (3) also raises an important question about the status of the concept of a **word** (which we shall take up in Section 6.6).

When you have finished your two analyses, see how your analysis compares with mine, as shown below in Figure 6-2.

Solutions

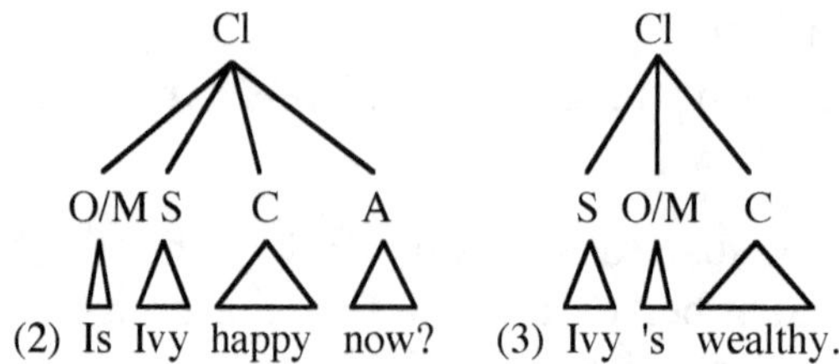

Figure 6-2: Two more examples with O/M

You will probably not have had any problems this time, but these examples include phenomena that raise two questions that need answering - and both occur quite frequently when the Main Verb is a form of *be*. We shall now look at these two matters.

6.4 Qualities as Complements

In both (2) and (3) we have a new type of Complement: a word that expresses the **quality** of the thing that is the referent of the Subject. The question is: 'If *happy* and *wealthy* are to be analyzed as **Cs**, what is it that they have in common with *reporters* in *They are reporters*?'

The answer is that, just as 'being a reporter' means 'being a member of the class of reporters', so 'being happy' means 'being a member of the class of those who are happy' - and *wealthy* means 'being a member of the class of those who are wealthy'. The purpose of uttering (2) is therefore to ask whether Ivy is now a member of the class of those who are happy, and the purpose of uttering (3) is to tell us that Ivy belongs to the class of people who are wealthy. So the 'qualities' expressed in *happy* and *wealthy* in fact refer - though only indirectly - to 'things', and each of the words *happy* and *wealthy* is, in terms of its meaning, a **quality** of a **thing** - and so, at the level of form, what is termed in traditional grammar an 'adjective'. (In contrast, *gently* in our first example of *We shall simmer them gently* is, in terms of its meaning, a **quality** of a **situation**, and, at the level of form, a 'manner adverb'.)

6.5 Qualities (and things) as the expression of 'affective' meaning

We have just met the concept that a Complement can be a **quality**, and we have seen that it is typically expressed through an 'adjective'. Before we move on, we shall note a few further points about qualities as Complements - and in so doing we shall meet another strand of meaning.

First, notice that such qualities are quite often 'tempered' by a word such as *very, fairly* or *terrifically.* So (3), for example, could be expanded to *Ivy's very wealthy, Ivy's terrifically wealthy* or even *Ivy's more wealthy than Fiona is.* In the Cardiff Grammar such adjectives are seen as functioning as the pivotal element - called the **apex** - of a unit called the **quality group.** [45]

Second, the 'qualities' that are expressed in such groups vary in an interesting way in the types of meaning that they express. Some, such as *happy* and *wealthy* in (2) and (3), express a relatively 'pure' **experiential** meaning, while others reflect THE

---

45 Note that here I am simply MENTIONING the 'quality group'; our interest in it is as a unit that may fill the Complement of a clause. However, even though there are no chapters of this book whose function is to describe the **quality group** - or the **nominal group**, which will be mentioned shortly - you can learn a lot about them from Appendix 1. See Tucker 1998 for the fullest treatment (in any theoretical framework) of the quality group, and Fawcett 2007b for an introduction to one aspect of the nominal group. And see my *Functional Syntax Handbook* for full descriptions of both.

PERFORMER'S FEELINGS about the object, as in (4). The technical name for this type of meaning is **affective** meaning.

(4) Ivy is absolutely wonderful!

Notice that we could replace *wonderful* in (6) by any of the following 'affective' words, and the clause would still be expressing essentially the same meaning of 'strong approval':

amazing, fabulous, great, marvellous, superb, terrific etc.

Alternatively, the Complement may express a meaning of 'disapproval', if we use one of these:

awful, dreadful, horrible, lousy, nasty, terrible, etc.

But perhaps the most interesting way in which affective meaning is used in English is when it occurs in the very large set of adjectives that express a **blend** of **experiential** and **affective** meaning - again showing either 'approval' or 'disapproval' - such as *kind* in (5), and other adjectives such as:

beautiful, brave, generous, handsome, important, clean and
ugly, cowardly, mean, cruel, trivial, dirty.

(5) Ivy is very kind.

Because (i) this book focusses on the clause and (ii) the element that a quality group fills most frequently is a Complement in a clause whose Main Verb is a form of 'being', I have been illustrating these meanings as ones that occur in a quality group that fills a **Complement**. But such 'affective' and 'experiential-affective' expressions also occur quite frequently as a quality group that fills a **modifier** in a **nominal group**, such as the underlined portions of the following (where the first line gives examples of purely **affective** meanings and the second line gives examples of **experiential-affective** blends):

a <u>very nice</u> guy, an <u>absolutely fabulous</u> TV series, a <u>lousy</u> book;
a <u>really kind</u> person, a <u>mean</u> act, an <u>economical</u> car

All of these can occur in most of the many places that a nominal group occurs, but they are particularly frequent as the Complement of a clause.

Similar combinations of 'experiential' and 'affective' meaning can be found in certain nouns, such as *hero*, *idiot, weed* and *dirt*, but the natural home of expressions of affective meaning is the quality group.

Finally, we should note that there are adjectives, such as *new*, *gentle* and *disappointing*, which may at first sight appear to be 'objective' - and so, supposedly, 'purely experiential' - but which in fact carry affective connotations of either 'approval' or 'disapproval' in a given culture that are quite powerful.

As will be clear, there is a strong underlying presence of 'affective' meaning in many words that at first appear to be 'experiential' - and the subtle use of such words is a potent force in the language of persuasion (e.g. in advertisements of holidays in *luxury apartments overlooking a beautiful beach,* or the speech of a politician who refers to *our brave soldiers in Afghanistan*). The affective attitude that the Performer wishes the Addressee to adopt is communicated all the more effectively for being partially hidden behind an experiential meaning. This aspect of its use makes it important to build it explicitly into one's model of language as a strand of meaning. It has its place in the present framework in its own right.[46]

---

46 **Comparison with the Sydney Grammar** Perhaps as a consequence of the emphasis in Halliday's linguistics on 'language and society' rather than 'language and the individual', 'affective' meaning has received relatively little attention in his framework (where it is treated as a minor strand of 'interpersonal' meaning). In contrast, it has been there from the start in what was to develop into the Cardiff Grammar, i.e. (i) Fawcett 1973/81:152-4 (where, however, it is still subsumed under 'expressive' meaning), and (ii) Fawcett 1980, where it is recognized as one of the eight major components of meaning.

However, recent work by Jim Martin, Peter White and others on analyzing the expression of 'appraisal in texts has gone a long way to fill this gap in the Sydney Grammar (e.g. Martin 2000, Martin and White 2005). Note (i) that their descriptive framework includes evaluation in terms of 'validity' as well as 'affect', and (ii) that the general function of 'evaluation' MAY BE MEDIATED THROUGH ANY STRAND OF MEANING (e.g. via 'experiential' meaning in *I like that*). Martin and White's descriptive framework for 'appraisal' must therefore OPERATE AT A HIGHER LEVEL THAN THE SEMANTICS OF THE LEXICOGRAMMAR. In Fawcett forthcoming 2010, I suggest that their framework is the equivalent, broadly, of one of a set of a dozen or so higher 'microplanners' that predetermine the selection of meanings in the semantic system networks.

Let me summarize. In this section, we have met another kind of meaning - **affective** meaning. It is a type of meaning which typically - but not exclusively - occurs as the Complement in a clause. So we can now say that we have met at least some representatives of the following strands of meaning: the **experiential**, **interpersonal** and **affective** strands.[47]

6.6 Contractions

Before we move on, there is an aspect of the detail of (3) - i.e. *Ivy's wealthy* - that requires a brief comment. It concerns **contractions** - and these are the fourth 'related concept' that arises out of our consideration of the use of forms of *be* as a Main Verb.

In *Ivy*'s *wealthy* the single letter *s* - together with the preceding apostrophe - stands for the full form *is*. You can test this claim by changing it into a 'polarity seeker', i.e. into *Is Ivy wealthy?*

Conversely, we can change (2), i.e. *Is Ivy happy now?* into the 'information giver' *Ivy's happy now*.

Luckily, very few contractions are a source of problems in sentence analysis. In (3), for example, it is easy to work out that the *'s* must be the **M**, because we expect every clause to have a **M** (99.99% reliable, with only very rare exceptions).

In general, we can say that the presence of an apostrophe (') is a warning (i) that one (and occasionally more) letters of the equivalent full form is missing - and (ii) that what follows the

---

One problem to which work on 'appraisal' has led is that some scholars now appear to assume that it is the ONLY method of text analysis that is needed! There are two dangers in this: (i) that other equally important strands of meaning will be ignored, and (ii) that the 'renewal of connection' which Firth reminded us we should constantly make (1968: 24) will be lost. This is the 'connection' between the categories for 'appraisal' and the evidence for them from the level of form. In the twenty-first century we need to be able to make this connection explicit in rules that relate (i) the decisions by the performer of a text in the 'appraisal' algorithm (or algorithms, in the plural) to (ii) features in the semantic system networks - and so, via realization rules, to linguistic forms.

47 In Chapter 12 we shall meet an element of the clause which always expresses a purely 'affective' meaning, i.e. the Affective Adjunct. It is therefore a 'purer' example of affective meaning in the clause than affective meaning in a Complement, because the Complement is typically a PR and so has an experiential meaning in the structure of the clause.

apostrophe is a SEPARATE ELEMENT of syntax. Some of the most frequent cases are:

forms of the verb *be*:	*'m* for *am*	*'s* for *is*	*'re* for *are*
the auxiliary verb *have*:	*'s* for *has*	*'ve* for *have*	*'d* for *had*
modal verbs:	*'ll* for *will*	*'d* for *would*	

Note that *'s* is ambiguous between *is* and *has*, and *'d* between *had* and *would*. However, none of these contractions is likely to cause you problems.[48]

6.7 Aside: the case of 'apostrophe *s*' as a 'genitive'

While we are considering 'apostrophe *s*', we should note that it can have a third meaning, as well as being the contracted equivalent of the two full forms identified above. This is the genitive *'s*, as in *Ivy's* in *Ivy's car*. As with the two earlier types, the apostrophe marks the start of a separate element, but in this case THERE IS NO EQUIVALENT FULL FORM - at least, not in Modern English. So the genitive *'s* is unlike those cases, in that it is not a contraction.

For a set of analyzed examples of the construction in which this element occurs, see the summary the 'genitive cluster' in Appendix 1.

6.8 Summary

This chapter began by identifying the unique behaviour of the word - or in fact words - that are the most frequent ones to function as the Main Verb in English - the forms of *be*. (We shall come to the other uses of forms of *be* at later points in the book.)

This led us into considering a number of more general matters that occur frequently in clauses where the **M** is a form of *be*:

(i) the concept of a 'class of things' and whether it can be a **referent**;

(ii) the occurrence of **qualities** as Complements when **M** is a form of *be*;

---

48 Another frequent contraction is the use of *n't* for *not*, as in *isn't*, etc. We shall introduce this in Section 9.4 of Chapter 9.

(iii) the use of words that express **affective** meaning in a Complement when **M** is a form of *be* (and in nominal groups); and finally

(iv) the use of **contractions** when M is a form of *be* (and elsewhere).

Some of these phenomena also occur in clauses that don't contain a form of *be* as **M**, but they all occur particularly frequently in clauses that do. And they are all useful concepts to have covered by this point in our survey of the English clause.

Chapter 7
Interlude: a systemic functional grammar for the structures introduced so far

7.1 Overview

In this chapter we shall have a break from learning about new structures and their meanings. Instead, we shall take a look at a **systemic functional grammar** as a whole - if only a very small one. But it can generate the structures of all the examples that we have considered so far, and this will be sufficient to show you how a SFG actually works.

Here is the grammar itself:

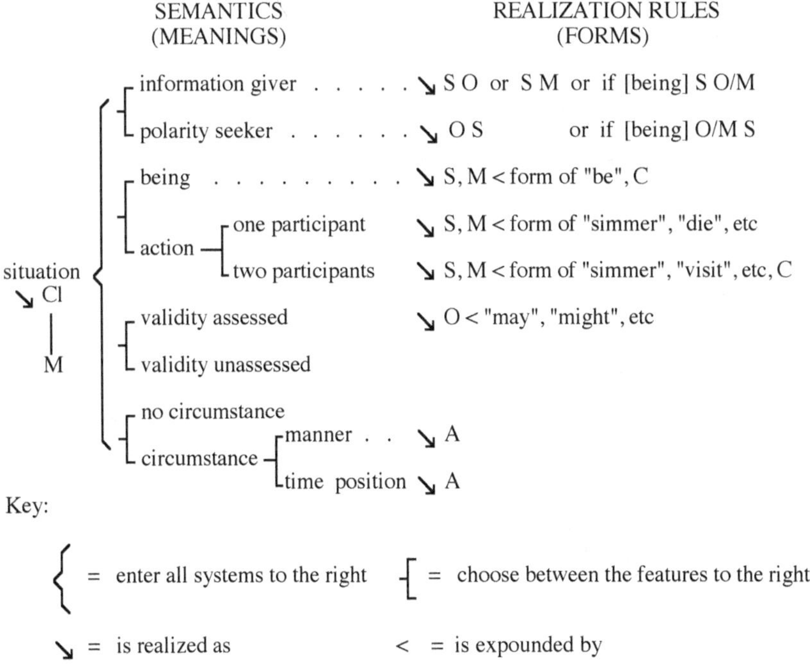

Figure 7-1:
A very small systemic functional grammar for the English clause

This little grammar provides a very informal introduction to a few of the central choices in a system network for the English clause, together with their realizations in structure. As you can see in Figure 7-1, the system network has just six systems, while the full grammar that is implemented in the computer in the COMMUNAL Project currently has over a thousand - and indeed several thousands more when we include, as we should, the system networks that generate lexical items (the nouns, lexical verbs, adjectives and manner adverbs of the language).

It is only because the coverage of this little grammar is limited to just those elements of the English clause that are described in Chapters 3 to 7 that I can present it in this highly simplified form, without distorting it too seriously. A grammar that was any fuller would be too complex to display on a single page. And to save space I have even omitted the NAMES of the system networks. However, you may be able to recognize that the first two systems in the network as embryonic versions of the system networks for MOOD and TRANSITIVITY.

This informal and very limited little grammar is therefore very far indeed from being a complete grammar of English. Yet it should serve its purposes - which are:

1 to give simple examples of THE TWO MAIN COMPONENTS of a systemic functional grammar AND THEIR OUTPUTS (as described in Chapter 2 and summarized there in Figure 2-3); and
2 to give you a sense of HOW THE GRAMMAR WORKS - and so how the structures of the clauses that we have been analyzing in Chapters 3 to 7 would be generated in a fully explicit computer model of language - and so perhaps also, in some very broadly analogous manner, by the human mind, when it communicates with another through language.

The little grammar in Figure 7-1 has TWO components, just as has Figure 2-3 in Chapter 2 - even though they are not shown here in two different boxes (as is done in Figure 2-3). The first component of the grammar is the **system network** of semantic features on the left side of Figure 7-1. This displays some of the main choices in the 'meaning potential' of English, i.e. in its **semantics**. The second component of the grammar is the set of informally expressed **realization rules** for these semantic features, and they are shown on the right side of Figure 7-1. Each such realization rule states the way in which a feature from the network - i.e. a MEANING - is expressed at the level of FORM. In this very introductory grammar, almost all the meanings are expressed in **syntax**, but in a few cases the rules give examples of the **items** that would **expound** the **elements** specified there (to use the correct technical terms, as introduced in Chapter 5) - with the items being shown in double quotation marks.

This little grammar, small though it is, provides in outline form for all the structures introduced in Chapters 3 to 7 - and so for many of the most frequent structures in the English clause.

7.2 How to use the system network

Let me begin by explaining more fully the concepts of 'system' and 'system network'.

A **system** consists of (i) two or more **semantic features**, of which you must select one, and (ii) an **entry condition** - which is itself a semantic feature (or more than one, in more advanced grammars that have complex entry conditions). A system is symbolized by a right-opening square bracket, and it means 'or'. As an example, look at the simple system in Figure 7-1 in which the entry condition is [action] and the two features between which you must choose are [one participant] and [two participants]. (Note that in running text we indicate semantic features by placing them in square brackets.)

So what is a **system network**? Clearly, it is a network of systems - but how are the systems related to each other? The answer is that there are several possible relationships, and here I shall introduce just the two most important ones. Firstly, one system may be **dependent** on another. For example, the system in Figure 7-1 in which the choice is between [one participant] and [two participants] is 'dependent' on the one in which the choice is between [being] and [action] - because it is entered when one of those features - i.e. [action] - is selected. The main way in which a small network such as that shown in Figure 7-1 can be developed into a larger and more adequate one is through this relationship of 'dependence', because it is this that enables the grammarian to add more 'delicate' systems to the network.

However, the first bracket to the right of [situation] is different. It is not a square bracket but a curly one, and it symbolizes 'and'. This use of 'and' brackets is the second most important way in which system networks can be developed to cover more of the meanings of a language. As you can see, in using the system network in Figure 7-1, there are three points at which you have to return to the curly bracket to start down another pathway to the right through the network. In this small network the pathways are only one or two features long, but in the full grammar a pathway may consist of a dozen or so features.

A system network, then, is simply a 'network' of 'systems', connected to each other by 'and' and 'or' relationships. In order to use the one in Figure 7-1 to generate clauses, you start at the left with the feature [situation], and you then move through the network to the right. As you do so, you collect one semantic feature from each system that you encounter. When you reach a terminal feature at the end of a pathway, you return to the 'and' bracket and start on the next sub-network below the one you have just traversed.

Now try using the network in Figure 7-1. It will be helpful if, as you work your way through it, starting from [situation], you make a list of the features you have chosen.

The meanings of most of the features should be clear. As we have already noted, the first system is a rudimentary system network for MOOD, and the second is an equally rudimentary one for TRANSITIVITY.

However, it may be useful to say that the third system is for a very different type of meaning, i.e. CORE VALIDITY. **Validity** is one of four types of meaning that are expressed through **modal verbs** - verbs such as *may, might, will, would, shall* and *should.* Choices in the validity strand of meaning express THE PERFORMER'S ASSESSMENT OF THE 'VALIDITY' OF THE PROPOSITION THAT IS EXPRESSED IN THE CLAUSE. (There was in fact an example of this in the clause *Ivy might visit Fred* in Chapter 4.) This type of 'validity' is called 'core validity' because it is found at the 'core' of the clause, in the Operator, and it is the most frequently used of the various system networks in the **validity** strand of meaning. We shall meet examples of other types of 'validity' in Chapters 12 and 14.[49]

---

49 **Comparison with the Sydney Grammar** There are three differences to point out. Firstly, in the Sydney Grammar 'validity' (under the name of the 'probability' type of 'modalization') is treated as a sub-component of meaning within the 'interpersonal' component'. (So too are two other types of meaning that are treated in the Cardiff Grammar as strands of meaning in their own right - 'negativity' and 'affective' meaning - both of which we shall meet in due course.) In the Cardiff Grammar, however, we restrict 'interpersonal meaning' to those meanings that assign 'communication roles' to the Performer and the Addressee (as described in Section 3.4 of Chapter 3). This is because the type of meaning that tells the Addressee the degree of confidence that the Performer has in a proposition is significantly different from the type of that assigns communication roles such as 'information giver', 'information seeker' and 'proposer of action' - as also are 'affective meaning' and 'negativity'.

The second difference concerns the ways in which the two grammars deal with various types of meaning that have traditionally been brought together under the cover term of 'modality'. First, we need to distinguish clearly between **forms** and **meanings** - and specifically between 'modal verbs' (which is a set of verb forms, including *may, might, will, would, shall, should, can, could, must* and *ought*) and the types of meaning that they express (together with other forms). Chapter 4 of my *Functional Syntax Handbook* describes the four different types of meaning that are expressed through modal verbs: (i) **validity** (the 'probability' type of 'modalization' in *IFG* terms); (ii) the **experiential** meanings of 'control and disposition' ('modulation' in *IFG* terms): (iii) certain meanings of 'time' (so **experiential** meanings, such as *shall* in *We shall simmer them gently*); and (iv) certain **interpersonal** meanings in the system network for MOOD (several of which we shall meet in Section 11.3 of Chapter 11). Coincidentally, Halliday distinguishes 'four types of meaning' that are sub-types of 'modality' in the revised picture of 'modality' that he gives in the second edition of *IFG* (Halliday 1994: 355-62, e.g. Figures 10-12 and 10-13). However, the two sets of 'four types of meaning' should not be confused.

Consider now the four types of meaning that Halliday distinguishes. His four - all of which he presents as **interpersonal** meanings - are: (i) 'probability' (= our 'validity'); (ii) 'usuality' (e.g. *always, sometimes, never*) which corresponds closely to our 'usuality', as found in Section 12.2 of Chapter 12, but with the important difference explained below; (iii) 'obligation' and (iv) 'inclination' (the last two both being types of 'modulation'). Halliday's 'obligation' and 'inclination' correspond to our 'control and disposition', except that they are treated here as types of 'experiential' meaning - just as they were in Halliday's earlier (and in my view more insightful) treatment of this area of meaning (1970/76a). (For more examples of the range of meanings expressed in modal verbs, see Chapter 4 of Fawcett forthcoming 2011a.)

Here, then, we have recognized a fourth strand of meaning to put alongside the **experiential**, **interpersonal** and affective strands.

I have in fact also mentioned the **thematic** strand (in Chapter 3, very briefly) but we shall not include it in our growing list of strands of meaning until it is introduced properly, which will be in Section 8.5 of the next chapter.

Finally, Halliday's inclusion of 'usuality' as a type of 'modality' - and so as a type of 'interpersonal' meaning - raises a major issue that requires comment. Interestingly, the new description of 'modality' given in *IFG* doesn't appear, as it logically should, in the main chapter on 'interpersonal' meaning, but in the one on 'grammatical metaphor'. Why? I suspect that it is because one of Halliday's four types of 'modality' is 'usuality' - and this is a type of meaning this is usually (sic!) treated as a type of 'temporal' meaning (and so here as a type of 'experiential' meaning). Given the context of the description - in a chapter on 'grammatical metaphor' - we might expect to find Halliday suggesting that 'usuality' is - or can function as - a 'grammatical metaphor' for 'probability' - i.e. for the sub-type of his 'modality' that corresponds to our 'validity'. Compare *She sometimes has a glass of sherry before lunch* and *She may have a glass of sherry before lunch.* But in fact Halliday simply presents 'usuality' straightforwardly as a sub-type of 'modality'. In contrast, the Cardiff Grammar - unexcitingly but perhaps more appropriately - treats 'usuality' as one of several types of temporal Adjunct, and so as close in meaning to 'Periodic Frequency' Adjuncts such as *once a day* and *five times a year*.

However, the Cardiff Grammar does have a way of recognizing that there are **conceptual equivalences** between meanings of 'usuality' and some types of 'validity'. See Fawcett forthcoming 2010 for the first published account of the Cardiff Grammar's use of the concept of 'equivalences'. This important concept provides a 'cognitive-interactive' approach to many of the phenomena that Halliday has noted under the broad umbrella heading of 'grammatical metaphor'. While appreciating the insights that Halliday provides into the possible historical development of the various constructions that have been described in these terms, there are many advantages, when thinking synchronically - i.e. when describing what today's native speakers of English 'know' (unconsciously) to be the options available in the language - in modelling knowledge of this aspect of the language's resources in terms of 'conceptual equivalences'. In so doing, the Cardiff Grammar offers an alternative approach that has the enormous advantage of avoiding adding to the overall model of language a complete additional level of system networks. And this is what the concept of 'grammatical metaphor' entails, in the hypothesis outlined - but not described s fully enough for us to be able to evaluate it - in Halliday and Matthiessen 1999.

It will be probably be some years before we systemic functional linguists agree about what is the optimal way of describing these phenomena.

7.3 Generating a 'selection expression' of semantic features

Do you have a list of the features that you have selected? If you have followed all of the possible pathways to their terminal features, you will have generated a **selection expression** (to use the technical term) of between five and seven features (depending on your choices). This set of semantic features constitutes the **semantic description** of the 'situation' ('situation' being the semantic unit that corresponds to the syntactic unit of the clause).

If, for example, you chose the FIRST feature in every system, you should have generated the following selection expression:

> [situation, information giver, being, validity assessed, no circumstance].

One possible output from this selection expression would be *Ivy may be clever.*

But if you chose instead the SECOND feature in each system, you will have collected the following seven features:

> [situation, polarity seeker, action, two participants, validity unassessed, circumstance, time position].

In this case a possible output would be *Did you visit her this morning?* (See Section 7.5 for a note on the problem of where *did* comes from.)

In the next two sections we shall see exactly how these two selection expressions generate the structure of outputs like these.

7.4 Applying the realization rules

The second stage (and for our purposes the final stage) in the process of generation is to apply the **realization rules**. One informal way to indicate these is to use a little diagonal arrow, and you can see that this convention has been used in Figure 7-1.[50]

---

50 The arrow can be thought of as representing the movement through the model of language summarized in Figure 2-3, from (i) a semantic feature in the top left box to (ii) its representation as part of the structural output at the bottom right of the diagram.

Most of the realization rules in the network apply to a 'terminal' feature, and they can therefore be placed to the right of the feature to which they apply. But the realization rule for [situation] is different, in that it is shown directly below the feature. Since this rule is required in every case, we shall take it as an example. What it says is: 'First insert into the structure that is currently being built a clause (Cl), and then insert Main Verb (M) as an element of it.' And the other realization rules similarly specify that the various elements that we have met in Chapters 3 to 7 are introduced to the structure in the sequence shown.

7.5 Generating the structure of a clause

We shall now apply the realization rules for the first of the selection expressions that we noted in Section 7.3. If you apply them in the order in which you would choose the features, you will generate a clause (Cl) with the following elements:

Subject + Operator + Main Verb + Complement

Or, in more familiar terms, as in Figure 7-2:

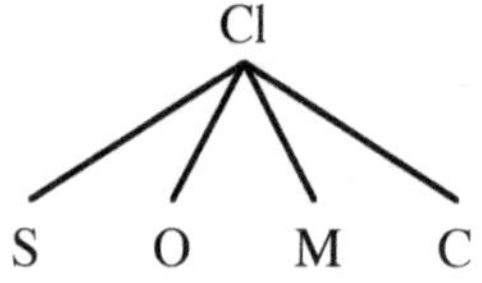

Figure 7-2:
The clause structure generated from the first selection expression

And a typical string of items that **expounds** these elements (to introduce the correct technical term) would be - using the items suggested in the realization rules and the familiar name of 'Adam' - the example shown in (1):

(1) Adam may be hungry.

Before we leave the realization rules, I should point out that those given in Figure 7-1 contain a little problem to which we have no solution - so far. This is the problem for our second selection expression of features noted in Section 7.3, i.e. the problem of how to provide the Operator that is always required when [polarity seeker] is chosen - if you don't ALSO choose one of [being] or [validity assessed]. So far, it is only if you choose one of these two features that the grammar generates an Operator. We shall find the solution to this problem in Chapter 9.

If you would like to re-enforce your understanding of how a SFG works, it would be a good idea to traverse the network again, making different choices this time. The final output of your choices might be, apart from (1) above, a structure like one of those exemplified in (2) to (4):

(2) Paula is a doctor.
(3) Did Paula visit her nephew yesterday?
(4) Might her patient die?

Altogether, this little network generates 36 different selection expressions, and 24 different structures (not 36, because the grammar generates an **A** for either [manner] or [time position].

7.6 Summary: some limitations of this little grammar

Now I must point out a few more of the limitations of the informal little grammar in Figure 7-1.

The first is that it merely illustrates the order in which the elements are to be placed in the clause, rather than explicitly specifying the **place** in the clause for each.

Another is that, when it specifies that a **Main Verb** is to be used, it should also specify (i) the conditions under which it should and should not have a 'tense form', and (ii) if it should, whether it is to be 'past' or 'present' (e.g. it wouldn't have a 'tense form' if a modal verb is generated, as in *Adam may be hungry*).

Yet another limitation is that the little grammar doesn't tell us what units are to fill the Subject, Complement and Adjunct. These units would need to be generated by further passes through a different part of the overall system network. In the case of a Subject the unit would probably be a nominal group such as *he, Adam* or *her nephew* - i.e. one that realizes the meaning of 'thing' (rather than 'situation', as in the units generated by the grammar in Figure 7-1).

And the system for [circumstance] is misleading, in that it implies that you must choose between [manner] and [time position], when in fact a clause can contain both.

Finally, the features in the system network don't have probabilities on them - as system networks should.[51]

The full grammar, however, does all these things (and many more). In other words: (i) it has realization rules that locate an **element** at a numbered **place** in the clause; (ii) other rules generate the actual **items** that **expound** the elements; (iii) others provide for the complex interaction between various types of **time** meaning and the various types of meanings in 'modal verbs', etc; (iv) other rules ensure that the grammar will **re-enter** the system network to generate **nominal groups** (and where appropriate other units, including **embedded clauses**) in order to fill elements such as the **Subject**, **Complement** and any **Adjuncts**; (v) the full grammar provides for more than one Circumstance to be generated for a clause; and (vi) yet another set of rules generates appropriate **intonation** or **punctuation** - and there are many other types too.

This little grammar is therefore far too small to be useful for any practical purpose, and it is also too limited to be used as part of an argument for preferring a SFL to other ways of modelling language. But it has succeeded, I hope, in its task of illustrating the characteristics of language which have led systemic functional grammarians to use the insightful combination of **system networks** and **realization rules** to model language.[52]

---

51 **Comparison with the Sydney Grammar** While Halliday would agree that the overall probabilities that features will be chosen should be represented in system networks, very few system networks drawn by systemicists who work in the framework of the Sydney Grammar do in fact supply them. In contrast, most system networks drawn by those who use the Cardiff Grammar approach include the probabilities.

52 Notice that this type of grammar does NOT attempt to summarize in one diagram THE POTENTIAL STRUCTURE OF THE CLAUSE AS A WHOLE. It is precisely because a 'phrase structure' grammar is inadequate for this task that the concept of the 'syntactic transformation' was brought into the picture. But this is essentially a 'sticking plaster' approach, and the SFG approach is to start instead from the concept that, when certain meanings are chosen in the system network, they are typically expressed by quite SMALL CONFIGURATIONS OF ELEMENTS - in just the way that we saw when we looked at the structures that realize meanings

This meaning-oriented approach to language provides a way to capture both the **meanings** of language and, through the realization rules, their manifestation as **syntax** - and, in the fuller grammar, also in **items** and **intonation** or **punctuation**. And it does so in a way that gives a greater sense of having explained language than a purely structural approach could ever do, because it embraces - and gives an equal place to - both meaning and form.

In terms of our developing picture of the strands of meaning found in the English clause, we have now added **validity** to the **experiential**, **interpersonal** and **affective** strands of meaning.

In the next chapter we shall return to the pattern of most earlier chapters, and meet some further elements of the clause - and, through them, further strands of meaning.

---

of TRANSITIVITY and MOOD in Chapter 3. If you examine the elements that get generated as a result of choices in the network in Figure 7-1 - i.e. those listed under the heading of REALIZATION RULES in the column on the right - the same picture emerges. It is SPECIFIC CONFIGURATIONS of elements, such as **S O** or **S M C**, that express the different types of meaning.

A further reason for not trying to generate all of the elements of a clause by one rule is that, in naturally occurring texts, Adjuncts occur in so many different places in the structure of the clause that it would be inordinately clumsy to try to characterize the resulting variations in clause structure simply as a set of possible strings of elements. (See Chapter 12 for an introduction to the rich variety of Adjuncts that occur in English, and their varied positions in the clause.)

Chapter 8
Three types of Auxiliary Verb, and one type of 'Theme', a 'covert' PR and 'New'

8.1 Auxiliary Verbs (X)

Please cover the solution on the opposite page so that you don't see it before you do the analysis task suggested below.

In this chapter I shall introduce three sub-types of another clause element: the **Auxiliary Verb** (or Auxiliary, for short). It is represented by **X** (and not **A**, since this is used for 'Adjunct').

The Cardiff Grammar recognizes many different types of Auxiliary, this being one of its major extensions of existing grammars (including Halliday's *IFG*). Here I shall introduce just the three most frequent types, but we shall meet several more in Section 14.3 of Chapter 14.

The first two types of **X** that we shall consider both express 'time' meanings. See Chapter 4 of *The Functional Syntax Handbook* for (i) a full discussion of the interestingly different set of meanings that each realizes, and (ii) the reasons for replacing the names used for them in traditional grammars by those used here.

8.2 The Auxiliary Verb that expresses the meaning 'retrospective'

The first type of **X** is exemplified by *has* in (1):

(1) King Henry has attacked Rouen. [53]

Using *Preliminary Guidelines 1* from Chapter 4, try analyzing (1). You will find a small problem with this analysis task, but it probably won't stop you from reaching the right solution.

---

53 Most examples in this chapter refer to King Henry V of England's successful siege of Rouen in 1418-19, which left him in control of much of France.

Solution

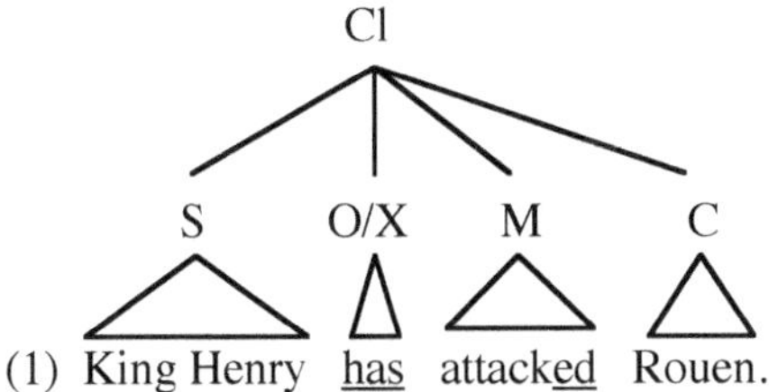

Figure 8-1: a clause with a 'retrospective' Auxiliary

As you can see, the **X** is conflated with **O** and shown as **O/X**. In this way it is like the conflation of **M** with **O** as **O/M** that we met in Chapter 6.

Now let's look more closely at the 'retrospective' Auxiliary. The meanings that it expresses are more complex than you might think, and here we shall limit ourselves to its most typical use, i.e. to express a type of 'pastness' that looks back from a point in time, usually the present moment. Hence the term 'retrospective'.

There are three points to note about its structure:

(i) It is always expounded by a form of the verb *have* - so it is always *have, has, had,* or *having*. This makes it very easy to identify, as the *Guidelines* in Chapters 9 and 15 will show.

(ii) If (a) this is the first Auxiliary in the clause and (b) there would otherwise be no Operator, **X** is conflated with **O**, and so shown as **O/X**.

(iii) One of the challenges of English syntax for the builder of generative grammars is how to model elegantly the way in which the meaning of 'retrospective' is realized - and, as we shall see, a similar problem arises with the meanings that are realized in the other two Auxiliaries that we are about to consider. The problem is the fact that the meaning is expressed not only in the Auxiliary *have* but also through the use of the 'past participle' form of the following Auxiliary - or, if there isn't one (as in the present case), in the 'past participle' form of the Main Verb. So in (1) the expression of the meaning 'retrospective' is begun in the Auxiliary *have* and completed - usually - by the 'past participle' on the Main Verb, as is shown by the underlining in (1).[54]

8.3 The Auxiliary Verb that expresses the meaning 'period-marked'

As before, please cover the solution on the opposite page so that you don't see it before you do the analysis task suggested below.

The second type of Auxiliary is as shown in (2):

(2) King Henry is besieging Rouen.

The core meaning expressed in this Auxiliary is that the event that is being referred to is marked as 'lasting for a period of time'.

In structural terms, it is remarkably similar to (1):

(i) Like the meaning of 'retrospective', the meaning of 'period marked' is always expressed by a form of the same verb - but in this case it is a form of the verb *be*, and so one of *am, is, are, was, were, being* or *been.*

(ii) Like the 'retrospective' **X**, this **X** gets conflated with **O,** if (a) it is the first **X** and (b) there would otherwise be no **O**.

(iii) Finally, this **X** too typically requires the use of a second element to expresses its meaning. In this case it is the suffix *-ing* on the following **X** or **M**, as shown in (2). The traditional term for this is the 'present participle' form of the verb.

We shall now put both 'time' Auxiliaries in the same clause, and we'll add a 'Duration' Adjunct to make it sound more natural:

(3) King Henry has been besieging Rouen for six months.

Now try analyzing (3) - which is a little more complex!

---

54 One exception to this generalization is when another Auxiliary follows it, in which case the suffix *-en* is added to the second Auxiliary, as we shall see in the case of *be* + *en* in (3). Another exception occurs when the elements of the clause after the 'retrospective' **X** are ellipted, as in B's response to A in: A: *Has he besieged Rouen yet?* B: *Yes, he has*. This pattern also applies to the other two Auxiliaries that will be introduced here.

Solution

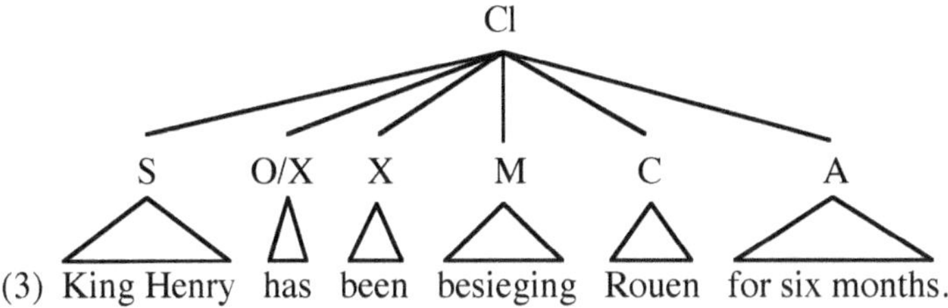

Figure 8-2: A clause with two 'time' Auxiliaries

8.4 The Auxiliary Verb that expresses the meaning 'passive'

The meaning of the third Auxiliary is very different. Its meaning is that the Process expressed in the Main Verb is one that is 'happening to' the referent of the Subject. In other words, the Subject is typically a 'passive' Participant in the Process (rather than an 'active' one). The labels used in traditional grammar to describe a clause that has or does not have this meaning are 'passive' and 'active' - and the element itself is called the 'passive Auxiliary. But there is a lot more to say about the meanings associated with this **X**, as the next few sections will show.

You can see an example of this third type of Auxiliary in (4):

(4) Rouen was besieged by King Henry for six months.

While the **meaning** of this third type of Auxiliary is very different from that of the first two, at the level of **form** it is remarkably like those in (1) and (2).

(i) As in (2), the **X** is expounded by a form of *be.*
(ii) As in both (1) and (2), the **X** is conflated with **O** if there isn't an **O** already.
(iii) Like (1) - but unlike (2) - the following **M** has the form of the 'past participle'.

But there is one major difference - and since it is one which raises an interesting little problem, I suggest that you discover what it is by trying to analyze (4) for yourself.

And remember not to turn the page until you have attempted the analysis!

Solution

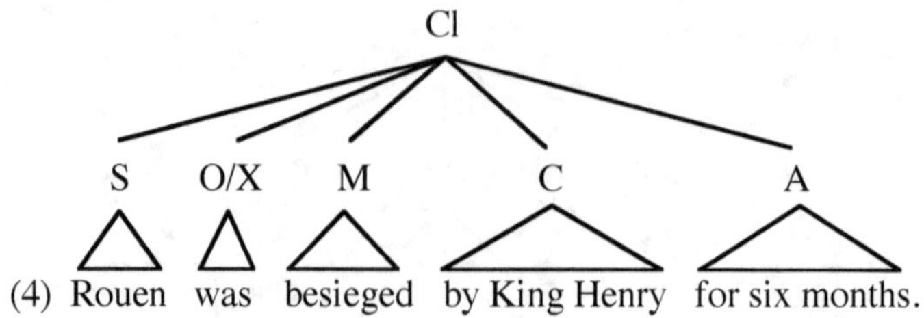

Figure 8-3: A clause with a 'passive' Auxiliary

As you will have discovered, the small problem is that, strictly speaking, the Participant who is the 'besieger' is not *by King Henry* but only *King Henry*. However, in an analysis in terms of the elements of clause structure, *by King Henry* is indeed the Complement - even though THE PR DOES NOT OCCUPY ALL OF THE COMPLEMENT. (We shall meet a similar case in Chapter 13.) And, as Chapter 10 will show, there are also many cases of Complements that are filled by prepositional groups where the whole group is the PR.[55, 56]

From a functional viewpoint, the next question to ask is: Why does the Performer of a text-sentence choose to make the clause 'passive'? There is no single answer, but there is always at least one of the three reasons that I shall give in the next few sections - and, as we shall see, sometimes two of the reasons are involved.

8.5 The SUBJECT THEME system: the first source of the 'passive' Auxiliary

In around 20 per cent of cases, the reason for the introduction of the 'passive' Auxiliary is that it is generated as a by-product of a choice in the SUBJECT THEME system. So this section is about a type of 'Theme', and so introduces another strand of meaning.

---

55 In the full grammar, we show the Participant (here an Agent) as conflated with the **completive** of the prepositional **group** that fills the Complement. For a description of the prepositional group, see Appendix 1.

56 The 'passive' **X** is usually a form of *be*, but occasionally a form of *get*. But then it cannot also be **O** - like some other **X**s. The test in Chapter 15 lists them.

The SUBJECT THEME system is entered in the generation of around 70-80 per cent of clauses (depending on the type of text), and this makes it the most frequently used of all of the several different types of system network that express a **thematic** meaning. So it is important to understand its role in the clause.

The 'Subject Theme' of a clause is the aspect of the meaning of a typical Subject that tells the Addressee 'what the clause is about'.[57] For example, in each of (1), (2) and (3) in the previous sections, the Subject Theme is *King Henry* - but in (4) it is *Rouen.* In other words, if the Performer decides to present the Participant that typically comes SECOND as the Subject Theme, the result is that the 'passive' Auxiliary is introduced to the clause. Compare the 'passive' version in (4) - which is repeated here - with the far more frequent 'active' version in (5):

(4) Rouen was besieged by King Henry for six months.
(5) King Henry besieged Rouen for six months.

The question of which Participant is to be the Subject Theme arises whenever a Process has two Participants, EITHER OF WHICH CAN BE MADE THE SUBJECT THEME. As you can see, the event of 'King Henry's besieging Rouen' can be reported with the Participant that is the 'besieger' ('King Henry') as the Subject Theme, as in (5), or with the Participant that is being 'besieged' ('Rouen') as the Subject Theme, as in (4).[58]

---

57 Indeed, it is this aspect of the typical meaning of a 'Subject' that originally gave the element its name - even though, paradoxically, it is NOT this aspect of its meaning that defines it - as we saw in Footnote 37. (The way to IDENTIFY the Subject is the *Mood Test*, as we saw in Chapter 4, and a much improved version of it will be presented in the next chapter.)

58 **Comparison with the Sydney Grammar** In the Cardiff Grammar the words *by King Henry* in (4) function as a Complement, as Figure 8-3 shows. The reasoning that underlies this analysis is that 'King Henry' is a Participant in the Process of 'besieging', whether or not he is also the Subject. In contrast, *for six months* is a Circumstance of Duration, so it is not predicted by the Process, and so is an Adjunct.

But in the Sydney Grammar the words *by King Henry* would be treated as an Adjunct, just as *for six months* would. The reason Halliday gives in *IFG* (1994: 80) for this analysis is that 'an Adjunct is an element that has not got the potential of being Subject'. This definition is supposedly in contrast with the definition of a Complement, which, supposedly, is an element that does have this potential. The problem is that it quite frequently does not, i.e. in the frequent case when a Complement is an 'Attribute' (a PR), as in *King Alfred was a noble king* and *Its fleece was white as snow* (to cite the examples that Halliday uses, as he makes precisely this point). It is not clear why he allows the definition to stand, given the clear evidence against the generalization that he himself brings. In other words, his definition of an Adjunct has two weaknesses: (i) it is a statement about what it is not rather than what it is (which is understandable, given the wide range of functions that Adjuncts serve) and (ii) it depends on a faulty generalization. I shall shortly suggest that there is in fact a more fundamental reason why Halliday takes the position he does.

If we were operating purely at the level of form, Halliday's statement that 'an Adjunct is an element that has not got the potential of being Subject' would be true, because we cannot say **By King Henry besieged Rouen.* But in a functional description of a language our analysis needs to recognize the fact that the role played by 'King Henry' in the event of 'besieging' is the same in both (4) and (5). So the question we need to ask is this: Is the fact that a PR that is predicted by the Process is expressed as a **prepositional group** (or more accurately, in this case, WITHIN a prepositional group) a sufficiently strong reason to treat what would otherwise be a Participant Role as a Circumstantial Role?

In the Cardiff Grammar the answer is that it is not. Indeed, in this example the case for claiming that the prepositional group *by King Henry* is not a Circumstance is particularly strong, because *by* has no meaning in its own right. It is merely the 'passive marker' that is introduced automatically whenever a PR that typically occurs as the second (or third) PR in a clause is 'promoted' to be the Subject Theme. So the word *by* is not there as the result of a choice in a system to have a meaning realized in *by* (rather than one realized in *through* or *round* etc), but merely as a by-product of the decision to make 'Rouen' the Subject Theme. So cases such as this bring out particularly clearly that the fact that the role of 'King Henry' in the Process of 'besieging' really is that of a Participant rather than a Circumstance.

In my view, the reason why Halliday treats a prepositional group as an Adjunct - and so *by King Henry* in (4) as an Adjunct rather than a Complement - is, essentially, that he always has done so, and that he feels that he had a good reason when he first did so. So what was that reason? In the very early days of the theory, in the late 1950s and early 1960s, he made the generalizing assumption that each **class** of **group** typically fills a given **element** of the **clause** - i.e. that nominal groups typically fill Subjects and Complements, and that a prepositional group typically fills an Adjunct. But note that this was in the period BEFORE he made the three revolutionary suggestions (as described in Section 1.3 of Chapter 1) which resulted in the concept that a language consists essentially of a system network of choices between meanings. But in the framework of the explicitly functional theory of SFL we need to ask: Is it valid to use such assumptions as the basis for identifying the role of a clause element? If you take the position that it is, you will find yourself in conflict with a different criterion - and one, moreover, that is explicitly functional. The general question that we should be asking about criteria in identifying an element in a clause is this: Is its function to be determined 'from below' - i.e. by the evidence of the internal structure of the unit that fills it - or is it to be determined by the role that the element plays in the clause - i.e. through its relationships with the other elements of the clause? Since this criterion and Halliday's earlier one are frequently in conflict, it is simply not possible to answer 'Both'.

In the Cardiff Grammar we use the second criterion, precisely because it is an explicitly functional one. When functional and formal criteria are in conflict, we place functional criteria above formal criteria - but only as long as this doesn't lose contact with the level of form. And we ensure that this doesn't happen by writing realization rules that relate every meaning that we build into the lexicogrammar to its realization at the level of form. This, then, is why we take the position that A COMPLEMENT IS - OR INCLUDES - A PARTICIPANT THAT IS PREDICTED BY THE PROCESS. (This criterion, which I introduced informally in Chapter 3, will be expanded upon in Chapter 10 and formalized as a standard test in Chapter 15.)

Using this criterion gives very different results from the results produced by using the criterion of the internal structure of the unit that fills the clause element - i.e. the criterion that states that 'if the unit is a prepositional group and it fills a clause element that element must be an Adjunct'. The latter would show that 100% of those prepositional groups that function as clause elements are Adjuncts. In contrast, the analysis of texts in terms of the Cardiff Grammar criterion of predictability by the Process shows that only about 32% of prepositional groups fill Adjuncts, whereas 52% of them fill Complements - e.g. in examples such *Ivy is in London today*, where the Location *in London* is predicted by the Process of 'being' (in its 'locational' sense). And prepositional groups also fill the qualifier in a nominal group quite frequently, as Halliday recognizes - as well as several elements of other units, as Appendix 1 shows.

Let me summarise the argument. If you accept the view advocated here that 'predictability from the Process' is a valid criterion for identifying a PR, and that we should mark the status of such an element at the level of form by labelling it as a Complement (if it isn't a Subject), then you cannot at the same time argue that all (or even most) prepositional groups fill Adjuncts - unless, of course, you are prepared to use the circular argument that, if a prepositional group fills an element of the clause, it must be an Adjunct. But to take that position would have the considerable disadvantage of failing to distinguish between *by King Henry* and *for six months* in (4). It would be putting form before function.

As I pointed out earlier, the *IFG* view that 'any clause element that is filled by a prepositional group is an Adjunct' goes back to the 1960s, when Halliday still saw the lexicogrammar as operating purely at the level of form. And, like a good many other parts of the Sydney Grammar's description of English, it has remained as it was at that time ever since. That this is the case is demonstrated at many points in these footnotes.

8.6 The centrality in the grammar of SUBJECT THEME

The system of SUBJECT THEME is one that applies to the vast majority of the types of Process that have two or three Participants. It doesn't apply to ALL types of process - e.g. not to a Process of 'being', as in *Adam is hungry* or *Adam is in Buenos Aires*, and not to 'having' in its 'possession' sense. But it does apply to most two- and three-role Processes.

Despite its general applicability, however, we tend not to notice how central this system is in the grammar of English. There are two reasons for this. The first is that, in those cases in which both of the two relevant Participants are overtly present - which is over 99 per cent in most types of text - THE 'TYPICALLY FIRST' PR IS SELECTED AS THE SUBJECT THEME SO FREQUENTLY THAT WE BARELY NOTICE THAT A CHOICE IS INVOLVED. The second reason is that when this happens there is no overt marker that a choice has been made in the SUBJECT THEME system. But when the 'typically second' Participant is selected to be the Subject Theme there are two 'overt markers': the presence of (i) the 'passive' Auxiliary and (ii) the preposition *by* (as in Figure 8-3). The result of the combination of the two factors identified here is that we are hardly aware that the referent of the Subject has been given the additional function of being the **Subject Theme** AS THE RESULT OF A CHOICE BY THE PERFORMER. Yet in most English clauses the choice is there.

Figure 8-4 functions as a reminder of this fact. It reproduces Figure 4-2 from Chapter 4, but it additionally indicates that the Subject serves the third function of being a type of Theme. Thus our old friend 'Ivy' is the Subject Theme of the clause - as well as being both (i) a Participant in the TRANSITIVITY structure and (ii) part of the expression of the MOOD meaning of 'polarity

---

In conclusion, then I suggest that, in an explicitly FUNCTIONAL grammar, the fact that the realization of a Participant happens to be in the form of a nominal group in one case and a prepositional group (or 'prepositional phrase') in another should be subordinate to the fact that the referent in both cases is a PR that is predicted by the Process. (Two similar cases are noted in Footnotes 75 and 77.)

seeker'. The Subject, then, is one of the most **multifunctional** elements of the clause.[59]

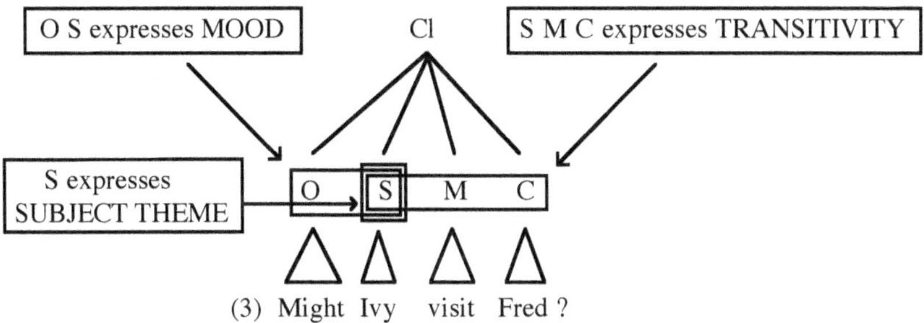

Figure 8-4: TRANSITIVITY, MOOD and THEME in the structure of a simple clause

We have now added a fifth strand of meaning to our steadily developing picture of the strands of meaning found in the English clause. So we have now identified the **experiential**, **interpersonal**, **affective**, **validity** and **thematic** strands of meaning.[60]

---

59 In Section 10.2 of Chapter 4 of my *Functional Syntax Handbook*, however, I demonstrate that the Operator can simultaneously serve five different types of meaning. Figure 17-2 in Chapter 17 of this book illustrates the use of four of them (the fifth being the 'informational' meaning of 'Contrastively New', which is introduced in Section 9.5 of Chapter 9.)

60 **Comparison with the Sydney Grammar** We need to start with a little history. One of Halliday's most important contributions to Linguistics in the late 1960s was to develop a descriptive framework for English and other languages which demonstrated clearly that we need to distinguish, as separate variables, the concepts of **thematic** meaning and **informational** meaning. While it quite frequently happens that the Subject Theme of a clause (e.g. *she*) is presented as 'recoverable' (and so is marked as 'Given' in an *IFG*-style analysis of the 'information structure' of a clause) Halliday's great insight was to recognize - and then to demonstrate - that THE THEMATIC AND INFORMATIONAL STRANDS OF MEANING ARE IN PRINCIPLE INDEPENDENT. His descriptions of these areas of English grammar are now widely reproduced in standard works such as Quirk et al 1985 (so usually without acknowledgement - a practice that is the ultimate accolade for a new idea).

We have just met the most frequent type of 'thematic' meaning, and we shall shortly meet the most frequent type of 'informational' meaning.

It is not surprising, then, that in virtually all examples of fully analyzed clauses (e.g. those in 'The "silver" text' on pages 368-85 of Halliday 1994),

Halliday shows TWO lines of analysis for these two types of meaning: one for 'thematic' meaning and one for 'informational' meaning. In practical terms, then, Halliday clearly recognizes the independent existence of these two strands.

However, in his verbal descriptions and his summary diagrams of the nature of language, he always locates these two strands of meaning within a single 'functional component' (or 'metafunction'), which he terms the 'textual' component. Interestingly, he originally included both types of analysis under the 'cover term' of 'theme' (Halliday 1967b: 199, 1969/72/81:141). In Halliday 1968 (p. 211) the name became the 'discoursal component', and by Halliday 1970a (pp. 160-6) he had changed it to the 'textual component' - and so it has remained ever since. He suggests that what these two types of meaning have in common is that both serve an 'enabling' function (i.e. they are said to 'enable' the expression of 'experiential' and 'interpersonal' meanings). It is true that they both have a role to play in determining the sequence in which elements occur in the clause, but describing the relationship between these strands and the others as 'enabling' has the unfortunate effect of appearing to downgrade their importance in relation to those other strands of meaning - something that was clearly NOT Halliday's intention.

The Cardiff Grammar, however, takes to its logical conclusion Halliday's innovative proposal that each of these two strands of meaning is (i) an important type of meaning in its own right and (ii) independent of the other. In other words, it recognizes that each of the two makes a contribution to the total meaning of the clause that is as significant in its way as, say, the 'experiential' or the 'interpersonal' strand. Our experience of using this approach in the Cardiff Grammar - for both describing and generating text-sentences - is that there is no advantage in treating the two strands as 'sub-components' of an overarching 'textual' component. Indeed, the danger in this is that they may be thought of, wrongly, as one 'strand of meaning' (as they were in the original Prague School approach, from which Halliday developed his new approach in the late 1960s). The fact is that each strand conveys its own distinctive type of meaning, such that no account of the meaning of a clause - whether spoken or written - is complete without a description that includes both. And this fact is best expressed by avoiding the introduction of 'textual' as a 'cover term' for both. We might say, then, that in recognizing each of the two strands of 'thematic' and 'informational' meaning in their own right, the Cardiff Grammar is more 'Hallidayan' than Halliday's own grammar.

There is a second important difference from the Sydney Grammar to which I must now draw your attention. Like the matter that we have just considered, this is a matter of both **description** and **theory**. This difference is that, while Halliday presents his analyses of the 'thematic' strand of meaning in a clause as consisting of a 'Theme' and a 'Rheme', the concept that there is an element of the clause called the 'Rheme' is rejected in the Cardiff Grammar. We simply mark any element that is one of the various types of 'Theme' as the type that it is, and, since there is nothing to be said about the elements that occur within the part of the clause that an *IFG* analysis would label as the 'Rheme' (other than

8.7 A covert Agent (or other PR): the second source of the 'passive' Auxiliary

However, in the vast majority of cases in which the clause is 'passive' - about 80 per cent - the reason is that the Performer has chosen a very different kind of meaning. Compare (4) with (6):

(4) Rouen was besieged by King Henry for six months.
(6) Rouen was besieged for six months.

---

what is covered in the analysis in the 'informational' and other strands of meaning), we do not label the 'post-Theme' part of the clause at all. Indeed, to label the clause elements that are NOT types of 'Theme' collectively as the 'Rheme' gives the misleading impression that there is a clause element with this name, when the evidence is that there is no such element. Our experience in developing the Cardiff Grammar is that the concept of 'Rheme' is simply not needed at all - either in the description of a text or in the generation of a text-sentence. Interestingly, the generative version of the Sydney Grammar reflects a similar position. The diagram on p. 109 of Matthiessen and Bateman 1991: 109 simply leaves unlabelled the part of the clause that is not the 'Theme' - very much as is done in the Cardiff Grammar representation of the strands of meaning (e.g. Figure 17-2 in Chapter 17) - except that the Cardiff Grammar analysis is in terms of features from the system network, while the Sydney Grammar analysis is in terms of clause 'functions' (i.e. clause elements). The point is that the absence of the concept of 'Rheme' is not missed in either generative model. (See Section 2.2 of Chapter 2 of Fawcett 2009 for reasons why it isn't needed for modelling 'text development', as suggested in Danes 1974, which complement the reasons given above.) The concept of 'Rheme' is rather like the appendix in the human body: a left-over from an earlier stage in the development of the current model - i.e. that stage being the pioneering work of the Prague School on which Halliday drew in developing what we now see as the two 'thematic' and 'informational' strands of meaning (e.g. as described in Vachek 1966).

While this point is important for making good SFL **descriptions** of languages, it is also important for SFL **theory**. Its theoretical significance lies in the fact that it is a further piece of evidence that it is not clause-length STRUCTURES for each strand of meaning that are conflated, as Halliday's description of English in *IFG* implies, but individual ELEMENTS of those structures. In other words, it is only SOME of the elements of the clause that express two, three, four or even five types of meaning simultaneously, and not every element - nor even most elements. See Fawcett 2000a: 122-35 for a full examination of this central issue in SFL theory - and, more generally, Fawcett 2000a for (i) a full history of the theory of syntax in SFL and (ii) a statement of the theory of syntax that I consider to be required for SFL in the twenty-first century.

Examples such as (6) occur when the Performer decides to omit from a clause with a two-role Process THE PARTICIPANT THAT IS TYPICALLY PRESENTED FIRST. So in (6) P has decided not to mention 'King Henry' (or whoever the 'besieger' was) at all. In such cases we say that the Participant is **covert**.

These two questions arise: (i) Should the covert PR be represented in the structure, and, if so, how? and (ii) What causes a Performer to decide to make a PR covert?

The answer to the first question is that a covert PR should indeed be represented, since its referent is part of the message. And the way in which it should be shown is as in Figure 8-5:

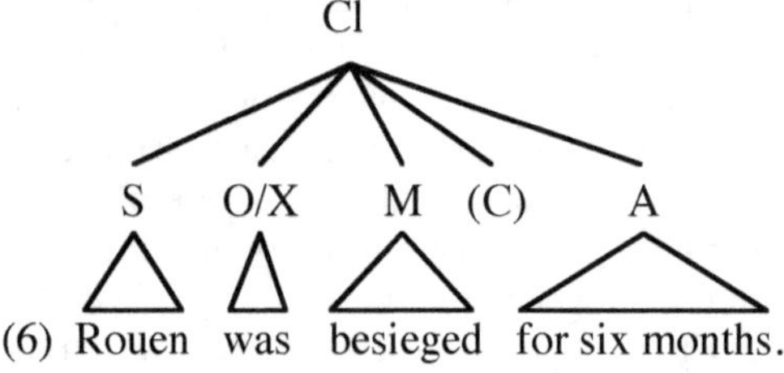

Figure 8-5: The analysis of a covert Participant Role

The second query concerns the reasons why a Performer chooses to make a PR covert. This takes us into the question of how a Performer plan the details of her contribution to the discourse. Strictly speaking, an account of such 'discourse purposes' is far beyond the scope of this book (since our topic is the functional syntax of the clause). Nonetheless, I shall attempt a brief summary, because it is in the process of planning the details of the discourse that the explanation of the syntax is to be found. (Here I am using the term 'discourse purpose' in a wide sense that covers many aspects of the Performer's discourse planning.) The answer is that there is no single, overarching 'discourse purpose' that explains why a Performer decides not to present a PR overtly. The decision depends on a range of widely differing factors. The four main discourse purposes for choosing this option are:

1 **To avoid assigning responsibility** One of the most interesting and most frequent reasons for making a PR covert occurs when the covert Participant is a human being who is functioning as an Agent (a type of Participant that will be described more fully in

Chapter 10). In such cases the reason for omitting the Participant is quite often TO AVOID ASSIGNING RESPONSIBILITY for the event to that person. A typical example would be a military commander who reports to his superiors, after an attack by his soldiers on a village where they thought terrorists were hiding, *Sixteen women and children were killed as part of the collateral damage.* Here, then, the Agent in the action of 'killing' - i.e. the men under the command of the Performer - is conveniently left unstated. The use of a covert PR in this way is often ideologically significant, as in this case - but it need not be, and probably is not in (6). And the other three reasons that we are about to meet are not normally ideologically significant.

2 **Recoverability** In this type the PR is covert because the referent is so clearly RECOVERABLE FROM THE CONTEXT that it doesn't need to be specified - and this is probably the reason for the use of a 'passive' **X** in (6). So here the discourse purpose is to avoid excessive redundancy (a little redundancy being good).

3 **Lack of information** In this type P simply lacks the information to identify the PR. In other words, P could have chosen to add *by someone*, but chooses instead to leave the PR without even the vaguest identification.

4 **Irrelevance** In this type, the PR is left unidentified because it is irrelevant to P's concerns and/or goals in the discourse (as in *Ivy's cat has just been run over*).

As you can see, any of these four reasons may lead to the choice to leave a PR covert by using the 'passive' construction.

We have now met two reasons why the 'passive' Auxiliary gets introduced, and the next section introduces the third. It involves the concept of 'Unmarked Newness'.

8.8 'Unmarked Newness': the third source of the 'passive' Auxiliary

The first thing to note about this third reason for using a 'passive' Auxiliary is that it is often hard to know whether it really is the reason! The problem is that, because it looks and sounds like the type of example that we were considering in Section 8.4, i.e. (4), it is sometimes hard to tell whether the Performer's reason for using this construction is to have a PR as the Subject Theme (as in Section 8.4) or to have a different PR marked as 'New Information' - or possibly both.

Here - for reasons that will soon be clear - we shall consider (7) instead of (4) - this simply being (4) without the Adjunct *for six months*:

(7) Rouen was besieged by King HENry.

Since this third reason for having a 'passive' Auxiliary is also relevant at other points in understanding how the English clause works, it will be useful to give a brief explanation of it here.

The next few pages are therefore about **Unmarked Newness**. I shall begin with six key concepts, and then I shall add three more. Taken together, they explain (i) the meaning of the most frequent of the three major ways in which a clause element may come to be marked as **New Information**, and (ii) one of the major roles of intonation in the operation of the grammar - even, as we shall see, in the grammar of written texts. This, then, is part of yet another strand of meaning: the **informational** strand.

To understand this strand of meaning, we must start by considering what happens in a **spoken text**. Then, when we have a clear picture of this, we shall go on to consider the fascinating problem of how a reader of a **written text** extracts from the written words what we may call, informally, the 'information structure' of each of its text-sentences.[61]

1 Every spoken sentence consists of one or more **intonation units**. If you read (7) aloud you will probably read it in a way that tells the listener that it is all one intonation unit.

---

61 **Difference from the Sydney Grammar** While the term 'information structure' is frequently used in *IFG*, there is in fact no 'structure', in the strict sense of the term. The generative version of the Sydney Grammar identifies, in each information unit, ONLY ONE ELEMENT, e.g. the 'New' element (in (7) that is conflated with *King Henry*. The Addressee (and also the analyst) may well be able to INFER from other evidence (e.g. the use of *he, she, it they, them* etc) that certain stretches of a text-sentence are probably 'Given'. So when, in analyzing a text-sentence in the *IFG* manner, an analyst writes 'Given' below an element or a string of elements, THIS IS MERELY AN INFERENCE FROM THE TEXT, not part of the grammar itself. Thus the status of 'Given' is very like that of 'Rheme', as described in Footnote 60.

2 Every intonation unit (at the level of **form**) is the realization of an **information unit** (at the level of **meaning**). So (7) has one information unit.
3 Every intonation unit has one **Tonic**. This takes the form of a strong pitch movement known as a **Tone**. Example (7) would typically be spoken with the Tonic on the capitalized syllable (i.e. *HEN*) and, since the MOOD of (7) is 'information giver', the Tone would be a **fall**.[62]
4 In the case of **Unmarked Newness** - which is the type of 'Newness' we are considering here - THE TONIC AUTOMATICALLY FALLS ON THE LAST 'NEW' WORD IN THE UNIT - so typically on the last word with an inherently 'strong' syllable (i.e. probably a noun, adjective, adverb or lexical verb).
5 This marks the element on which it falls as **New Information** - or simply **New** - i.e. information that P is presenting to A as material that P believes A does not already know.
6 Note the word 'AUTOMATICALLY' in 4 above - i.e. the Performer cannot simply decide to put the Tonic on one element rather than another. An information unit is only given 'Unmarked Newness' if another option - the more dramatic meaning of 'Contrastive Newness' - is NOT chosen. So 'Unmarked Newness' is the result of a DEFAULT PROCEDURE that is followed when P chooses NOT to present any element as 'contrastively new'. This option, which is described in Section 9.5 of Chapter 9, is selected in only a small minority of information units (often under one per cent, but with a higher frequency in spoken texts). So 'Unmarked Newness' is by far the more frequent type - and the only way that P can exploit this pattern is to place an element at a position in the clause where it has a good chance of receiving the automatically inserted Tonic. (A third type of 'Newness is introduced in Section 12.5 of Chapter 12.)

---

62 The **Tone** with which a Tonic is spoken is the realization of fine choices in the MOOD network of the clause - i.e. its **interpersonal** meaning. But since we are concerned here with the **informational** strand of meaning we shall not explore Tones any further here; for the Tones used in the Cardiff Grammar see Tench 1996.

Let me summarize so far. If the option to mark an element as 'Contrastively New' is NOT chosen, the Tonic is placed on the last word in the information unit with an inherently 'strong' syllable, and that element is thereby marked as 'New Information'. In (7), the fact that the Tonic falls on *HEN* signifies that the clause element *King Henry* refers to something that is 'New Information'.

Now we come to the way in which Unmarked Newness may lead to the use of the 'passive' Auxiliary. How does it do this? The answer is that if P makes 'King Henry' a Complement (rather than a Subject) 'King Henry' has a fairly good chance of being the last element in the clause, and so of being marked as 'New'.

To complete the picture of 'Unmarked Newness' in English, I should add these three supplementary points to our summary:

7 Being the Complement doesn't make it 100 per cent certain that 'King Henry' will be marked as 'New Information', because there could be a following Adjunct (e.g. *for six months*) - and in this case the unmarked Tonic would probably fall on *months*.
8 Any words that occur AFTER the Tonic are marked as 'Given Information' - i.e. P is presenting them as 'recoverable' by the Addressee, as with *in it* in *Did you put SUGar in it?*
9 The elements of the information unit that precede the element marked as 'New' MAY OR MAY NOT also be 'New'.

Interestingly, then, the last point states that the message we receive from the intonation - whether as the Addressee or as text analysts - is unspecific in this respect. The 'Newness' may be limited to the element on which the Tonic falls (here 'King Henry'), or it may extend right back to the very beginning of the intonation unit (which coincides in (7) with the beginning of the clause). Or it may stop at any element between the two. In other words, as text analysts, we have to work with the fact that the message sent by the intonational component of the English language is, for the stretch of the intonation unit that precedes the Tonic, unclear. What is certain, however, is that the word on which the Tonic falls is **New Information**.

Does this vagueness matter? Not very much. The reason is that the language has other ways of conveying the meaning of 'recoverability' (or 'givenness'). Let's start from (7). Here it seems virtually certain that the 'New Information' extends all the way back to the start of the clause. This is because it doesn't contain any words that realize the meaning 'recoverable information'. But it would have, if the sentence had been *It was besieged by King Henry*, because here the word *it* signals the meaning 'you know which one', i.e. the meaning of 'recoverable information'. But that would still leave the words *was* and *besieged* in an unclear state. The key point is that, even when the sentence is in its natural context as part of a text, the analyst can do no more than make an intelligent guess about the extent of the 'Newness'.[63]

Finally, consider the situation in which (7) occurs as part of a **written text**. Interestingly, the 'informational meanings' of an intonation unit are 'read into' it by skilled readers - drawing, of course, on the evidence of the preceding text as well as that within the clause itself. And the only way, logically, in which this can be done is if the Addressee produces a SILENT version of 'reading the sentence aloud' in which A can 'hear' the intonation with which the clause would have been spoken, if it had been read aloud.

Let me summarize where we have got to. We can now see that the Performer's motivation to use a 'passive' construction could have been the wish to present 'King Henry' as **New Information**.

Unfortunately, however, we cannot be sure of this. The reason is that the Performer of *Rouen was besieged by King Henry* is simultaneously presenting the French city of 'Rouen' as the **Subject Theme**. It could therefore have been P's wish to have 'Rouen' as the Subject Theme that led to the use of the 'passive' version of the clause. In a single sentence that is extracted from its source text it is usually hard to decide which is the motivation, but

---

63 **Comparison with the Sydney Grammar** For the description of English intonation used here, see Tench 1996. Tench's model is based fairly closely on Halliday's description of English intonation, e.g. as presented in Halliday 1967c and 1970b, but it is an advance on it in a number of ways - just as the description of the forms and meanings of functional syntax presented here is an updated version of Halliday's description of these phenomena.

Tench 1996 is, however, a description of intonation for the text analyst and not a generative model of intonation. The fully formalized generative version of the model of intonation for the Cardiff Grammar (which incorporates some minor changes) is described and illustrated in Fawcett 1990 and 2004a.

when we see a sentence in its context we are normally able to tell quite easily which of the two reasons is the right one - or whether both apply.

In this section, then, we have met the 'unmarked' type of 'Newness', and this is the type that is used in upwards of 90 per cent of intonation units. It is, as we have seen, the type that is generated as the default - i.e. if the meaning of 'Contrastively New' is NOT chosen. We shall meet this second important type of 'Newness' in Section 9.5 of the next chapter - and we shall meet a third type of 'Newness' in Chapter 12.

8.9 Summary

In the last few sections we have looked at the three reasons for using the 'passive' form of a clause. And, as a result, we have now met TWO MORE STRANDS OF MEANING: the **thematic** strand and the **informational** strand. The first affects the choice of elements that come at - or near - the START of the clause in English, and the second affects the choice of an element that may well come at the END of the clause.

This means that we have now identified one or more of the types of meaning within each of the following six strands of meaning: the **experiential**, **interpersonal**, **affective**, **validity**, **thematic** and **informational** strands.[64]

Let us now return to the Auxiliaries themselves. We shall summarize the three new elements introduced in this chapter in diagram form. Please look at Figure 8-6, on the next page. It illustrates the following facts:

---

64 **Comparison with the Sydney Grammar** As we saw in Footnote 61, Halliday always analyzes the **informational** strand of meaning as a separate strand from the **thematic** strand in his diagrams that analyze clauses - rather as we do here. Yet at the same time he describes them both as being in the 'textual' metafunction. The Cardiff Grammar simplifies matters by treating the 'informational' strand of meaning as a strand of meaning in is own right, on a par with the **experiential**, **interpersonal**, **affective**, **validity** and **thematic** strands of meaning. Its distinctive function is to present certain elements as 'New' to the Addressee (or, as we shall see in the next chapter, as 'Contrastively New').

1 All three **X**s can occur in the same clause.
2 If there isn't a word that expounds **O** already, the first **X** takes on the role of the Operator and is conflated with **O**.
3 We represent the **covert Participant** by placing **C** in round brackets at the place where it would occur if it was overt.[65]

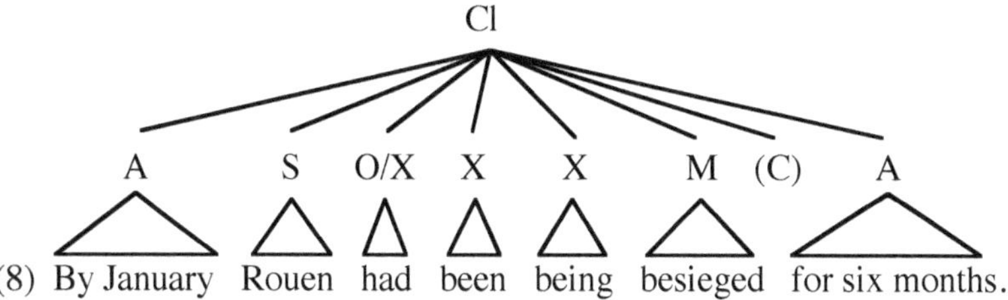

Figure 8-6: A clause with three Auxiliaries

It will by now be clear that the realization of the meanings that are expressed in the three Auxiliaries is quite a complex matter - especially when there is more than one such Auxiliary in the same clause. A further complication is that, in a full model, we must allow for Adjuncts to intervene between them. It is a particularly difficult task for the researcher who is building a generative grammar to provide for the various types of complexity that the Auxiliaries introduce, because of the suffixes and other changes of form that they require in a following element - especially when we extend the model to handle irregular lexical verbs.[66]

---

65 **Comparison with the Sydney Grammar** In the Sydney Grammar the Auxiliary Verbs are treated as elements of the 'verbal group', and this in turn fills the 'Predicator', which is an element of the clause. In the Cardiff Grammar the Auxiliary Verbs are themselves elements of clause structure, just as the Main Verb is. **X**s are very frequently conflated with **O**, and for this to be able to happen they need to be elements of the same unit as **O**. So, since **O** is a clause element, the **X**s must be too. See Footnote 27 for other arguments for treating all elements that would be elements of the 'verbal group' in the Sydney Grammar as elements of the clause.

66 All these problems have been overcome in the Cardiff Grammar, and implemented in the computer. See Fawcett, Tucker and Lin 1993 for an overview of the generation of this spoken text-sentence: */ but you MUST/1- have been at the meeting /*. See Fawcett 2000b and 2000c for a full critique of Halliday's concept of the 'verbal group' as described in *IFG*.

For the text analyst, however, there is good news. This is that when we are analyzing text-sentences we only need to identify the Auxiliaries as **X**, in the way shown in Figure 8-6. We can ignore the suffixes and past participle forms of **M**, because they follow automatically from the analysis of the Auxiliary.

The three Auxiliaries that we have introduced here are the most frequent **X**s - but they are not the only ones. Several other types will be introduced in Section 14.3 of Chapter 14.

However, one result of the enrichment of our picture of the elements of the clause introduced in Chapters 6 and 8 is that they make it necessary to extend the *Mood Test* to take account of these new factors. This we shall do in the next chapter - but only after adding several further reasons for revising it.

Chapter 9
POLARITY, 'Contrastive Newness' and *Preliminary Guidelines* with an improved *Mood Test*

9.1 The types of Operator met so far

In our first example, back in Chapter 3, the Operator was expounded by the modal verb *shall*. Then in Chapter 6 we found that a form of *be* that is functioning as the Main Verb can be conflated with the Operator, and in the last chapter we found that an Auxiliary can as well. So there are already two reasons why we need to update Step 2 of the version of the *Mood Test* in Chapter 4. Now we come to several other reasons to update it.

The two questions that this chapter addresses are:

1 What happens, on those occasions when we need an Operator to form a 'polarity seeker', if there isn't one?
2 Are there any other meanings which require the presence of an Operator - and if so what are they?

In answering these questions, this chapter introduces the new strand of meaning that expresses **negativity** (through the POLARITY system), and then it adds 'Contrastive Newness' to the **informational** strand of meaning. The chapter concludes with revised *Guidelines* that include a more comprehensive *Mood Test*.

9.2 The problem of a clause with no Operator

Try analyzing (1) below - and, as you do, try to apply the *Mood Test* that was introduced in Chapter 4. As in earlier analyses, you may encounter a little difficulty, but do your best.

(1) Adam visited Paula last week.

Don't turn the page until you have attempted the analysis!

Solution

You will probably have been able to analyze (1) quite easily, and your analysis is likely to be as shown in Figure 9-1.

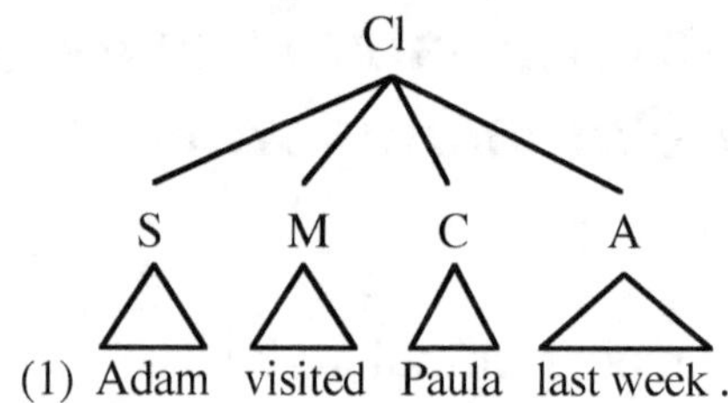

Figure 9-1: The analysis of Example (1)

But were you able to apply the *Mood Test*? You were not. The problem comes in Step 2. It is that, since there is no Operator in (6), there is no element which you can use, with the Subject, to form a 'polarity seeker'.

Clauses such as (1) in fact occur very frequently in texts, especially in narratives - as the underlined **M**s in the following example show:

Paula walked down to the shops and Adam went with her. Paula bought a pair of jeans for Adam, and then they went to the library and Paula borrowed a book. After that they visited Phoebe *in her new flat. Phoebe and Paula had a nice cup of tea, and Adam had some orange squash.*

Since this form of the Main Verb is so frequent, it is clearly important that the *Mood Test* should cover such cases.

9.3 Introducing a form of *do* as a default Operator

So how is the 'polarity seeker' that is equivalent to (1) formed? Up to this point we have found that, when we needed an Operator to change the meaning of a clause from 'information giver' to 'polarity seeker', there was already an Operator in the clause to enable us to do it. But in this case there isn't. The answer to our question, as you will probably have discovered for yourself in analyzing (1), is that we simply introduce a form of the verb *do* as an Operator - as in Figure 9-2.

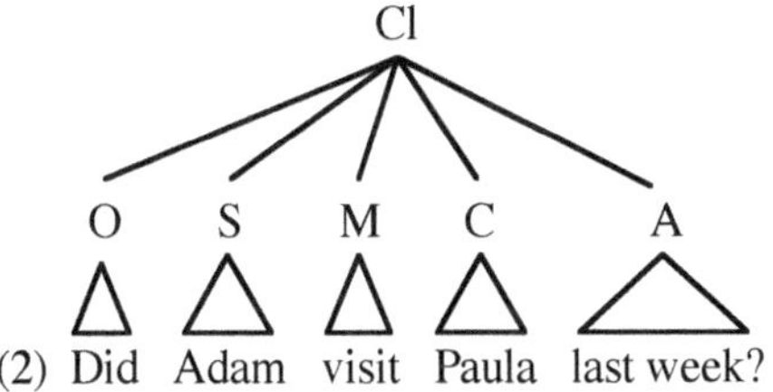

Figure 9-2: The 'polarity seeker' equivalent of (1)

The key point is that it is ONLY WHEN NO OTHER MEANING HAS BEEN CHOSEN THAT IS EXPRESSED IN AN OPERATOR that a form of *do* is introduced. In other words, the form of *do* is introduced AS A DEFAULT. The forms of *do* that can function at **O** are simply:

do, does, did.

The fact that we find it necessary to provide a word that will function as the Operator is interesting in itself - because it shows how important it is to have the structure of **O S** when expressing the meaning of 'polarity seeker' in English.

However, there are two other equally frequent reasons why a form of *do* may be introduced as a default Operator, and we shall now consider each of these in turn.

9.4 Negation: a second reason for having an Operator

We have already met the concept of POLARITY briefly, in Chapter 4. Clauses may be 'positive', as in *Adam ate the ice-cream*, or 'negative', as in *Adam didn't eat the ice-cream.*

However, there are TWO frequent ways of expressing negation:

(i) the 'unmarked negative', realized as *n't*, and
(ii) the 'strong negative', realized as *not*.

Here we need to consider them both. They have interesting similarities and differences.

We shall take the 'unmarked negative' first - as in (3):

(3) Adam didn't visit Paula last week.

Try analyzing it, so you discover its structure for yourself.

Don't turn the page until you have attempted the analysis - and, when you do, cover the two solutions lower down the page.

Solution

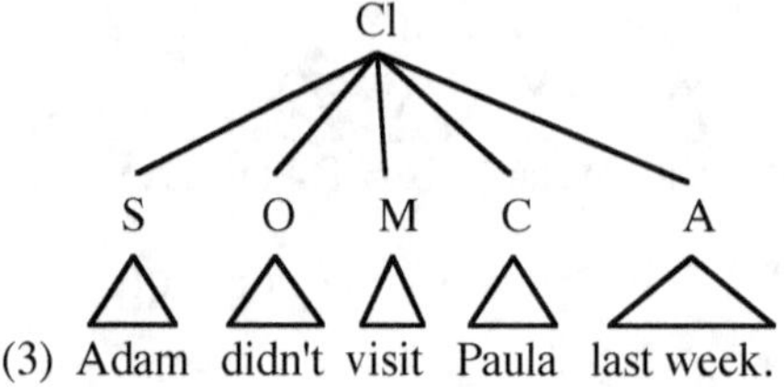

Figure 9-3: The 'unmarked negative' equivalent of (1)

Notice that the item *n't* is NOT a separate element of the clause, as you might at first think, but an integral part of the Operator.[67]

To remind ourselves that the Operator is not necessarily just **O**, try analyzing (4) and (5) (spoken on a visit to a wild life park):

(4) They aren't dangerous.
(5) They aren't being friendly.

This will also be an exercise in analyzing forms of *be*.

Solutions

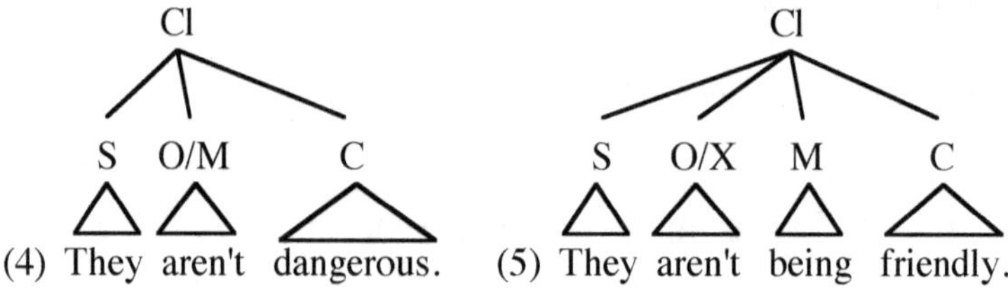

Figure 9-4: Conflation plus 'unmarked negation'

The analysis of **O/M** in (4) and **O/X** in (5) demonstrates that the suffix *n't* is also added to the Operator WHEN IT IS CONFLATED WITH ANOTHER ELEMENT. The test of this claim is that, if you

---

67 In this book we are focussing on the **syntax** of the clause, and it is a matter of **morphology** that the item *n't* is a **suffix** that is added to the **base** of the **word** that expounds the Operator. There is no need to analyze the base and suffix as separate elements, because they always function as a single syntactic element, i.e. the Operator.

change (4) into *Aren't they dangerous?*, the **O/M** functions as a single element. And the same is true when it is an Auxiliary that is conflated with the Operator, such as the **O/X** in (5), which becomes *Aren't they being friendly?*

It is tempting to think that the reason why the Operator is introduced for the 'unmarked negative' is that it is needed to provide a **base** to which the **suffix** *n't* can be added. But this cannot in fact be the explanation - and for the following interesting reason. This is the fact that the Operator is not only required for the 'unmarked negative' of *n't* but also for the 'strong negative' of *not*, as in (6):

(6) She did not accept his excuse.

In other words, native speakers of English don't say **She not accepted his excuse*, but *She did not accept his excuse* (Here I am using the useful convention that an asterisk indicates a grammatically unacceptable sentence.)

In the case of a clause with a 'strong negative', then, the word *not* functions as AN INDEPENDENT ELEMENT. It is easy to identify this element when you are analyzing clauses, because it is always the word *not*. This new element is called the **Negator**.

How can we demonstrate that the word *not* is NOT part of the Operator (in the way that we have seen that *n't* is part of it)? The obvious test, you might think, is to convert the example into a clause that has the form a 'polarity seeker'. Let's try it. The result is as in (6) in Figure 9-5.

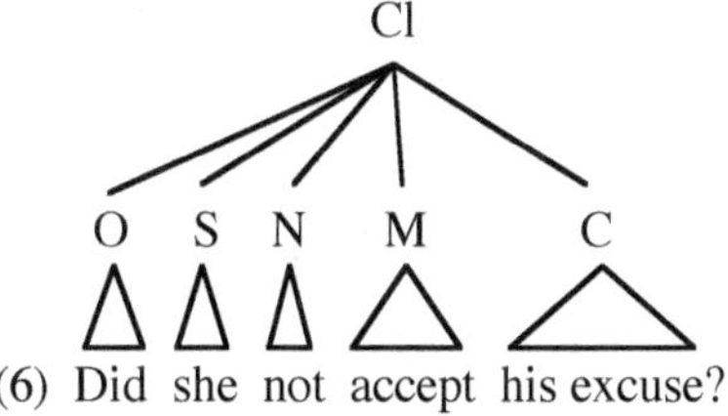

Figure 9-5: Why the Negator is not part of the Operator

However, there is a little problem here. Notice that I have just used the words 'a clause that HAS THE FORM OF a polarity seeker'. I have had to use these words rather than simply saying 'a clause that is a polarity seeker', because there is a problem with the logic of saying that we are applying the 'polarity seeker' test to a clause that is 'negative'. Let me explain.

The problem is that a clause that has BOTH the structure **O S** AND the item *n't* as the suffix on **O** does not normally function as a 'polarity seeker', but as something else (a point that I'll come back to in a moment). In other words, since the purpose of uttering a 'polarity seeker' such as *Did she accept his excuse?* is precisely to discover the polarity of the proposition expressed in the clause, it follows that A 'POLARITY SEEKER' DOES NOT HAVE 'POLARITY'.

Why, in that case, does the test work for 'positive' clauses? The reason is the unusual way in which the meaning of 'positive' is realized. The meaning 'positive' is in fact realized by THE LACK OF AN OVERT MARKER OF THE MEANING OF 'NEGATIVE'. So the realization of 'positive' is that there is no realization!

In a 'negative' clause, however, there IS a realization of the meaning 'negative' (typically in the form of *n't* or *not*), so that when we apply the test we end up with a clause that actually contains a marker of 'negativity' - and it is this prevents it from being interpreted as a 'polarity seeker'.

The solution to the problem is to make all clauses to which this test is to be applied (i) an 'information giver' and (ii) 'positive' - and this, you will find, is stated as part of the revised *Guidelines* in Section 9.6.

The interesting side effect of the fact that there cannot logically be a 'negative' 'polarity seeker' is that a clause with both **O S** and *n't* such as *Didn't she accept his excuse?* is available to be used to express a rather different meaning. Such a clause is a **confirmation seeker**. And a clause with *not* such as *Did she not accept his excuse?* is usually one too.[68] (We shall come back to the question of the meaning of a 'confirmation seeker' in Chapter 11,

---

68 I say 'usually', because it is possible for a clause containing the Negator *not*, such as *Did she not accept his excuse?* to mean 'Is it or is it not the case that she did not accept his excuse' - i.e. to be a 'polarity seeker' where the proposition is 'negative'. Compare 'double negatives' such as *She can't have not seen us*, which show that both the meaning of the Operator and the meaning of what follows *not* can be negated. In rare cases, therefore, a clause may contain more than one Negator.

when we expand our current rather restricted picture of the forms and meanings of MOOD.)

Let's return for a moment to the 'unmarked negative' form *n't*. Virtually every word that can function as **O** can accept the suffix *n't*. The only exceptions are *am* and its contraction *'m*, which require the **Negator** in an 'information giver', as in *I am not rich* and *I'm not rich*. But in the version of an **O S** structure with *n't* the word *aren't* is used instead of **amn't*, as in the 'confirmation seeker' *Aren't I lucky?* (This is in contrast with the 'exclamation' *Aren't I lucky!* which we shall meet in Section 11.2 of Chapter 11.) Note too the unusual contracted forms of *will* and *shall*, when followed by *n't*, as *won't* and *shan't*.

Finally, there is the question of how we should analyse the words *Yes* and *No*. We saw in Section 4.9 of Chapter 4 that:

Yes means 'If I said this clause in full it would be **positive**,' and
No means 'If I said this clause in full it would be **negative**.'

In such cases, then, the function of *Yes* or *No* is to express:

(i) the POLARITY of the clause ('positive' or 'negative'),
(ii) the MOOD of the clause (always 'information giver'), and
(iii) the TRANSITIVITY of the clause (the semantic feature for which is 'transitivity recoverable' - the Process and PRs typically being recoverable from the 'polarity seeker' to which *Yes* or *No* is the response).

No single element covers all these meanings, but the one that comes closest to the crucial meaning is the **Operator**. It is, after all, the element to which the suffix *n't* is attached, and the element that must be present when the Negator *not* is used. We therefore show the analysis of both *Yes* and *No* as a **clause** that has the single element of the Operator.[69]

Negativity is a very different type of meaning from any that we have met so far. It is not simply a variant of MOOD, because most

---

69 In this book we are limiting ourselves to the simple clause, but it may be useful to say that in a response such as *Yes, he is* each of *Yes* and *he is* is a separate clause. The two clauses function alongside each other in a single sentence, just as two co-ordinated clauses do.

choices in the MOOD network - but not all, as we have just seen - select independently in the POLARITY system. An 'information giver' is a 'giver' of 'information', whether it is 'positive' or 'negative'. So here we are adding **negativity** as a seventh strand of meaning that the clause expresses - alongside the **experiential**, **interpersonal**, **affective**, **validity**, **thematic** and **informational** strands. (Now there is only one strand of meaning to come - and for this we shall have to wait till Chapter 12.)

9.5 The 'Contrastive Newness' of 'polarity correction': a third reason for having an Operator

Consider the following scrap of conversation, which concerns the question of how Fred feels about Fiona - and notice the use of a form of *do* in Paula's response.

(7) Adam: Fred doesn't like Fiona.
Paula: He DOES like her.

Why doesn't Paula simply say *He likes her*?[70] Paula's response introduces two more new concepts:

(i) the Operator is expounded by a form of *do,* and
(ii) a **Contrastive Tonic** (shown by capital letters) is placed on it.

By placing a Contrastive Tonic on the Operator Paula presents its meaning of 'positive' as being not merely 'New' information (i.e. the type that we met in Section 8.8 of Chapter 8), but as being **Contrastively New** information. This, then, is a second type of **informational** meaning. And, as we saw in the last chapter, it is when 'Contrastive Newness' is NOT chosen (as is the usual case) that the default generation of 'Unmarked Newness' occurs.

The effect of marking an element as 'Contrastively New' is always to signal that THE PERFORMER IS CORRECTING A POSSIBLE MISAPPREHENSION BY THE ADDRESSEE. In the present case it is a misapprehension about the POLARITY of the clause, i.e. Paula is emphasizing that her statement about 'Fred's liking Fiona' is

---

70 Notice that, whether Paula says *He DOES like her* or *He likes her*, she will replace the names used in Adam's original clause by pronouns rather than repeat the names.

'positive' and not 'negative' (as she thinks Adam may mistakenly believe).

This use of forms of *do* is often referred to as 'emphasis', but that is a rather inadequate description of its function. Its function is always to correct a possible misapprehension by the Addressee.

For three further examples of 'Contrastively New' elements, consider the alternative responses by Paula in the following little dialogue:

(8) Adam: Fred doesn't like Fiona.
(9a) Paula: (But) IKE likes her. [correction concerns **S**]
(9b) (No;) he LOVES her! [correction concerns **M**]
(9c) (No;) he likes IVy. [correction concerns **C**]

As these examples suggest, virtually any element in the clause has the potential to be made 'Contrastively New'.

This generalization even includes the last element - which you might think we have covered already (in Section 8.8 of Chapter 8). But this isn't so. Contrast the way in which Adam would be likely to say *Fred doesn't like Fiona* in (8) and the way in which Paula would say *He likes IVY* in (9c). Adam's intonation in (8) would typically have a slowly falling pattern, with a final fall on the **Tonic** in *FiOna*, and it simply expresses the meaning of unmarked 'New'. But in (9c) there is a low start, followed by a high fall on the **Contrastive Tonic** in *IVy* - in which *he likes* is presented as 'recoverable' and *IVy* as 'Contrastively New'.

9.6 *Preliminary Guidelines 2*

Now that we have introduced (i) the use of forms of *be* as a Main Verb, (ii) the three main Auxiliaries, and (iii) the various reasons for using forms of *do* as the Operator, it is time to revise Step 2 of *Preliminary Guidelines 1* to take account of these. The other steps, however, will still involve intelligent guesswork, until we have made fuller studies of the other elements of the clause and the various strands of meaning that they express. The *Full Guidelines* for the simple clause will be given in Chapter 15.

0 **Preparation:** If the clause to be analyzed does NOT have the structure of an **information giver** that is **positive**, first re-express it as one.

Example
Fiona saw him. This is already both an 'information giver' and 'positive', so it doesn't need to be re-expressed.

1 Find the **Process** and so the **Main Verb**. (No tests yet.)

Example
Intelligent guess: The Process is 'seeing', so **M** is *saw*.

2 ***The Mood Test***

2.1 **Find the Operator**, if there is one. So far, it is

EITHER	(i)	a modal verb such as *may, might, shall, should, will, would, can, could, must*	as **O**
OR	(ii)	*do, does* or *did* (used in a 'polarity seeker', 'negation' and 'polarity correction')	as **O**
OR	(iii)	*am, is, are, was* or *were*, expressing a Process of 'being',	as **O/M**
OR	(iv)	*am, is, are, was, were, have, has* or *had*, expressing an 'Auxiliary' meaning,	as **O/X**

Example
In *Fiona saw him* there is no **O**.

2.2 Re-express the **information giver** as a **polarity seeker**, i.e. as seeking the answer *Yes* or *No.* If the clause has no Operator, supply *do, does* or *did,* as appropriate, as **O**.

Example
Re-express *Fiona saw him* as *Did Fiona see him?*

2.3 Now you are in a position to identify the **Subject (S)**.

The Subject is the word (or words) which, by occurring before or after the Operator, tells you whether the clause is an 'information giver' or a 'polarity seeker'.

Example
We know that the word *did* is the Operator, so *Fiona* must be the Subject - because, by occurring after *did*, it shows that the MOOD of the clause is 'information seeker'.

So in *Did Fiona see him?*, *did* is **O** and *Fiona* is **S**.
So *Fiona* is also **S** in the original clause *Fiona saw him.*

In other words, typically:
S O or S O/X or S O/M or S M means 'information giver', and
O S or O/X S or O/M S means 'polarity seeker'.

3 **S** is a Participant (99% reliable).
Now find any other Participant, and label it **C**. (No tests yet.)

4 Find any Adjuncts and label them **A**. (No tests yet.)

9.7 A summary of MOOD so far

The improved version of the *Mood Test* in Step 2 above can also stand as a summary of what we have noted so far about MOOD. Although we have so far identified only the two meanings of 'information giver' and 'polarity seeker', they are two of the most important choices in the network - and I have also mentioned the 'confirmation seeker'. Our focus has been on learning to recognize a variety of types of Operator, as summarized in the improved *Mood Test*, and we are now familiar with both the simple version, when **O** is expounded by a modal verb or a form of *do*, and the two 'conflated' versions of **O/M** or **O/X**. We shall expand the present rather skimpy picture of the choices in MOOD in Chapter 11. Indeed, some readers may be surprised by the extent to which the MOOD system will be expanded.

But first, in Chapter 10, we shall focus on gaining a good overview of the most important patterns in the TRANSITIVITY part of the 'experiential' strand of meaning.

Chapter 10
An overview of the syntax of TRANSITIVITY: Participants as Subjects and Complements

10.1 Four questions

The main purpose of this chapter is to give a clear picture of what Subjects and Complements are, and how to recognize them. The questions to be answered are:

Question 1: What is a Subject - as well as being (i) an element that helps to express the MOOD meaning and (ii) a type of THEME?

Question 2: What is the significance of labelling part of a clause as a Complement - rather than as an Adjunct?

Question 3: How many Complements can there be in a clause?

Question 4: What types of Complement is it useful to recognize at this stage?[71]

---

71 Traditional grammars make a distinction between 'Objects' and 'Complements' and, within 'Objects', between 'Direct Objects' and 'Indirect Objects'. Some grammars also make a further distinction between 'Subject Complements' and 'Object Complements'. Yet here we shall treat them all as 'Complements'.

This question then arises: If SFG doesn't recognize such distinctions, how does it account for the phenomena that these distinctions were set up to describe? The answer is that SFG uses an even fuller and more discriminating set of functionally motivated categories - one which makes such distinctions redundant in English. (However, we should note that the traditional distinctions (or equivalent categories) still have a role to play in describing inflectional languages like French and German, in which the contrasts in 'case endings' at the level of form do not match the semantic distinctions between Participant Roles.)

The 'more discriminating set of functionally motivated categories' is the set of types of **Participant Role**, versions of which are used in both the Cardiff Grammar and the Sydney Grammar (such as Agent and Affected, Carrier and Attribute, and Cognizant and Phenomenon, to cite just three configurations from the Cardiff Grammar's set of PRs). Once these are introduced there is no longer

In order to answer these questions, however, we must first have a clear picture of what a P**articipant Role** is.

10.2 How to identify a Participant Role

Till now, we have been using the term 'Participant' informally, without defining it. The full name for this concept in SFL is **Participant Role**, and Participant Roles are contrasted with **Circumstantial Roles**. The abbreviations for these are PR and CR.

We have already met three types of CR:

1 *gently* in (1) in Chapter 3 and *very carefully indeed* in (1) in Chapter 5 are 'Circumstances of Manner';
2 *now* in (2) in Chapter 6, *yesterday* in (3) in Chapter 7, *by January* in (8) in Chapter 8 and *last week* in (1), (2) and (3) in Chapter 9 are all 'Circumstances of Time Position';
3 *for six months* in (3), (4), (5) and (8) in Chapter 8 are all 'Circumstances of Duration'.

All CRs are expressed as Adjuncts (though it is not the case that all Adjuncts express CRs, as we shall see in Chapter 12).

Here we shall concentrate on the problem of how to be sure that an element is a PR and not a CR. So we shall begin by asking:

What is a Participant Role (PR)?

And the answer is:

A PR is a role that is 'expected' by the Process.

---

any need for terms such as 'Direct' and 'Indirect Object', etc. However, in this introductory book we shall not distinguish between the different types of PR; it will be a sufficient challenge to learn to recognize when an element is functioning as a Participant Role (and so is **S** or **C**) and when as a Circumstantial Role (and so is **A**). See Footnote 76 for an indication of the difficulties.

Interestingly, the distinction between the different Participants is one that is used at THREE LEVELS OF REPRESENTATION in the Cardiff Grammar. Thus we find (i) **participants** such as **agent** (with a lower case initial letter) in the representation of the event in **logical form** that is the input to the lexicogrammar; (ii) references to these participants in the semantic features in the **system networks**, and (iii) an equivalent set of Participant Roles (shown by their initial upper case letter, such as **Agent**) in the **functional structure**. In the full representation of the functional structure the names of the specific types are shown (typically conflated with the **S** and **C**) - as in Figures 17-1 and 17-2 in Chapter 17.

Or, to express it a little more precisely:

> **A Participant Role is a role which we expect to occur in the clause, as a result of knowing what the Process is.**

(I shall explain in Chapter 13 why I have written 'which we expect to occur' rather than simply 'which occurs'.)[72]

We are now in a position to answer the first three questions.

10.3 Answers to the first three questions

Answer to Question 1 (which was 'What is a Subject - as well as being (i) an element that helps to express the MOOD meaning and (ii) a type of THEME?):

> **Typically, the Subject (S) is a PR** (over 99% reliable).

Answer to Question 2 (which, put simply, was 'What is a Complement?'):

> **A Complement (C) is any PR that is not S**. (This generalization is 100% reliable when we are only analyzing the elements of clauses, as we are doing here, but will be

---

72 It is tempting to say that it is the Main Verb (rather than the Process) that 'expects' the PRs - and in around 70-95% of cases (varying with different types of text) it would do no harm to work on this assumption. But if we did we would find that we had two additional problems.

The first is that quite a few verb forms are ambiguous, so that ONE FORM CAN CO-OCCUR WITH TWO (OR MORE) SETS OF PRS. As we shall shortly see, Figure 10-1 provides examples of this. So it is the Process - i.e. the SENSE of the lexical verb at **M** rather than its FORM - that must be our guide.

The second additional problem is that, in English, the expression of the Process is very frequently spread over **M** AND ONE OR MORE OTHER ELEMENTS, i.e. (i) the **Main Verb Extension (MEx)** - of which there may be two and very occasionally three - and (ii) the **preposition** of a following prepositional group. The three possible combinations of these are traditionally termed 'phrasal verbs', 'prepositional verbs', and 'phrasal-prepositional verbs' (e.g. in Quirk et al 1985). Chapter 13 introduces this important set of constructions. They are essential to a full understanding the concept of 'Process' as it is realized in English, and they are appearing with increasing frequency in most types of text – formal, written and technical as well as casual, spoken and non-technical.

expressed in different terms in the test given in the *Full Guidelines* in Chapter 15).[73]

In other words, a Complement is a PR because it 'complements' the Process - in the sense that it is needed to 'complete' the meaning expressed in the Process.[74] So, typically, both the Subject and any Complement in the clause are PRs (99% reliable).

This means that, when the Subject is a PR - as it typically is - it has the following THREE functions:

1 a TRANSITIVITY function in expressing a Participant Role,
2 a MOOD function (i.e. it tells us whether the clause is an 'information giver' or a 'polarity seeker', through its relation to the Operator or Main Verb), and
3 a THEME function (as we saw in Section 8.5 of Chapter 8).

This brings us to **Question 3** (How many Complements can there be in a clause?) It will now be clear that we need to answer this question in terms of the number of PRs, so we shall re-express it as Question 3a:

Question 3a: How many Participant Roles can be associated with a Process?

The answer to Question 3a is:

The vast majority of Processes have TWO associated PRs,
a small number have ONE associated PR,
a small number have THREE associated PRs, and
a very few - i.e. those expressing 'environmental' Processes) - have NO PRs
(e.g. *It*'s *raining*, where *it* does not refer to anything).

---

73 This important modification is needed because, in cases such as the underlined portions of *Ivy was seen* <u>*by Ike*</u> and *Ivy looked* <u>*at Ike*</u>, the PR is not in fact conflated with the **C**. Instead, it is conflated with the 'completive' of the 'prepositional group' that fills the **C**. See Appendix 1 for a summary of the internal structure of the prepositional group.

74 The one exception, which accounts for the fact that this statement is only 99.99% valid, is the 'experientially empty' *it* found in examples such as *Ike resented it that Ivy had visited Fred.*

Let's now answer the original Question 3, which was about the number of Complements. This is the version of the answer that you need to have in mind when analyzing a clause.

Because the Subject is typically a PR (over 99% reliable), we can say that, typically:

The vast majority of clauses have ONE Complement,
a small number have NO Complement
(including ones expressing 'environmental' Processes), and
a small number have TWO Complements.

In the next section we shall meet Figure 10-1, and we shall see that it illustrates examples of clauses with one, two and three PRs - and so clauses with zero, one or two Complements.

Question 4 asked: What types of Complement is it useful to recognize at this stage? This is a question that is best answered by illustrating the types, so I shall delay the answer until Section 10.5, i.e. after we have studied Figure 10-1 in the next section.

Figure 10-1 summarizes, in a single diagram that displays a set of KEY EXAMPLES, everything said so far in this chapter - and a good deal more. So the notes on Figure 10-1 in Section 10.5 will answer Question 4, and the further notes on Figure 10-1 in Section 10.6 will then bring out some further important patterns in the semantics and syntax of TRANSITIVITY in English.

10.4 A summary diagram for TRANSITIVITY

Figure 10-1 shows ALL the main types of Process in English that have either one PR or three PRs, and MOST of the more frequent of the very many types of Process that have two PRs.

The two-role Processes shown here have been chosen because they have an interesting semantic relationship with the example in the neighbouring column - as you can see for yourself.

Figure 10-1 therefore provides a visual summary of practically all that we have learnt so far about TRANSITIVITY. In fact, if you can internalize the information summarized in this diagram - together with the accompanying notes - you will have passed a crucial milestone in building an adequate picture of the TRANSITIVITY structures of English clauses. It provides a simple framework that can guide you to making good analyses of many important aspects of English texts - including making a start on the question of what units may fill the Complement.

I suggest that you now take a few minutes to 'read' Figure 10-1 for yourself, noting the similarities and contrasts between adjacent examples, both vertically and horizontally. Then, when you have done that, read the notes that follow it in Section 10.5, because it is these that provide the answer to Question 4. Finally, go on to the additional points that are made in the notes in Section 10.6.

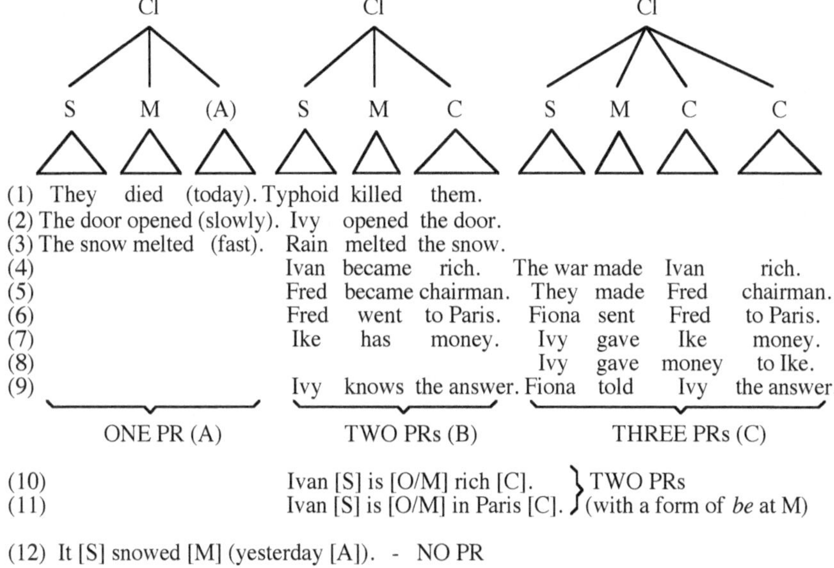

Figure 10-1
A summary of the major types of Processes and Participant Roles

The notes in the next two sections refer to the examples in Figure 10-1 both by numbers - (1), (2), (3), etc - which indicate the row they are in, and by letters - (A), (B) or (C) - which refer to their place in one of the three columns. Apart from (12A), all the examples in Column A have one Participant Role, all those in Column B have two, and all those in Column C have three. For the use of brackets in Column (A) see Note 7 in Section 10.6.

10.5 Types of Complement

These notes provide a first answer to Question 4: What types of Complement is it useful to be able to recognize at this stage?

1 While the referents of **S** and **C** in Rows (1), (2) and (3) are all 'things' of one sort or another - e.g. *they, typhoid* and *them* in Row (1) - the two examples in Row (4) remind us that with some types of Process the PR can be a 'quality', such as *rich.* They are both 'attributive' Processes, because in both the Complement is being presented as an 'Attribute' of the Subject (the 'Carrier'). We met examples that had an Attribute as the Complement in Chapter 6, and an example of this type is given in Row (10). Note especially the example in the third column (4C), which shows that in such processes an Agent can be a brought into the picture as an 'agent of change', making it a three-role Process - and so a clause with two Complements.

2 If you now compare Rows (4) and (5), you will see that the two patterns with a **quality** as the Attribute as the **C** also occur with a **thing** as the **C**. The PRs are the same for both - though there are certain lexical verbs that almost always occur with a 'quality' rather than a 'thing' (e.g. *turn* in *The leaves have turned red)*, and certain other lexical verbs that can only occur with a 'thing' (e.g. *elect* in *They elected Ivy (as) chairperson*).

3 Please look now at Row (6). This illustrates the important fact that a PR is not necessarily a 'thing' or a 'quality'. It may also be a 'place', such as *to Paris* or *there*. The two examples in Row (6) in fact have a similar relationship to the two examples in each of Rows (4) and (5); both are 'directional', but the second introduces an Agent. So a PR can answer the question 'Where?' (including 'Where to/from?' - as also does the 'locational' Process in Row (11).[75]

---

75 **Comparison with the Sydney Grammar** While the Sydney Grammar treats *to Paris* and *in Paris* in (6B), (6C) and (11B) as Adjuncts, the Cardiff Grammar treats them, as Figure 10-1 shows, as Complements. The grounds are that these two PRs - a 'Location' in (11B) and the type of 'direction' termed a 'Destination' in (6B) and (6C) - are predicted by the Processes of 'being',

4 Now look again at (11) - and also at (10). While (11) is 'locational' and has a 'Location' as its **C**, (10) is 'attributive' and has a 'quality' as the 'Attribute' conflated with its **C**. (The reason for not including these two examples with the equivalent two-role Processes in Rows (4), (5) and (6) above is that their **M** is a form of *be*, and so also an **O**, and they therefore require the label **O/M** rather than **M**.) In these two types of Process the two PRs are nearly always overtly present (99% reliable). But what fills the **C**s varies greatly - between 'things', 'qualities' and even 'situations' in 'attributive' Processes, and between 'places' in 'space' and in 'time' in 'locational' Processes, as in *Her birthday is in November.*

5 An important extension to the concept of a Complement is that some Processes expect an 'event' - and so typically a CLAUSE - as their Complements. This pattern occurs particularly frequently with 'mental process' clauses such as those shown in Row (9), where *the answer* in each of (9B) and (9C) could be replaced by a clause such as *Ike is there* (often preceded by the Binder *that*). Clauses also occur quite frequently as **C**, e.g. the underlined Complement in *He knows what he wants,* and occasionally as **S**, e.g. the underlined Subject in *Eating people is wrong*. This crucial concept of a 'clause within a clause' is a major source of the richness and complexity of syntax. The full analysis of such a sentence is given in Figure 17-1 in Chapter 17. And a careful and imaginative reading of the 'clause' page of Appendix 1 will quickly provide you with further examples of embedded clauses - e.g. those introduced by a **Binder (B)**.

There is a great deal more that could be said about the units that fill Complements and their meanings, and for this I refer you to *The Functional Syntax Handbook* and *The Functional Semantics Handbook.*

'going' and 'sending' respectively. The situation is fairly similar to that described in Footnote 58, except that in this case there is no question that the preposition (*in* or *to*) is part of the PR. Here, then, as in Footnote 58, we treat these cases as Complements, because they function as Participants in the Process. See the similar cases with the Process of 'giving' that is covered in Footnote 77.

10.6 Some major patterns in TRANSITIVITY

The following further notes on Figure 10-1 explain how it provides an overall summary of the main TRANSITIVITY structures of English.

1 Rows (2) and (3) illustrate an uncomfortable fact for the syntax analyst. This is that there are many lexical verbs which can occur with EITHER ONE OR TWO PARTICIPANT ROLES. This is in contrast with Row (1), where essentially the same meaning is expressed in two different verb forms, depending on whether there is one PR or two. The fact is that the same 'structural ambiguity' illustrated here with *open* and *melt* occurs with many other verbs: (i) with *boil*, *bake* and *simmer,* and most other 'cooking' verbs; (ii) with *break* and *crack* and most other verbs expressing the idea of 'destroying' (but not, interestingly, *destroy* itself), and also with many others. What do they all have in common? The answer is that they are all Processes of 'changing'. The examples in Column (A) simply describe that Process of 'changing', but those in Column (B) additionally have a PR, which tells us who or what CAUSED the Process of changing. This PR is an **Agent.** So, in the examples in Column (B) of Rows (2) and (3), each of *Ivy* and *rain* is an Agent (and each of *the door* and *the snow* is an Affected). The problem is that we often find the same verb being used to refer to BOTH 'something changing' AND 'something causing something to change'. This is a type of ambiguity that the analyst must simply learn to look out for - but it is one that can be dealt with without too much difficulty, with a little practice. This is because the verbs belong to clear semantic classes, and it is easy to learn to recognize the most frequent problem cases.

2 The concept of **Agent** is one which also helps in understanding many of the other main types of TRANSITIVITY. As we have seen, an Agent is an entity that is being presented to the Addressee as the PR that CAUSES some 'event' (where the term 'event' includes 'state of affairs'), and it is therefore often a 'causer of change'. Usually the 'causer' of the change is a person, or a group of persons such as a committee. But

sometimes the Agent is an animal, or some object that is presented as acting in the way that animate beings do, such as a car or a computer. But an Agent may also be a natural phenomenon, as in (3B) or an event, as in (4C). (The Agents in Column C are discussed in the next note).[76]

3 The third column (C) of Rows (4) to (9) shows the main types of TRANSITIVITY which have THREE PRs - but it does NOT, of course, show all of the many verbs that occur with each type. It is an interesting fact that each type has an equivalent Process with TWO PRs - as the diagram neatly shows. This raises the following question: 'What do these three-role Processes all have in common?' The answer is that, in each case, an Agent acts as a 'third party' that CAUSES a 'changing event' to come about, which then results in a new 'state of affairs'. So the event in (4C), *The war made Ivan rich*, causes (4B), *Ivan became rich*, and so in turn (10), *Ivan is rich* (which has to be placed below because its Process is an **O/M**). Essentially the same pattern can be traced in each of Rows (5) to (9), except that in Rows (7) and (9) Column B skips the 'change' and simply reports the resulting 'state of affairs'. So in Row (7) *Ivy gave Ike money* brings about the state of affairs in which *Ike has*

---

76 **Comparison with the Sydney Grammar** As will be clear, this chapter is about distinguishing PRs from CRs, and not about TYPES of Participant Role (although I have allowed myself to introduce a few to illustrate the concept (Agent, Affected, Carrier, Attribute, Location and Direction). For a full account of types of PR, see Chapter 2 of Fawcett forthcoming 2011b, Neale 2002 and Neale forthcoming. But it may be useful to say that, in the Cardiff Grammar, we find that we can adequately characterize the different PRs by giving each a SINGLE label. Thus a PR such as *Ivy* in (2B) is not BOTH an 'Agent' AND an 'Actor', as in the Sydney Grammar, but simply an Agent. Because we use Halliday's earlier concept of 'Affected' (rather than the over-general term 'Medium' that replaced it), labels such as 'Actor' and 'Goal' become redundant, and there is no longer any reason to provide both an 'ergative' and a 'transitive' analysis of a clause (see Fawcett 1980, Neale 2002 and Neale forthcoming.) So the Cardiff Grammar is simpler in having just one analysis for each clause.

Note that analyzing a PR in terms of two types of TRANSITIVITY (i.e. with a 'transitive' and an 'ergative' analysis - e.g. 'Actor/Agent') as Halliday advocates, is a different matter from using a compound label, such as 'Agent-Carrier', as is done in the Cardiff Grammar whenever a PR passes the tests for both PRs.

money. And in Row (9) the effect of *Fiona told Ivy the answer* is that *Ivy knows the answer*.

4 We can summarize what we have learnt so far from examining Rows (4) to (9) by saying that, in each case, the Agent in the clause in Column (C) causes something (or someone) to 'be' something or somewhere, or to 'have' or to 'know' something. But note too that with the 'giving' type of Process shown in (7C) there are alternative sequences for the Complements: compare (7C) with (8C).[77] As a final point in discussing this set of examples, it may be useful to say that the Cardiff Grammar analyzes cases such as *The heat turned the milk sour, He got his hands dirty* and *He painted the shed green* in exactly the same

---

77 **Comparison with the Sydney Grammar** There are two differences to point out. The first is that the Sydney Grammar treats *to Ike* in (8C) as a Adjunct, while the Cardiff Grammar treats it, as Figure 10-1 shows, as a Complement. It is hard to see how this PR, which is an Affected-Carrier in both (7C) and (8C), should be treated as a Complement in (7C) and an Adjunct in (8C). Note that the preposition *to* is introduced automatically, as an automatic by-product of the decision to place the Agent at (or near) the end of the clause, where it is likely to receive the unmarked Tonic and so be marked as 'New Information' (cp Section 9.8 of Chapter 8). The reasoning that leads us to analyze this element as a Complement rather than an Adjunct is therefore essentially the same as that set out in Footnote 58. Yet the form-based criteria used in the Sydney Grammar demand that *to Ike* be analyzed as an Adjunct.

The second difference is that if, in (9B) and (9C), we replace *the answer* by a report of the contents of the answer - e.g. by *that she wouldn't marry him* - that part of the sentence would no longer be treated as part of the clause in the Sydney Grammar (as it is in the Cardiff Grammar), but as a separate clause that is dependent on the first part without being a part of it, in a relationship that Halliday calls 'hypotaxis'. And if the wording in (9C) were to be made explicit, as in *Fiona told Fred 'I'm frightfully sorry, but I'm afraid I can't marry you!'*, the Sydney Grammar would analyze the part in 'direct speech' as related to the first part by an unusual type of 'parataxis' - i.e. as being of equal status and, again, not as a part of it (which would be the Cardiff Grammar analysis). See Appendix 1 for examples of how the Cardiff Grammar handles such cases, but see Fawcett 2004b for the full set of reasons for preferring the Cardiff Grammar analyses to those of the Sydney Grammar. See also Fawcett 2000a: 271-2 for a brief summary of the contents of that paper. And for a survey of the criticisms of Halliday's proposals for 'parataxis' and 'hypotaxis' by other scholars see Appendix C of Fawcett 2000a, on 'The "rank scale" debate'.

way as (4C). In other words, a Process of 'painting the shed green' is essentially the same as one of 'making the shed green'. The only difference is that the verb *make* in (4C) doesn't tell us anything about HOW the change was brought about, but in *He painted the shed green* the verb DOES give us this information. This pattern of variation in the semantic specificity of a verb is a common phenomenon; for example the verb *made* in (5C) could be replaced by semantically richer words, such as *elected* or *appointed*, and *went* in (6B) could be replaced by *flew, drove* or *marched.* And *sent* in (6C) could be in fact also be replaced by *flew, drove* or *marched.* In other words, the present approach enables a single framework of concepts (i) to capture an insightful generalization and (ii) to explain a number of otherwise problematical examples.[78]

5 In Note 1 above I pointed out one type of **ambiguity** to look out for. There are others, such as the examples that we have just been considering. Now consider the verb *make*, as used in (4C) and (5C). Besides this THREE-role sense (in which someone makes something into something) there is a TWO-role sense, as in *They made a cake*. Many other high frequency verbs (such

---

78 **Comparison with the Sydney Grammar** Halliday treats the second of the two Complements in such examples as an additional (but in my view unnecessary) type of Circumstantial Role, termed a 'Product'. This suggestion may seem intuitively attractive at first sight, but it has two serious disadvantages. The first is that it loses the generalizations that are neatly expressed by relating the 'attributive' Processes in (4B) and (4C) and the 'directional' Processes in (5B) and (5C) - and so on. The second disadvantage is that, in *He moulded the army into a disciplined fighting force* (Halliday's example), *into a disciplined fighting force* is treated as a CR rather than a PR - despite the facts that (i) this PR is predicted by the Process and (ii) none of the examples given in *IFG* illustrate the concept that it occurs in clauses where it is NOT predicted by the Process. (Nor can I think of any possible ones.)

Halliday's example would therefore be analyzed in Cardiff Grammar terms as having the same PRs as (4C) - and so two Complements. This analysis allows us to capture neatly the semantic relationship of (i) *He moulded the army into a disciplined fighting force* to (ii) *The army became a disciplined fighting force* and (iii) *The army was a disciplined fighting force.* See Fawcett 1987 for the original and still the fullest published statement of the rationale for this approach to 'relational' Processes in English.

as *get, go, keep, leave, put* and *send*) are similarly ambiguous - sometimes with different numbers of PRs. So when you are analyzing a sentence you cannot simply decide from the form of a verb whether it has, say, two or three associated PRs; it really is important to work out - ON THE EVIDENCE OF THE PROBABILITIES FOR THAT VERB FORM AND THE LINGUISTIC CONTEXT - what the MEANING of the Main Verb is (i.e. the type of Process that it is) - and so the number of PRs to expect. With isolated examples, such as those in this book, this can be difficult, but it is much less of a problem with sentences that occur in their natural setting, i.e. in real texts.

6 Note the example of an 'environmental' Process with no PR at all in (12).

7 The final point concerns Adjuncts. The examples in Column (A) illustrate the fact that clauses that have only one PR are, in general, more likely to be given an Adjunct than clauses with two or three PRs - though Adjuncts do of course regularly occur with all TRANSITIVITY types. The point to note is that these Adjuncts are NOT 'expected' by the specific types of Process, in the sense described in Section 10.3. The brackets round *today, slowly* and *fast* show that these words are 'optional', in the sense that they are not predicted by the Process. So the example *They died (today)* in fact illustrates TWO clauses in one example: *They died*, and *They died today.*

10.7 Summary

Each of the twelve points in the last two sections is highly relevant to understanding the structure of English clauses. The notes in Section 10.5 provide the answer Question 4 - as far as it is possible to do, without starting on the major task of listing and defining the various TYPES of Participant Role. Full guidelines for identifying each type of PR are given in Chapter 2 of *The Functional Semantics Handbook* (Fawcett forthcoming 2011b).[79] And

79 When you are facing the problems of trying to decide (i) whether a possible PR is a Participant or a Circumstantial Role, and (ii) which type of PR it is, a particularly valuable source of insights is Amy Neale's *Process Type Data Base*

the notes in Section 10.6 point out several of the central patterns in TRANSITIVITY - without, however, embarking on the major task of identifying the major Process types ('action', 'relational', 'mental', etc). These are intimately bound up with the identification of the different types of Participant Role, and will therefore be left to *The Functional Semantics Handbook.*

Perhaps the most important fact that Figure 10-1 illustrates is the wide range of variation in the INTERNAL syntax and semantics of Complements - in contrast with Subjects. As we have seen, they can be 'things', 'qualities', and 'places' etc - and with some types of Process, such as many 'mental' processes - they may be full 'events', so that the Complement is filled by an embedded clause.

However, variations in the internal structure of Complements should always be treated as secondary to the main test - i.e. the semantic test of asking what the Process 'expects'. At this stage of learning about SFL - when what concerns us is the structure of the simple clause in English - you simply need to be able to decide which entities are PRs and which are not.

The *Full Guidelines* in Chapter 15 will provide you with tests that help in these decisions. They include a comprehensive set of tests that will enable you to identify the Process and its associated Participant Roles in virtually any clause - including some complexities in the expression of the Process in syntax that we shall come to in Chapter 13.

Figure 10-1 provides a clearer summary of this chapter than any summary in words can - so it might well be worth taking a further look at it before we move on to the very different topic that we come to in the next chapter.

(Neale 2002). This includes the analysis of a new set of recently identified 'relational' Processes in English, which we call 'matching' Processes. See Neale 2004 for the first published account of these.

Chapter 11
An overview of the syntax of MOOD

11.1 The pattern of the next few chapters

As in most of the book so far, this chapter and those that follow will introduce new structures and their meanings. However, while we shall meet several more elements, many of the new concepts will be (i) new **meanings** that various syntactic arrangements of familiar elements may express and - importantly - (ii) new **places** in the clause at which elements may occur.

Up to this point in the book, we have largely succeeded in keeping things simple by treating structures in terms of one strand of meaning at a time. But from here on it will become increasingly difficult to do this.

For example, the description of one type of MOOD in Section 11.2 of the present chapter will require us to recognize a second type of **covert Participant Role**. (We have already met one type in Section 8.7 of Chapter 8, and we shall meet another in Section 13.5 Chapter 13.)

And the concept of **thematizing** an element, which we first met in Section 8.5 of Chapter 8, comes up again in two sections of Chapter 13.

Finally, the concept of **Newness**, which we have already met in Chapters 9 and 10, is needed again in Chapter 12 when we consider Adjuncts - twice, in fact.

In other words, the plurifunctional nature of language, which we first met at the start of Chapter 3, is such that from here on it will no longer be possible to keep the realizations of the different strands of meaning separate from each other, as we examine the syntax associated with each.

Another change from this point on will be in the way I present analyzed examples. I shall occasionally use a new type of diagram: a **linear diagram** which has the advantage of saving space. However, this way of representing structure is of limited value. Its main weakness is that it can show the structure of ONLY ONE UNIT AT A TIME - and even then it doesn't show the structure as clearly as a tree diagram does. So it is only useful for times when we are interested in the structure of a single unit with a simple structure. For the task of making a full analysis of a text-sentence, such as the one illustrated in Figure 17-1 in Chapter 17, no linguist has yet proposed an adequate alternative to a tree diagram.[80]

I therefore recommend tree diagrams as the clearest and most elegant way of representing the full functional syntax of a sentence. How else, indeed, could we represent clearly all the different structural relationships in Figure 17-1 that we need to show, in order to illustrate the way in which the sentence is constructed? It simply could not be done without using a form of tree diagram.

11.2 MOOD meanings concerning 'information'

There are two main types of MOOD - those that express meanings to do with 'information' and those concerned with 'proposals for action'. In this section we shall broaden our currently limited picture of meanings that relate to 'information', and in Section 11.3 we shall meet the major types of 'proposal for action'.

We have already met (i) the **information giver** and (ii) the type of 'information seeker' which seeks from the Addressee the answer *Yes* or *No*, i.e. a **polarity seeker**. But what other types of 'information seeker' are there?

The second major type, besides the 'polarity seeker', is the **new content seeker**. The Performer's purpose in using it is to try to get the Addressee to complete a proposition by supplying new information about an element of the clause. (In traditional grammars this is often called a '*Wh*-question', because it typically begins with one of the words *who, what, which, where, when* or *how,* but it seems preferable, in a functional grammar, to use a functional name for it, rather than one that refers to the form of a class of words. Hence the term 'new content seeker'.)

---

80 For a discussion of the various possible ways to represent functional syntax in two-dimensional space, see pages 245-9 of Fawcett 2000a.

In a 'new content seeker', the 'new content' may concern a Participant or a Circumstance - i.e. an **experiential** (or occasionally a **logical**) element of the clause. Typical examples are:

(1) What are you reading? [seeking a Complement]
(2a) When will you finish it? [seeking an Adjunct]
(2b) Why did you choose it? [seeking an Adjunct]
(3a) Who's eaten my porridge? [seeking a Subject]
(3b) Who cooked it? [seeking a Subject]

You might be tempted to think that the occurrence at the start of the clause of the element about which information is being sought (the 'sought' element) is a second type of 'Theme' - one to place alongside the concept of 'Subject Theme' that we met in Section 8.5 of Chapter 8. But it is not, because the position of the 'sought' element is NOT the result of a choice in a THEME system, but the result of a choice in MOOD. In other words, the early place in the clause of the 'sought' element is simply part of the realization of the meaning of being a 'new content seeker'.

The 'linear analyses' of our five examples are as follows:

(1) What [C] are [O/X] you [S] reading [M]? with **O S**
(2a) When [A] will [O] you [S] finish [M] it [C]? with **O S**
(2b) Why [A] did [O] you [S] choose [M] it [C]? with **O S**
(3a) Who [S] 's [O/X] eaten [M] my porridge [C]? with **S O**
(3b) Who [S] cooked [M] it [C]? with **S M**

(Note that here '**O**' stands for '**O** or **O/X** or **O/M**'.)[81]

---

81 In some approaches to describing clauses, the analyst is expected to mark the '*wh*-element' with a superscript, like this: $\mathbf{S}^{\mathbf{wh}}$, $\mathbf{C}^{\mathbf{wh}}$ and $\mathbf{A}^{\mathbf{wh}}$. But this is not required in a Cardiff Grammar analysis, because the *wh*-word (which may also be *how,* as in *How many chocolates did she eat?*) is always there in the text below the element, so that the 'wh' superscript is in fact redundant.

However, we should note that the function of a *wh*-item is not necessarily to indicate that the element is being 'sought', as it is in (1) to (3b) above. It can also be a 'relating out' meaning, as in a 'relative clause' such as the underlined portion of *The person who has eaten my porridge will be sorry!* or a report of a quasi-reply, as in *Now I know who has eaten my porridge* (Fawcett 1996:335). But since these examples involve a clause that fills an element of a higher unit in the sentence, they are beyond the scope of this book, which is limited to the 'simple clause'. All such constructions are covered in Fawcett 2009b.

How would you apply the *Mood Test* to such examples? The solution to this problem is to re-express the clause as an 'information giver' as part of the preparation for applying the test. To do this, you simply replace the element containing the *wh*-item by *something, someone, somewhere* or *some time.* So, for example, you would re-express *What are you reading?* as *You are reading something.*[82]

---

82 **Comparison with the Sydney Grammar** In *IFG,* the occurrence of an element that contains a *wh*-item at the start of the clause is assumed to be a type of 'Theme'. This is one aspect of the general assumption made in *IFG* that 'if an element comes early in the clause it is a type of Theme' - an assumption in which **form** reflects **meaning** in an attractively simple one-to-one manner. But matters are in fact a little more complicated than that.

Clearly, it is not a coincidence that certain elements of the clause always occur near its start. Examples of such elements include: (i) a Linker such as *and* and *or*, (ii) a Binder such as *if, that* and *because*, (iii) a 'relative pronoun' such as *who* in *the man who came to dinner*, and (iv) an 'interrogative pronoun' (such as those we are considering now) - AND VARIOUS THEMATIZED ELEMENTS, such as a thematized PR, CR or other type of Adjunct. From a cognitive-interactive viewpoint, it is obvious that, in each of the above cases, the Addressee is greatly helped in the task of understanding the function in the current discourse of the clause that the element introduces IF THIS ELEMENT IS PLACED AT OR NEAR THE START OF THE CLAUSE. The question that needs to be asked about such cases is: Has this element been placed where it is AS THE RESULT OF A CHOICE IN A SYSTEM CONCERNED WITH 'THEME'? In other words: Has it been thematized? In the Cardiff Grammar, the answer in all of the above cases - other than those that I have described as 'thematized' - is 'No'. In each case the element is located at its place early in the clause AUTOMATICALLY, as a direct result of the decision to include that element in the clause.

We interpret the concept of 'Theme' in the following strict sense. We only treat an element as carrying the additional meaning of being a type of Theme IF THE ELEMENT HAS BEEN THEMATIZED AS THE RESULT OF A CHOICE IN A SYSTEM. The corollary is that if the option is NOT selected, the element would occur elsewhere in the clause.

Now consider the case of the 'new content seeker', starting with (1) and (2). Each of these is the realization, through having an early place in the clause and a *wh*-item, of the choice in the MOOD network of the type of 'information seeker' that is seeking a piece of 'new content' to complete a proposition. There is therefore no independent decision to thematize it. In other words, the early place in the clause of the element about which information is being sought is simply part of the realization of the meaning of being a 'new content seeker'.

There is a third - and much less frequent - type of 'information seeker', and this too seeks information about a piece of 'content'. But this type operates by providing two or more possible specifications of the piece of content that P is seeking information about, and asking the Addressee to say which is correct. For reasons that will be clear, we call this a **choice of alternative contents seeker**. (This is termed an 'alternative question' in traditional grammars.)

A typical example of this type of 'information seeker' is (4):

(4) Will [O] future generations [S] regard [M] Chomsky or Halliday [C] as the greatest linguist of the twentieth century [C]?
with **O S**

As Examples (1) to (4) show, there is a general pattern for the structure of 'information seekers' in which **O** precedes **S** - with the one exception that when the element about which the information is sought is the Subject, as in (3), its structure is the same as if it was an 'information giver'. It is the initial *wh*-word that signals that information is sought.[83]

The corollary of taking this position is that utterances such as *He said what?* (spoken with a rising tone) and *And then he said what?* (spoken with a falling tone) are not treated as 'new content seekers', are that they are generated from different features in the full system network for MOOD. Although they are no covered here, they are in the full description of English in my *Functional Syntax Handbook* and my *Functional Semantics Handbook.*

There is one apparent exception to the generalization that the meaning of being a 'new content seeker' is realized by placing the 'sought element' at an early place in the clause. This occurs when the 'sought' element is a PR that is also the Subject, as in (3a) and (3b). As the analyses to their right illustrate, neither conforms to the general pattern of **O S** that is set by (1) and (2). Why don't they? The answer is that, because the 'sought' element is the Subject, this PR is being thematized as the result of a choice in the system of SUBJECT THEME (in the way described in Section 8.5 of Chapter 8). But an element can only be thematized once, and the way in which English resolves this conflict is to use the thematization of a PR to function as the Subject as the one that determines the resulting structure. Indeed, in (3b) there isn't even an Operator. So the structures of (3a) and (3b) are identical to the equivalent 'information givers', i.e. *She's been eating my porridge* and *Mother Bear cooked it.*

83 Note that the *wh*-item in a 'new content seeker' is not necessarily the only item in the 'sought' element. Consider, for example, *What sort of car does she drive?*, *How many of the chocolates did she eat?* and *How long have you been waiting?*

We come now to a type of MOOD meaning that might at first appear to be an 'information seeker' but is not - and yet it certainly concerns 'information'. This is the **confirmation seeker** (which we first met briefly in Chapter 9). Here is a typical example:

(5) Isn't [O/X] she [S] feeling [M] better [C] yet [A]? with **O S**

Its meaning, as its name implies, is that the Performer is asking the Addressee to confirm that the information expressed in the clause is valid. It is typically used when P has just realized that something which P had believed to be valid may well not be valid - though P still hopes that it may be, and so seeks A's confirmation that it is. (Note the use of the word 'valid' rather than 'true', which reduces - somewhat - the philosophical problems of defining 'truth'.)

I shall now briefly introduce a second option in which P may seek a confirmation by A of information. This is the type of 'information giver' which has as its Adjunct a 'tag' clause which, IN ITSELF, functions as a 'confirmation seeker'. It is an **information giver plus confirmation seeker**, as in (6a) and (6b):

(6a) Ivy likes Ike, doesn't she? with **O S**
(6b) Ivy doesn't like Fred, does she? with **O S**

And there are other variations within this general type, including variations in meaning that are realized in intonation.[84]

---

84 **Comparison with the Sydney Grammar** The general approach to the meaning of such 'tags' is similar in the two grammars, but there appears to be a difference between the two in the structural relationship to the main clause that each proposes. The Cardiff Grammar analyzes cases such as *doesn't she* in (6a) as a clause that (i) is **embedded** as an **A** in the main clause, and (ii) is a **truncated clause**. It is 'truncated' in that it lacks all clause elements except **O** and **S**. And the reason for this is that the only strand of meaning that it needs to express is the 'interpersonal' meaning of [plus confirmation seeker] in the MOOD network.

The many internal variations within the **O** and the **S** of the embedded clause are required to conform to the semantics of the main clause, and in the generative version of the Cardiff Grammar these are elegantly generated from the semantic features that are chosen when generating the Subject and Operator (or Main Verb) of the main clause, by 'preselection' rules that are automatically applied. But for the grammar to be able to do this we need first to generate the main clause, and then to re-enter the system network to generate the 'tag'

Finally, we should note the unusual category of the **exclamation**. Essentially, exclamations are a type of 'information giver', and the syntax of the main type reflects this. But they are different from ordinary 'information givers' in the following way. What they give information about is the Performer's surprise at the 'quantity' of something - sometimes quite literally the 'quantity of something', as in (7), but more often the 'quantity of a quality', as in (8).

(7) What a lot of cake he ate! with **S O**
(8) How kind she is! with **S O**

But there are two other types of exclamation. One is another long-established type, but it is one that uses a variant of **O S** syntax, as in (9) below. And finally there is a recently developed type that is currently in very wide use among those who belong to the younger generation - and those who wish they did! - as in (10).

---

clause. And it is the above analysis of the structure that makes this possible. (As an aside, note that this Adjunct occasionally occurs medially in the main clause - though usually only in longer sentences. But it never occurs initially, so that in this respect it doesn't conform to the norm for Adjuncts - like a small number of other Adjuncts.)

In *IFG* the structural relationship between what is termed there the 'Mood tag' and the main clause is not clear. The diagrams simply place a 'Mood tag' such as *isn't it* after the main clause (1994: 77). The general tendency in *IFG* is to treat all clause elements whose status is in doubt as a type of Adjunct - e.g. *Yes*, *No*, and our Main Verb Extension (for which see Section 13.2 of Chapter 13) are Adjuncts in *IFG*. Yet the 'Mood tag' is never described as an Adjunct. The Sydney Grammar presents it as an element in its own right, and it functions in the 'primary structure' of the clause as a sister element to the 'Mood' element, such that a clause with a 'Mood tag' also has a 'Mood'. And each of the two has, as its 'secondary structure', the two clause elements of a Subject and a Finite (or Operator, in our terms). But this has a worrying effect on the full (i.e. 'secondary') analysis in *IFG* terms, because it gives the full clause two Subjects and two Finites. The obvious way to avoid this undesirable state of affairs is to treat the 'tag' as a clause that fills an Adjunct in the main clause. This analysis has been used for two decades of text description in the Cardiff Grammar without finding any problems.

Thus there are both descriptive and generative reasons for the analysis adopted here.

(9) Isn't that wonderful! [spoken with a falling tone] with **O S**
(10) How cool is that! [spoken with a falling tone] with **O S**

And there are a few other choices within this part of the overall MOOD network that occur regularly (though infrequently) - all of which are covered in Fawcett forthcoming 2011b.

The system network for MOOD, as we have developed it so far, can be represented as shown in Figure 11-1. Notice (i) that this version is much more adequate than the minimal one in the little generative lexicogrammar in Chapter 7, and (ii) that it embodies the further development of including general **probabilities** for each feature in each system - as all system networks should (other than the most introductory ones).

Finally, notice the feature [proposal for action] at the bottom of the network. This leads into the lower half of the network, and you will find the diagram that shows this at the end of the next section, in Figure 11-2.

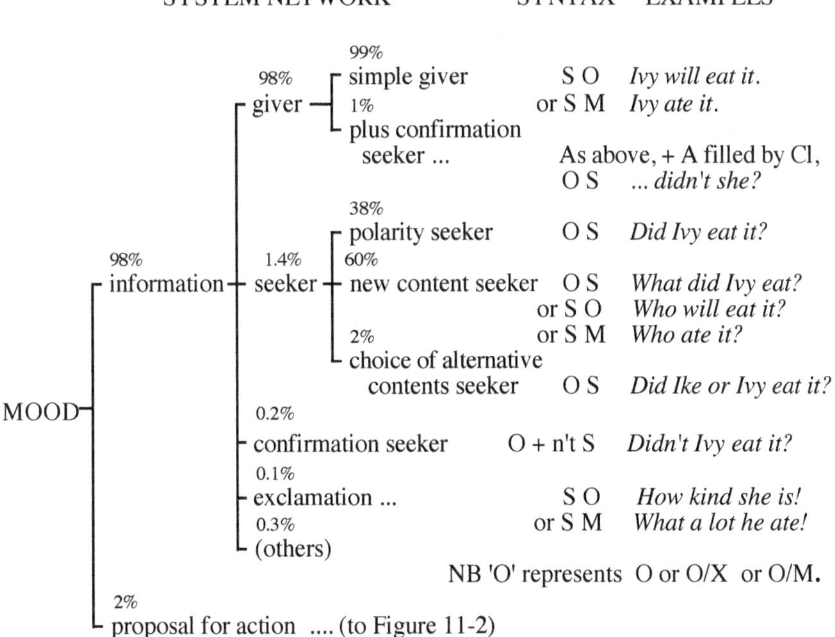

Figure 11-1: A simplified system network for the 'information' sub-network of MOOD

11.3 MOOD meanings that are 'proposals for action'

We shall look now at some of the major types of 'proposal for action' in English.

The Performer's 'proposal' is almost always for one of the following three types of 'action':

(i) action by the Addressee (A),
(ii) action by the Performer (P), and
(iii) action by P and A.[85]

Such 'proposals' range from bare commands through requests and tentative suggestions - and what they have in common is that they all make a proposal for some sort of future 'action'.

Here are simple examples of each type:

(11) Touch your nose!
(12) Shall I read it for you?
(13) Let's read it together!

We shall begin with the **proposal for action by addressee** type, since it is by far the most frequent. Example (11) is just one of the many ways in which the semantics of English provides options that are designed to get someone else to do something. It is a **simple directive**, and it is the most frequent of all the various types of 'proposal for action'. Interestingly, its realization in syntax is by leaving the Subject unrealized. And, since the Subject in such clauses is always a Participant Role (typically an Agent) this is a second type of **covert Participant Role**.[86] The reason why it is safe to leave the Subject unexpressed is that, given the agreement among users of English that a simple clause without a Subject such as *Touch your nose!* signals the meaning of a 'simple

---

85 There is also a fourth type: a 'proposal for action by outsider' (i.e. by someone other than the Performer or the Addressee, e.g. *Let Ivy do it!*

86 We met the first type in Section 8.7 of Chapter 8, when we were considering the 'passive' Auxiliary, and a third - and more problematical - type will be introduced in Section 13.5 of Chapter 13.

directive' to the Addressee, the referent of the unrealized Subject is easily recoverable.[87, 88]

The analysis of the 'simple directive' in (11) is therefore:

(11) ([S]) Touch [M] your nose [C]! with no overt **S** or **O**

Notice the use of both ROUND BRACKETS and SQUARE BRACKETS AROUND 'S' in (11). This is in contrast with the use of square brackets on their own in linear representations, as in Examples (1) to (5), which simply identifies the clause elements. The meaning of '([S])' in (11) is therefore that the Subject is **covert**.

In one type of 'simple directive', however, the Subject is made overt, e.g. in a strongly expressed directive such as *You watch your language!* And in other types the Operator is required, e.g. *Do take a seat!, Don't do that!* and - using both **O** and **S** - *Don't you speak to me like that!*[89]

We shall turn now to the types of 'proposal for action by addressee' that are NOT 'simple directives'. Interestingly, very many of the examples that we shall be looking at from here on have the structure **O S**. In this, then, they are unlike the 'simple directive' and like all the types of 'information seeker' introduced in the last section (with the exception of a 'sought Subject', as we noted at the time). The question to which this fact leads is this: Does this create a problem for the Addressee? In other words, is the amount of ambiguity in these forms of language seriously ambiguous? Should we really be analyzing these cases as 'polarity seekers' that require to be re-interpreted as a type of what Halliday has called 'interpersonal grammatical metaphor'? We shall consider this issue after we have examined the examples.

---

87 The 'Addressee' may be singular or plural, and may even include others who are associated with the Addressee but are not present.

88 Thus, like an 'information giver' and most types of 'information seeker', the meaning of this third major type of MOOD meaning is realized by one of the possible configurations of **S** and **O** - i.e. the 'zero' configuration in which NEITHER **S** nor **O** is present.

89 Note that, since the Operator is not predicted by the Process (as a Participant Role is), it would be misleading to show in the representation that there is a 'covert Operator'.

We shall begin with the many types of **request** that are available in English. Here there is a particularly wide range of variation between one individual speaker and another, with each having their favourite 'request forms'. But the modal verbs *can, could, will* and *would* (though not *shall*, *should*, *must* or *ought*) are all particularly widely used as exponents of **O** in requests, e.g. as in (14):

(14) Could [O] you [S] read [M] this [C] for me [A]? with **O S**

In this grammar, then - unlike some others (including Halliday's *IFG*) - such clauses are NOT treated as 'polarity seekers' about the Addressee's 'ability' (when *can* or *could* is used) or 'willingness' (when *will* or *would* is) to do something, but as **requests**. This position is supported by the fact that they cannot appropriately be responded to by *Yes, that is so* or *No, that isn't so.* Instead, they are requests that function by appealing to A's ability or willingness, and this is why, like other 'proposals for action by addressee', they often occur with the Adjunct *please*.

There is also an extraordinarily wide range of formulaic strings of words that introduce clauses that function as 'requests', such as *I wonder if you could read this*?, *Would you be so good as to read this for me? Would you mind reading this?* and scores of others, all of which we shall represent here by (15):

(15) Would you be so kind as to [F] read [M] this [C]?

Here, the letter 'F' stands for 'Formulaic Element' (see Appendix 1), and it signals a decision by the analyst to treat the string of words that precedes it as a fixed string (rather like the words in a compound nouns such as *washing up liquid* and *fork lift truck*). But note that this example, like many of the other 'request formulas', has a historical origin in a structure that consists of (i) a 'being' clause beginning with **O S** and (ii) a 'partial' embedded clause in which the process is 'reading'.[90]

---

90 See Tucker 2006 for a demonstration that such apparently formulaic strings of words also retain the ability to be generated through the full system network and so to accept minor variations, and Tucker 1996 for a demonstration of the way in which the Cardiff Grammar handles quasi-formulaic phenomena such as *I haven't the faintest/foggiest clue/idea about that.*

Finally, we should consider the third broad set of ways to get the Addressee to do something, i.e. making a **suggestion**. First, consider these two examples:

(16) Couldn't you finish it tomorrow? with **O S**
(17) Why don't you throw it away? *Why* with **O S**

Other types of suggestion using **O S** include *Can't you ..?, Shouldn't you..?, Mightn't you ...?* and *Oughtn't you to ...?* But other frequent types of suggestion use **F**, such as *What about* [F] *eating* [M] *it* [C]*?* Interestingly, some of these can also be used for the other major types of 'proposal for action' - unless, of course, they have the addition of *you* or *your* (which are both treated here as a Subject), as in *What about* [F] *you(r)* [S] *eating* [M] *it* [C]*?*

There is a final important point to note about one type of 'proposal for action by addressee'. This is that, if the 'action' is the sort that involves speaking - as it is in *Tell me your name!* or *Could you tell me your name, please?* - the Performer's **discourse purpose** in uttering these words is essentially the same as it would be if P were to say instead *What's your name?* Indeed, the response to any of the three sentences would probably have the form of *It's Ike* (or simply *Ike*) - and this is an informal demonstration that the two forms of language serve essentially the same function in discourse. Yet, in terms of their meanings in the **semantics** of English, *Tell me your name!* is just as much a 'proposal for action' as *Touch your nose!* is, whereas *What's your name?* is a straightforward 'new content seeker'. What such cases teach us is that we need a model of language and its use that distinguishes not only between (i) the syntax of the clause and (ii) its semantics, but also between (ii) the semantics of the clause and (iii) the **acts** in **discourse structure** that are performed through the meanings and forms of language, and which reflect the Performer's 'discourse purpose' at that point.

Having considered quite a wide variety of types of 'proposal for action by addressee', we shall now look at examples of the two main sub-types of **proposal for action by self** - with (12) being repeated from the start of this section:

(12) Shall I read it for you?
(18) May I see it?

More specifically, (12) is an **offer** and (18) a **permission seeker**, and their analyses are:

(12) Shall [O] I [S] read [M] it [C] for you [A]? with **O S**
(18) May [O] I [S] look [M] at it [C]? with **O S**

And to these we must add the third option of a **suggestion**, such as *What about ...-ing ...?* and *Why not ...?*, which, as we have just noted, can function here too - as also can *What about me/my reading it?*

Finally, we turn to the third category of **proposal for action by self and addressee**, as in (13) - which is also repeated from the start of the section - and (19).

(13) Let's read it together!
(19) Shall we read it together?

And their analyses are:

(13) Let [L] 's [S] read [M] it [C] together [A]! with **L S**
(19) Shall [O] we [S] read [M] it [C] together [A]? with **O S**

So the **agreement-seeker** in (19) follows a familiar pattern, but the **firm proposal** in (13) is rather different. You might at first assume that *let* (or even *let's*) should be analyzed as an Operator. But we must also be able to analyze related examples such as *Do let's (all) read it together!* in a principled manner. Such examples show that *let* should not be analyzed as the Operator, since the Operator is clearly required for *do.* So in such cases we introduce the **Let Element (L)**, as in the above analysis of (13).[91]

Interestingly, then, we find that this third broad type of 'proposal for action' can be realized EITHER through the structure **O S**, as in (19), OR through a completely different element.

---

91 **Comparison with the Sydney Grammar** Halliday's analysis in *IFG* is that *let's* 'is best interpreted as a wayward form of the Subject' (1994: 87). Our position is that the form *let's* INCLUDES the Subject in the form of the item *'s* - an analysis that is supported by the fact that it can be followed by *all* - and that it is more insightful to recognize the historical origin of this use of *let* by analyzing it as an element in its own right (as grammarians do in the case of Auxiliary Verbs).

And here too there is also a range of **suggestions**, including *What about (us/our) reading it together?*

I give below a simplified version of the 'proposal for action' sub-network for MOOD.[92] It therefore completes the system network for MOOD, the first half of which we met in Figure 11-1 of the last section.

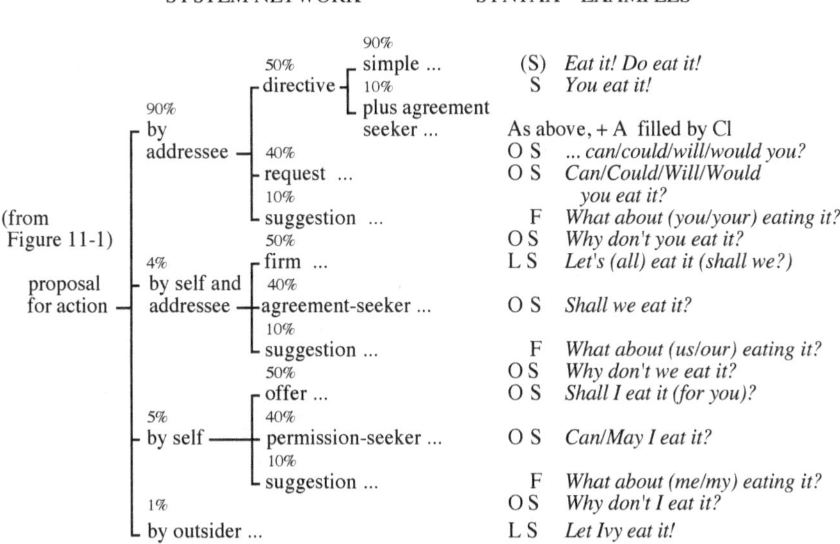

Figure 11-2: A simplified system network for the 'proposal for action' sub-network of MOOD

11.4 The meanings and forms of MOOD: a summary

Near the start of the previous section I raised the following two questions. Does the fact that many of the types of 'proposal for action' recognized here have the structure **O S** - which is typical of the 'information seeker' meanings that we noted in Section 11.2 - create a problem for the Addressee, i.e. the problem that they are ambiguous between different types of MOOD? And, if it does, should we analyze such cases as 'polarity seekers' (as was done in

---

92 Note that the fourth type of 'proposal for action' is a second sort that uses the **Let Element (L)**.

the early days of SFL), and then reinterpret them as cases of 'interpersonal grammatical metaphor' in which the 'real' meaning is that it is a 'directive'?[93]

---

93 **Comparison with the Sydney Grammar** This is what is still done in the Sydney Grammar today. In *IFG* the 'confirmation seeker' from Section 11.2 and most of the various types of 'proposal for action' distinguished in Section 11.3 would be analyzed as a 'polar interrogative', and then reinterpreted at a higher level of analysis as if it had been an 'imperative'. (The main exceptions are (i) the 'simple directive' and (ii) the type of 'proposal for action by self and other' realized by *let's*.) This reflects the fact that the system network for MOOD in *IFG* is essentially a network of options at the level of **form** rather than one at the level of **meaning**. In other words, the core of the system network for MOOD in Halliday and Matthiessen 2004 (p. 135) is essentially the same as it was in the early 1960s - i.e. as it was at the time BEFORE Halliday changed the theory by proposing that the system networks should be regarded as choices between meanings - rather than choices between forms.

The result of the fact that Halliday did not 'semanticize' the MOOD network (as he largely did in his revisions of the TRANSITIVITY network of the late 1960s and early 1970s) is that the Sydney Grammar has to invoke the problematical concept of 'grammatical metaphor' to explain how it is that a clause with the structure of a 'polarity seeker' - i.e. **O S** - can function as a 'proposal for action'.

One reason why 'grammatical metaphor' is a 'problematical concept' is that it requires enormous extensions to the descriptive apparatus of the Sydney Grammar. The way in which this additional complexity is manifested in *IFG* is that it requires TWO ANALYSIS OF THE MEANING OF EACH SUCH EXAMPLE. This is illustrated in several of the analyses of examples in 'The "silver" text', in Halliday's *IFG* of 1985 and 1994 (a particularly insightful appendix to the book that is missing –regrettably - from Halliday and Matthiessen 2004). The second manifestation of this additional complexity is the exploration in Halliday and Matthiessen 1999 of the hypothesis that a SFL model of language requires A FURTHER LAYER OF SYSTEM NETWORKS – i.e. a layer of system networks above the existing networks for TRANSITIVITY, MOOD, THEME, etc that are currently recognized in all systemic functional grammars.

We should be grateful to Halliday for identifying this range of problems, but we should avoid accepting unquestioningly his current proposal as to how they should be modelled. At this relatively early stage in the exploration of the 'two networks of meaning' hypothesis, those proposals should, from a scientific viewpoint, still be regarded as tentative. It is important that alternative solutions to these problems should be explored equally thoroughly. Linguists should note that the Cardiff Model uses alternative approaches to modelling many types of 'grammatical metaphor' - such as the one outlined here as a replacement for one type of 'interpersonal grammatical metaphor'.

The answer to the first question is 'No' - and we can therefore ignore the second. The reason why there is no problem of ambiguity is that each type of 'proposal for action' that has the structure **O S** is in practice clearly differentiated from each of the others (and so also from 'information seekers') by the COMBINATION of two further sources of evidence. These are: (i) the item at **O** (i.e. *shall, may, could* etc) and (ii) the item at **S** (i.e. *you* or *I* or *we* etc). For example, we know that if a clause begins with *Could you ....* it is overwhelmingly likely to be a 'request' - and NOT a 'polarity seeker' (where what is sought is information as to whether the Addressee had the ability to do something at some time in the past - which is, given the right context, a possible but unlikely interpretation). And the same principle applies to clauses that begin with *Shall I ...., May I ...., Shall we ...., Couldn't you ....* etc.

In evaluating the meanings of structures, then, we need to take account of the **words** that expound the elements as well as the **syntax** of the **elements**. It is the recognition of this principle that enables us to have a genuinely semantic system network for MOOD.

The contents of Figures 11-1 and 11-2 can therefore be taken as a summary of this chapter. I should emphasize again, however, that the system network for MOOD that they present is a considerably simplified version of the full network that is needed when working on the analysis of texts at the level of semantics (e.g. as in the analysis in Figure 17-2 in Chapter 17). This extends over six pages of closely drawn system networks, and it is presented in Fawcett forthcoming 2011b - much of the additional complexity being in the various types of 'proposal for action'.

Chapter 12
The syntax of Circumstances and other types of Adjunct

12.1 An overview of Adjuncts

Now that we have completed our overviews of TRANSITIVITY (in Chapter 10) and MOOD (in Chapter 11), it is time to look at the other main element in the clause: the **Adjuncts**.[94]

We have already met a few - in the examples in Chapter 3 to 10. These Adjuncts have had two things in common: (i) they have all been located tidily at the end of the clause, and (ii) they have all been Circumstantial Roles.

Although the picture of Adjuncts that these examples give has been limited, it has been fair. This is because (i) most Adjuncts do indeed express a 'circumstantial' meaning, and (ii) the most frequent position for this type of Adjunct is at or near the end of the clause. But it is now time to broaden the picture by describing and illustrating:

1 the range of functional types of Adjunct that occur in English,
2 the various places in the clause at which they may occur,
3 the meanings of those positions.

12.2 An overview of the functions served by Adjuncts

Let's start by considering the amazing range of functionally distinct types of Adjunct. We shall group them according to the different **strands of meaning** that they express. We shall find that three strands of meaning have no Adjuncts that express them, (though two - the thematic and informational strands - are involved

---

94 As those who are familiar with Quirk et al 1985 will realize, the term 'Adjunct' is used in SFG in a broad sense that includes the various types of 'Adjunct', 'Disjunct', 'Conjunct' and 'Subjunct' described in that great work.

in the meanings of THE PLACES IN THE CLAUSE WHERE THE ADJUNCTS OCCUR). But we shall at the same time introduce the eighth (and last) major strand of meaning, and two MINOR strands of meaning.

The list begins with Adjuncts that realize **experiential** meanings, of which there are about forty different types. Typically, any element in a clause that (i) expresses an experiential meaning and (ii) is not a Process, a Participant Role or an Auxiliary is a **Circumstantial Role (CR)**. This name explicitly contrasts this set of roles with the 'Participant Roles' (for which see Chapter 10).

Here, then, is a representative sample of the sixty functionally distinct types of Adjunct (most being fairly widely agreed ones):

1 **Experiential** meanings of forty types, frequent ones being:
  Time Position (e.g. *yesterday, in 2001*)
  Duration (e.g. *for two days, all week*)
  Repetition (e.g. *five times, twice)*
  Usuality (e.g. *always, sometimes, never*)
  Place (e.g. *in the garden*)
  Manner (e.g. *very clumsily, in a very clumsy manner*)
  Instrument (e.g. *with a knife*)
  Degree (as in *Ike loves her <u>very much indeed</u>*)
    .... and over thirty other types.
2 **Logical relations** meanings of ten types, including:
  Cause (e.g. *because he is ill, because of his age, therefore*)
  Grounds (as in *He's gone to sleep, <u>because his light is out</u>*)
  Purpose (e.g. *in order to see Fred, so as to see him*)
  Contrast (e.g. *whereas Ivy is poor, on the other hand*)
3 **Validity** meanings:
  Validity (e.g. *perhaps, definitely*)
  Report of Validity (e.g. *I think, it is said, allegedly*)
4 **Affective** meanings (e.g. *unfortunately, I'm afraid*)
5 **Interpersonal** meanings:
  Politeness (e.g. *please, if you please*)
  Confirmation Seeking Tag (e.g. *isn't she, shall we*)
6 **Inferential** meanings (e.g. *even, only*).
7 **Discoursal** meanings of eight types, including:
  Discourse Organizer (e.g. *firstly, in conclusion*)
  Topic Marker (e.g. *as for Ivy, talking about fishing*)

However, the plain fact is that no grammarian has yet provided a compete list of all the functionally distinct types of Adjunct in English - and this is despite the fact that English is almost certainly the most studied language in history.

Ongoing work in the framework of the Cardiff Grammar currently suggests that there are OVER SIXTY DIFFERENT TYPES OF ADJUNCT. It recognizes around forty Adjuncts that express a CR, and around twenty 'non-experiential' types of Adjunct - each of which can, in principle, occur in the same clause as any other.

The units that fill these Adjuncts vary greatly. For example, some CRs refer to 'things' (in a broad sense that includes 'times' and 'places' such as *the day after tomorrow* and *here*) and so use **nominal groups**. Many refer to 'a minor relationship with a thing', and so use a **prepositional group** (e.g. *in the park*). Many others refer to 'qualities' such as *very slowly*, and so use **quality groups**. And there is one (the 'Degree' Adjunct) that refers to the 'quantity' of the Process and so uses the **quantity group** (e.g. *very much*). And finally there are a few cases, such as some of the Adjuncts that express a 'Logical Relation' (e.g. *however* and *therefore*), where the word directly expounds the Adjunct.[95]

12.3 Interlude: the last major strand of meaning and two minor ones

Before we consider the question of the **places** at which Adjuncts may occur in the clause, let us use one of examples in the functional classification of the different types of Adjunct given in the last section to illustrate the final strand of meaning that is needed to complete our picture of the eight major strands of meaning in the English clause. Indeed, the classification of Adjuncts also includes examples of two minor strands of meaning that I have not mentioned so far, and we shall note these as well.

---

95 In the type of analysis used in this introductory treatment, we simply label all types of Adjunct as **A**. But in a full description of a text we would label them with their semantic role, e.g. as **A/TP**, **A/Dur** etc (standing for 'Time Position conflated with an Adjunct', 'Duration conflated with an Adjunct', etc) - as we do in the generative version of the grammar in the computer.

The eighth major strand of meaning is that of **logical relationships**. The reason why we have not met this type of meaning before this chapter is that it is typically realized as a logical relationship BETWEEN TWO CLAUSES - and since the topic of this book is the structure of **simple clauses** in English (rather than **clause complexes**, as they are termed in SFL) we have not needed to consider this type of meaning so far. Typical examples of clause elements that are used to relate two clauses are the **Linker** *and* in (1) and the **Binder** *because* in (2).

(1) Ike loves Ivy and Ivy loves Ike.
(2) They are happy, because they love each other.

Notice, however, that we could replace *because they love each other* in (2) by the Adjunct *therefore,* as in (3).

(3) They are happy, therefore (or 'Therefore they are happy')

So (3) illustrates the fact that the word *therefore* STANDS FOR a clause such as *because they love each other*. In other words, it functions as a 'pro-form' for a clause (just as a 'pro-noun' such as *she* functions as a 'pro-form' for a nominal group such as *Ike's girlfriend*). It is in this indirect way that a simple clause such as (3) comes to contain a meaning that inherently refers to TWO events. Other 'Logical Relations' Adjuncts include *however, moreover, similarly, on the other hand* etc.

So (3) is an example of the only type of meaning from the logical relations strand that is covered in this book.

For a few more examples of other 'co-ordinated' and 'dependent' clauses such as (1) and (2), see the 'clause' page of Appendix 1, and for a full introduction to the wide range of other types of logical relationship between clauses, see Chapters 12 and 13 in *The Functional Syntax Handbook.*

The list of types of Adjunct also includes the only example of an element of the clause whose exclusive function is to express **affective** meaning, i.e. in expressions such as *luckily*, *sadly*, *most unfortunately*, *I'm afraid* etc - as in (4).

(4) She was unfortunately rather late for the meeting.

Such 'Affective' Adjuncts tell the Addressee the Performer's evaluation of something, and in this respect they are like a

'Validity' Adjunct such as *probably.* But in this case it is the expression of P's EMOTIONAL RESPONSE to an event or an object.

Interestingly, such 'Affective' Adjuncts are only used relatively rarely. Why is this? We have already encountered a large part of the answer in Section 6.5 of Chapter 6, where we first met the concept of 'affective' meaning. We noted there that one of the most frequent ways in which 'affective' meaning is expressed is as part of the Complement in a clause whose Main Verb is a form of *be* (e.g. *Fiona is frightfully nice*, *Fred is rather nasty* etc) - and also as a **modifier** or even a **head** in a **nominal group** (e.g. *She's a very fine doctor* and *He's a rotter*).

But there is a second major reason why there is no need to have major resources in the clause for expressing 'affective' meanings. This is the widespread use of the combination of *I* as Subject with a Process that expresses 'emotion', as in *I love chocolate* and *I am pleased that Ike and Ivy are getting married.* (See Chapter 13 for the structure that allows us to treat *be pleased* as a Process.) And there are other resources too, such as the use of the **evaluative enhanced theme** construction, as in *It's great that they are getting married.* (For this construction, see Chapter 9 of Fawcett 2009, and also Chapter 23 of *The Functional Syntax Handbook.*)

Finally, we should note the two 'minor' strands of meaning that are represented by the last two types of Adjunct in the list in the last section. The first type is those Adjuncts whose role is to serve units of discourse that are, actually or potentially, longer than a single sentence. These are the **discoursal** Adjuncts such as *firstly, in conclusion* and *talking about plagiarism.* Such Adjuncts occupy a curious place in the grammar, because they function semantically in the overall structure of the discourse - and yet the language permits an Adjunct such as *firstly* to function INSIDE THE STRUCTURE OF THE CLAUSE - typically coming first, but also occurring at different places within it, as other Adjuncts do.

The second 'minor' strand of meaning is 'minor' because it is required for only a few Adjuncts. Yet they are unlike any of the eight major strands of meaning, in that they express a purely **inferential** meaning (*even, only* and *just* (in its 'only' sense).

We have now met the full complement of eight major strands of meaning: **experiential**, **logical relations**, **interpersonal**, **validity**, **affective**, **negativity**, **thematic** and **informational** - as well as two minor strands of meaning: the **discoursal** and the **inferential** strands.[96]

As you may have noticed, the above list rearranges the order of the major strands, so that they are no longer in the order in which we have met them. They are now sequenced in such a way as to make it easier to compare the EIGHT strands of meaning in the Cardiff Grammar (as shown in Figure 17-3 in Chapter 17) with the THREE (and often FOUR) shown in Halliday's diagrams.[97]

---

96 Some pieces of text serve what has been called a **metalinguistic** function. There are several types. One consists of expressions through which the Performer CORRECTS one form of words by replacing them with words with a different meaning, as in the underlined portion of *He is - or rather was - always open to new ideas*. Another type replaces one expression by another that seeks to CLARIFY it, e.g. *in other words*, *i.e.*, etc. Formerly I included this as a 'minor' strand of meaning (Fawcett 1980: 28 and 33), but now I consider that such meanings are best regarded as an aspect of 'ancillary grammar'. This is a 'grammar' that ignores the standard relations of syntax, interrupting units when the Performer wishes. Here, however, we shall ignore this aspect of language.

97 **Comparison with the Sydney Grammar** Thus the Cardiff Grammar recognizes EIGHT major strands of meaning, whereas Halliday's verbal descriptions of his model repeatedly talk of THREE (and sometimes FOUR) major functional components (or 'metafunctions'). In his 'three-functions' model, the three are: (i) the **ideational** metafunction (which is a cover term for his **experiential** and **logical** metafunctions); (ii) the **interpersonal** metafunction (which includes our **interpersonal**, **validity**, **affective** and (in some of his writings) **negativity** meaning; and (iii) the **textual** metafunction (which includes our **thematic** and **informational** strands of meaning).

But there is a problem with the *IFG* account of the relations between the 'ideational', 'experiential' and 'logical' components. Throughout the forty years of the life of SFG, the 'experiential' component has always been associated with the unit of the clause (and with 'lower' units). And in the early years the 'logical' component was always presented as a 'sister' component - with the two being treated together as the 'ideational' component. But in *IFG* the 'logical' component is presented as being 'above the clause' (the main title of Chapter 7), on the grounds that it contains system networks that apply to the 'clause complex' (or 'sentence') rather than the clause. And the 'clause complex' counts as a 'higher' unit on Halliday's 'rank scale' of units. Thus, for Halliday, 'logical' meanings apply to the clause complex, whereas 'experiential' meanings apply to the clause. It is therefore hard to see why these two metafunctions should continue to be treated as sub-components of one 'ideational' metafunction. Indeed we may reasonably ask: Does the use of the term 'ideational' serve any useful purpose at all? I suggest that it does not. In

Note, however, that this rearrangement should not be taken as implying that it is useful to regard them as sub-components of Halliday's three or four categories. On the contrary - two decades of experience in analyzing texts in the framework of the Cardiff Grammar has driven home the message that it is only through the recognition of these eight types of meaning that the role of each is sufficiently foregrounded in the semantic analysis of a text-sentence (as in Figure 17-2 in Chapter 17). The limits of the human mind are such that the omission of any one of these eight from the framework for the primary level of a semantic analysis can easily lead to the analyst's ignoring the very strand (or strands) of meaning that are the key to explaining what is going on in a text. And surprisingly often this turns out to be the 'affective' or 'validity' strand of meaning.[98]

12.4 An overview of the places filled by Adjuncts

We shall now return to the Adjuncts themselves - and to the challenging question of the **places** in the clause at which they occur.

We need to start by recognizing that almost all types of Adjunct can occur at SEVERAL DIFFERENT PLACES IN CLAUSE STRUCTURE.

---

practice, its use seems to lead to confusion, in that one quite frequently finds experienced Sydney-oriented systemic linguists using the term 'ideational' when they really mean 'experiential'. It would make the overall model simpler - and so easier to use - to abolish the term 'ideational' - and so also the concept that one 'metafunction' can be a sub-component of another. As I have remarked earlier, our experience in operating the Cardiff Grammar is that umbrella terms such as 'ideational' and 'textual' have no role to play - whether in a framework for text description or in a generative grammar in the computer. And the same is true of the 'interpersonal metafunction', which is used in the Sydney Grammar as a cover term for no fewer than four strands of meaning in the Cardiff Grammar. Such cover terms simply raise problems that are avoided when the types of meaning found in a language are considered in terms of the eight strands of meaning used here.

98 It has been the growing awareness of the importance of these two strands of meaning in the explanation of texts that has fuelled interest in the 'appraisal' approach to text analysis, as found in the work of Jim Martin, Peter White and their colleagues (Martin 2000, Martin and White 2005), as described in Footnote 46.

There are three main 'zones' of the clause at which Adjuncts can be found. However, the different functional types of Adjunct - such as the twenty that we identified in Section 12.2 - vary greatly in the probabilities with which they occur in these three main zones. And there are even variations WITHIN a few of these functional types, such as the variations within the Validity Adjuncts (where, for example, *perhaps* and *possibly* have very different probabilities).[99]

The present section will address this question: Where, in terms of the structure of the clause, are these three zones located? And the next section but one will answer this second question: What is the meaning of placing an Adjunct in one or these 'zones' rather than in another?' As the second question suggests, THE POSITION OF THE ADJUNCT IN THE CLAUSE EXPRESSES A TYPE OF MEANING.

Here are four examples which, between them, illustrate the main variations in place to be considered below:

(5) In the morning Ike usually eats an apple for breakfast.
(6) Last week, however, he unfortunately lost his appetite.
(7) Ivy has always very much preferred porridge.
(8) She simmers it gently, for a few minutes.

I suggest that you try analyzing these examples before I discuss them - and that you should follow the *Guidelines* from Chapter 9.

In this analysis task, you will face the additional problem that five of the ten Adjuncts consist of more than one word - as they often do in real texts. But I expect you will cope with that little complication satisfactorily - and your analysis skills may even be so good by now that you hardly notice it as a problem!

The analyses are given in Figure 12-1 (on the next page), so you should complete your analyses before turning the page.

---

99 Indeed, one of the major challenges to those attempting to build generative grammars for English, whether on paper or in the computer, is the very great variation in the places in the clause at which Adjuncts of various types can come. In the generative version of the Cardiff Grammar we have developed techniques for modelling these variables.

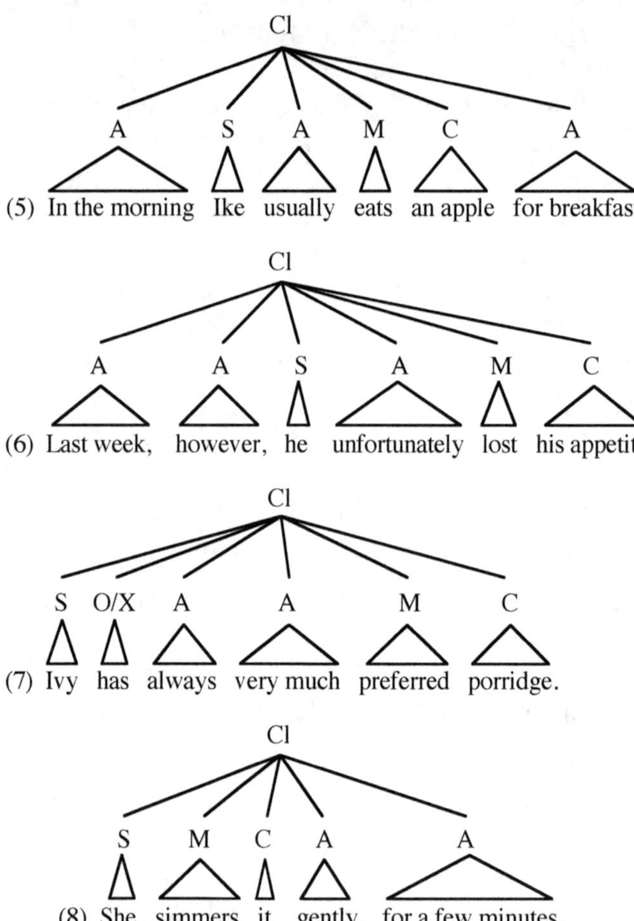

Figure 12-1: Some places in the clause at which Adjuncts occur

The key point about the places at which Adjuncts occur in the English clause is that for most Adjuncts there are THREE major choices (with minor variations within each).[100] Each expresses a different type of 'prominence' (in a broad sense of the term), as illustrated in (5) by *in the morning, usually* and *for breakfast.*

---

100 The positions of Adjuncts in English are often significantly different from those other languages, even closely related ones such as Dutch and German.

The three primary choices in the PROMINENCE system are [thematized], [integrated] and [potentially new], as follows:

1 When an Adjunct is placed at or near the start of the clause (e.g. to 'set the scene' for what follows), it is said to be **thematized**, e.g. *in the morning* in (5), and both *last week* and *however* in (6).[101]

2 When an Adjunct occurs medially in the clause, it is said to be **integrated**, e.g. *usually* in (5), *unfortunately* in (6), and both *always* and *very much* in (7).

3 When an Adjunct is placed at or near the end of the clause, it is described as **potentially new**, e.g. *for breakfast* in (5), *gently* and *for a few minutes* in (8) - as well as all the Adjuncts that have appeared in the examples earlier in the book. The Adjunct is said to be 'potentially new', because it is quite likely - but not certain - that it will receive the unmarked **Tonic** - i.e. the major pitch movement that typically falls on the last strong syllable in the intonation unit, which would in turn signal that the Adjunct is **New Information**.[102]

---

101 In grammars that use transformational rules to move elements about, a 'thematized' Adjunct is considered to have been moved by a transformational rule to its current place in the clause from its supposed 'original' place. But in SFG we pride ourselves on managing without such psychologically improbable rules. So the use of 'thematize' as a verb (as here in the term 'thematized') does not refer to the **movement** of the Adjunct, but to a procedure in the **realization** of a semantic element (the Circumstance) at the level of syntax. It is therefore NOT to be thought of as the movement of an element from its 'original' place in the clause to a 'new' place.

What happens in a SFG is this: the choice of the feature 'thematized' is made in the system network, and a realization rule then locates the element at the appropriate place in the structure of the clause. Indeed, it is one of the great attractions of SFG as a model of language that it doesn't first build one structure and then convert it into another (and another and another, etc), as in a transformational generative grammar; it gets the syntax right at the first attempt.

102 Strictly speaking, in the first variant of the third option (which will be described in Section 12.5) the Adjunct is given its own information unit, with the result that the Adjunct is not 'potentially new', but 'new'. This is because in this case it is certain to be marked explicitly as New Information.

I shall say a bit more about the MEANING that an Adjunct acquires when it occurs in each of these three 'zones' in the clause in Section 12.6.

Interestingly, even when the text is written, the 'information structure' of the clause is 'read into' it by skilled readers. But this, as will be clear, can only be done via a silent reading of the intonation with which the clause would be spoken if it were to be read aloud.

12.5 A third type of Newness

Within each of these three broad types of positionally-realized meaning there are two further types of variation.

The most important type is one which allows the Performer to give the Adjunct yet another type of prominence. This is achieved by using **intonation** or **punctuation** to give the Adjunct its own **information unit**. Most of what was said in Section 8.8 of Chapter 8 about the concept of an information unit applies here too. In other words, since (i) every intonation unit has its own **Tonic**, and (ii) the Tonic explicitly signals that the word it falls on is 'New', the effect is to mark the Adjunct itself as **New Information**. The difference from the first type of 'Newness' is that this type is not generated as a 'default', but is the result of a choice in a system.

In the case of a **thematized** Adjunct, this additional type of 'prominence' is combined with the type that the Adjunct has through is place in the 'thematized' zone. In (6), for example, *however* has been given the added prominence that comes from having a separate information unit, and it is thereby explicitly marked as **New Information**.[103]

Similarly, an **integrated** Adjunct can also be given its own information unit, as in *She is, almost certainly, the fastest woman in the world.*

---

103 Interestingly, the preceding Adjunct - i.e. *last week* - benefits from this decision, in that it automatically receives a Tonic as a by-product of the decision to present *however* as New. Alternatively, the Performer may in principle have also decided to present *last week* as New as well - though this seems less likely.

Finally, as (8) illustrates, a similar decision may be taken with an Adjunct that comes at the end of the clause, and so is **potentially new**. (In this case the 'Potential Newness' of the Adjunct *for a few minutes*, which is realized through its place at the end of the clause, is over-ruled by the choice to make it 'New'.)

The second type of variation is simply the use of more precise places within the three main 'initial', 'medial' and 'final' zones of the clause. Examples of analyzed clauses that illustrate these 'finer variations' are those in Figure 12-1:

(6), which has two **thematized** Adjuncts,
(7), which has two **integrated** Adjuncts, and
(8), which has two Adjuncts that are **potentially new** (both of which actually do express new information in this case).

For each of these pairs of Adjuncts, the grammar requires two **places** in clause structure at which to place the two types of Adjunct. (Notice that, since there are sixty functionally distinct types of Adjunct, many more places than two are needed in each zone, in order to handle all possible combinations of Adjuncts.)

To summarize: the types of 'prominence' available to Adjuncts are realized (i) by their position in one of the three zones in the clause and (ii), as an optional extra, as it were, by assigning to the Adjunct a separate information unit (realized in either intonation or punctuation).

12.6 The meanings of the three main types of 'prominence'

We shall now address the third question with which this chapter began, i.e. we shall look at the **meanings** of each of the four types of 'prominence' that an Adjunct may be given.

The primary choices in the PROMINENCE system are, as we have seen, [thematized], [integrated] and [potentially new].

We shall start with the concept of a **thematized Adjunct**. The question is: What does it mean when we say that an Adjunct has been 'thematized'? The answer is best expressed in terms of a cognitive-interactive model of the use of language. It is that, when a Performer thematizes an Adjunct, it becomes the first element of the event that the Addressee encounters (or at least a very early element) as he listens to (or reads) the text-sentence. And the result of this is that A automatically begins his 'decoding' of the clause with this element. It is this PRIORITY IN THE PROCESS OF INTERPRETATION that gives a thematized Adjunct its own particular type of prominence. In the 'travel' metaphor that Halliday sometimes uses to characterize the meaning of 'Theme', it is the 'point of departure' of the message (1994: 37).[104]

However, while this is the MEANING of 'thematized', this does not tell us the REASON why P has chosen to thematize it. There could in principle be as many reasons as there are types of Adjunct - and there are certainly a good many. Here I shall suggest four reasons that apply in the case of some types of Adjunct that are thematized relatively often.

(i) One such reason has been aptly named SCENE-SETTING, and this is indeed the usual reason for thematizing both 'Time position' and 'Place' Adjuncts.

(ii) A story-teller can add DRAMATIC EFFECT to an event by stating the Manner in which a Process occurs before saying what that Process is, as in *Slowly the door opened, ...* or *Suddenly a gunshot rang out....*

(iii) In other cases, P may wish to foreground her EVALUATION of the event. She may do this either in terms of how she feels about it, with an **Affective Adjunct** such as *luckily* in *Luckily, Fred will be there*, or in terms of her assessment of its validity, with a **Validity Adjunct** such as *perhaps* in *Perhaps Fred will be there.*

---

104 **Comparison with the Sydney Grammar** While the Sydney Model of language and its use is very strongly oriented to the SOCIAL and the CULTURAL rather than the COGNITIVE, the Cardiff Model is a COGNITIVE-INTERACTIVE model. In other words, it sets 'social interaction' within a cognitive model of two (or more) communicating minds, and is therefore both 'cognitive' and 'interactive'. But it is also 'social' in the broader sense, in which social and cultural beliefs are seen as important influences on choices in language. I first outlined the basic principles of the overall framework in Fawcett 1980, but please consult Fawcett 1993 and, more fully, Fawcett forthcoming 2010 for a description, with a worked example, of the current Cardiff Model of language and its use.

(iv) When the Adjunct expresses a LOGICAL RELATIONSHIP with an earlier proposition, as with *however* in (6), this too is likely to be thematized, so that the logical relationship between the present clause and the preceding proposition is clear to the Addressee.

Now let's consider the characteristics of an **integrated Adjunct**. The choice of the feature [integrated] provides a very different type of 'prominence'. When an Adjunct is 'integrated', it has the type of 'prominence' - or 'status' that comes from being at the heart of the clause, i.e. between the Subject and the Main Verb - or, more specifically, between the Operator (if there is one) and the Auxiliaries (if there are any). The first three of the examples in Figure 12-1 illustrate Adjuncts that are 'integrated', with (7) having two. But note that Adjuncts can in fact occur between most elements of the clause - though typically not between a Main Verb and the Complement that it predicts, unless it is a Manner Adjunct that describes a 'movement' Process, as in (9).

(9) She [S] ran [M] quickly [A] into the hall [C].

The third type of 'prominence' that an Adjunct may be given is to make it a **potentially new** Adjunct. This occurs when it is placed at the end of a clause, and in this position it is likely to receive the **unmarked Tonic** and so be marked explicitly as **New Information** - as in the case of *for breakfast* in (5) and *gently* in (8). In such cases, therefore, the motivation is to locate the element at a place in the clause where it is likely to receive the unmarked Tonic (i.e. the reason is the same as the third reason why 'passive' clauses get generated, as described in Section 8.8 of Chapter 8).

12.7 Summary

Adjuncts may be **thematized**, **integrated** or placed near the end of the clause and so be **potentially new** - and they may also be given the additional prominence of having their own information unit, and so also being presented as **New Information** in their own right. In these last two ways, then, the **informational** strand of meaning plays a major role in the way a Performer uses Adjuncts in the clause.

I have so far not given you any tests for identifying Adjuncts. Up to now you have been working on the assumption that, since you can identify all the other elements of the clause satisfactorily, those that are left over must be Adjuncts. This negative criterion has probably served you fairly well in your analyses of clauses up to this point in the book, but you would probably prefer to have positive tests as well. Since Chapter 15 will consist of a complete set of *Guidelines* for clause analysis, I shall delay the introduction of the relevant tests till that point.

For further examples of the places in the clause at which Adjuncts may occur, you could consult the diagram for the clause in Appendix 1.[105]

---

105 **Comparison with the Sydney Grammar** There are many differences between the two grammars with respect to the concept of 'Theme', and these are set out in full in Fawcett 2009. Here I shall restrict myself to just two that directly affect the concept of thematized Adjuncts - plus the more general point to which the discussion leads.

In *IFG* Halliday states that 'a clause, in its guise as a message, is a two-part structure, consisting of Theme + Rheme' (1994: 52-4). Here, then, he is presenting the notion of 'the Theme' as an element of the structure of the clause. But a problem arises when more than one element is thematized, as in the case of the two Adjuncts in (6). From the description of similar examples in *IFG*, it seems clear that, for Halliday, the two Adjuncts constitute a single element of the 'thematic structure' of the clause. He terms this type of Theme a 'multiple Theme' - and he then goes on to identify seven different clause elements that may occur within 'the Theme', all of which would otherwise function as direct elements of the clause. (As an aside, I should point out that some of these, such as the Linker (e.g. *and*) and the Binder (e.g. *because*) would not be regarded as 'thematized' in the Cardiff Grammar - the reason being that they cannot occur in any other place in the clause, so that their initial position is not the result of a choice in a system network to thematize them, as is the case with true Themes.)

The situation is therefore that Halliday continues to refer to the string of elements in a 'multiple Theme' as if they were all part of a single element called 'the Theme'. The nature of this 'part-whole relationship' is left unspecified, and it is not consistent with any relationship that is recognized in the theory (other than 'delicacy in description'). Yet I know of nowhere in Halliday's writings where he gives the reasons why we should view examples such as (6) as containing a single (if 'multiple') Theme, rather than two distinct Adjuncts.

From the 1970s onwards I myself have treated each thematized element as having been thematized IN ITS OWN RIGHT - and this approach, over many years of use in both the description of texts and the modelling of sentence generation in the computer, has proved to be a model that (i) captures the facts observed in the data of real texts economically and insightfully; (ii) raises no additional problems; and (iii) avoids certain difficulties that arise in the *IFG* approach (one of which we shall examine below).

In a recent survey of approaches to 'Theme', Thompson (2007: 672) similarly finds the concept that a multiple Theme is a single Theme troubling. He offers his own analyses of three examples with 'multiple Themes' (based closely on Halliday's analyses in *IFG*), and then goes on to point out that such an analysis 'implies that Theme is not a constituent but rather a region of the clause, a thematic "zone", in which different types of ideational and/or interpersonal meaning may exist'. And he continues: 'This implication, however, sits uneasily with a method of identifying Theme that relies on an analysis of clause constituents.' Exactly so. Yet there is no other method; it is the one that we all use, including Halliday. The logical conclusion, I suggest, is that we should dispense with the notion of 'a multiple Theme', and recognize instead the concept of 'multiple Themes' - i.e. 'Themes' in the plural, so implying the presence near the start of the clause of more than one different types of Theme.

Let us turn now to a second point of difference. Consider Example (5) in the main text. Here, in a Cardiff Grammar analysis, we would recognize (i) the Adjunct *in the morning* as a thematized Circumstantial Role and (ii) the Participant Role of *Ike* as the Subject Theme. It should surely be boringly uncontroversial to suggest that, in this clause, the Performer has decided both (i) to thematize the CR of *in the morning* so that it can 'set the scene' in terms of the time of the event, and also (ii) to select *Ike* rather than *an apple* to be what the clause 'is about', i.e. its Subject Theme.

But unfortunately this analysis is NOT uncontroversial. The problem with it, from the *IFG* viewpoint, is that it permits there to be TWO DIFFERENT SORTS OF EXPERIENTIAL THEME IN A SINGLE CLAUSE. The problem that I and many other systemicists have is to understand why this is a problem! The reason for the analysis just given is, of course, that there are two systems, each dealing with a different type of experiential meaning, in which these choices must have been made. And, while it is true that both are 'experiential' meanings, the type of experiential meaning that is expressed in a thematized 'experiential' Adjunct (a CR) is very different from the type expressed in a Subject Theme (a PR). One is typically 'scene-setting'; the other is 'what the clause is about'. Yet for Halliday there is a principle - which he describes as a 'very general principle' - that 'the Theme always includes one **(and only one)** experiential element' (1994: 53, my emphasis). This means that, for Halliday, the PR *Ike* cannot be a type of Theme, since the CR *in the morning* has been thematized. Yet *Ike* WOULD be a type of Theme for him if the CR *in the morning* had NOT been thematized.

It is therefore clear that the system of SUBJECT THEME (or whatever name you wish to give it) that we met in Section 8.5 of Chapter 8 has been used in BOTH (i) *In the morning Ike usually has an apple for breakfast* AND (ii) *Ike usually has an apple for breakfast in the morning* - i.e. irrespective of whether or not the Adjunct *in the morning* is thematized.

As in the case of the treatment of a 'multiple Theme' as a single element, Halliday simply tells the reader how he views the structure, but gives no reasons for preferring this controversial and apparently illogical position to the alternative described here. Yet, as Thompson comments (2007: 674), 'the most common position in the literature, after Halliday's, appears to be the Subject hypothesis' (i.e. the hypothesis that 'everything up to and including the Subject' is a type of Theme').

The position set out above has been presented as self-evident by many scholars. The paper that has been the most influential in pointing the way forward was Angela Downing's 'An alternative approach to theme' (1991). Drawing on a detailed study of Themes in H.G. Wells' *A Short History of the World* (1922), she suggests that we need to distinguish between the two concepts of 'Theme' as (i) a 'point of departure' for the message and (ii) 'what the clause is about' (Downing 1991: 141) - so rejecting the 'one experiential theme per clause' hypothesis. I myself had earlier published system networks for English that showed the system for SUBJECT THEME as independent of the other systems that involved thematizing experiential elements (Fawcett 1973/81: 169 and Fawcett 1980: 157-64) - though I did not explicitly set out the argument for this approach, as I have here. And we find essentially the same position in Berry's proposal (1995: 79) that we need to recognize (i) 'basic ideational theme (realized by grammatical subject)' and (ii) 'additional ideational theme (realized by adjunct at pre-verb slot)'.

We have been considering in this lengthy footnote two important issues of both the DESCRIPTION OF ENGLISH and, insofar as a 'general principle' is involved, the THEORY OF LANGUAGE. These are issues on which many systemic functional linguists have pointed out (but perhaps too gently?) the logical inconsistency of the Sydney Grammar's position. Yet no advocate of that position has yet answered these criticisms by giving a reason for retaining the 'one experiential theme per clause' principle. The 'principle' has simply been repeated as if it were self-evidently 'true' - both in the second and third editions of *IFG* and in the many derived introductory textbooks. It has been especially disappointing to find this 'principle' being repeated in the Third Edition of *IFG* (2004: 79). The wording has been slightly revised but there is no change of content - and the arguments against the Sydney Grammar's position have again been left unanswered. Yet the two functions served in the clause by the two types of 'experiential' Theme in (5) are so clearly different that the mere assertion of the 'principle' without supporting evidence carries no force.

Chapter 13
The syntax of TRANSITIVITY: five more concepts

13.1 The five additional concepts

This chapter enriches and extends the concept of TRANSITIVITY in five ways - the first three of them being closely connected.

In Chapter 10 our focus was on the criteria for identifying **Participant Roles**, and we made the simplifying assumption that a **Process** is always realized as a simple **Main Verb (M)**. But in Sections 13.2 to 13.4 of this chapter we shall add three significant extensions to the picture presented so far, as we meet three ways in which the meaning of the Process may 'spill over' from the Main Verb, as it were, into other elements.

We shall then look at two further aspects of THE SECOND PR IN A TWO-ROLE CLAUSE. We have already met two types of **covert Participant Role** (in Section 8.7 of Chapter 8 and Section 11.3 of Chapter 11), and Section 13.5 introduces us to a third type. Unlike the two previous types, however, this is one that often causes problems in text analysis - though they can be significantly reduced if the analyst is alerted to the problem. And that is the purpose of Section 13.5.

Finally, Section 13.6 introduces a relatively unusual construction, in which the PR that is the Complement occurs in an unusual position in the clause. This is what is termed in the Cardiff Grammar the **Marked PR Theme** construction.

13.2 A Process that uses a Main Verb Extension (MEx)

There is an element of the clause in English which occurs very frequently, especially in spoken English. It is in fact one of the major growing points of the language. Yet most grammars do not even recognize it as an element in its own right, typically lumping it in with other classes of word as an 'adverb' - or even categorizing both these words and prepositions as ‘particles’ - and so avoiding the important question of whether the word is functioning as (i) the central element in English syntax that we shall here call the **Main Verb Extension (MEx)** - or (ii) a **preposition**.

The **Main Verb Extension** has this name because it functions as an ‘extension’ of the **Main Verb (M)**, so that the two elements JOINTLY express a **Process**. The combination of a **M** and its **MEx** is referred to in traditional grammars as a ‘phrasal verb’. In modern English there are over five thousand such ‘phrasal verbs’, many being among the most frequently used verbs of the language. It is this that makes the **MEx** a central element in English syntax.

However, the term ‘phrasal verb’ is an unfortunate one. The term ‘phrase’ (which is equivalent to the SFL term ‘group’) implies that its two elements constitute a unit that can fill an element of clause structure - but it cannot. We shall shortly see why ‘phrasal verbs’ cannot be modelled as filling **M**, and why, instead, the two words of a typical ‘phrasal verb’ function as two separate elements in the clause. [106]

In the following two sections we shall meet two further ways in which a single Process (at the level of **meaning**) is realized in more than one word (at the level of **form**). When we wish to refer to all three types we shall use the term **multi-word Process**.

It is time for some examples. Compare (1) and (2) below. You would find it easy to analyze (1) - but could you analyze (2a)?

(1) He [S] raised [M] the problem [C] again [A].
(2a) He brought up the problem again.

Clearly, *brought up* in (2a) means virtually the same thing as *raise* in (1). Many phrasal verbs have a roughly equivalent simple verb - just as *bring up* in (2a) has in *raise* in (1). Other such pairs

---

106 Unfortunately, the term ‘phrasal verb’ is so firmly established that we cannot avoid using it. However, since (i) there are two types of ‘two-word’ verb (as we shall shortly see) and (ii) the type that we are considering in this section may consist of MORE than two words, we shall use the term ‘phrasal verb’ as an informal way of referring to the **M** + **MEx** class of ‘two-word verbs’. But the concept of ‘phrasal verb’ is not used in the generative version of the grammar.

are (i) *take apart* and *dismantle*; (ii) *get away* and *escape;* (iii) *go in* and *enter* etc. But some have no equivalent simple verb. So, while the existence of a near-synonym is a strong indication that the two words express a single Process, it cannot be made a necessary condition. If it were, many clear cases would be ruled out (e.g. *turn off* in *He turned the radio off.*)

In a rather similar way, we cannot use the fact that many phrasal verbs are **idiomatic** to make idiomaticity a criterion for identifying a 'phrasal verb'. Many are indeed idiomatic, in that the meaning of the Process is different from the combination of the 'physical world' meanings of the two words - as with *bring up* in (2a). But there is a 'physical world' sense of *bring up* that behaves syntactically in essentially the same way, e.g. *Ike brought up Ivy's breakfast* (*on a tray*) - as well as the 'vomit' sense of *bring up.*

Phrasal verbs are typically (i) made up of words derived from Anglo-Saxon and (ii) used in speech and informal writing. In contrast, their one-word near-equivalents are (i) almost always derived from Latin, and (ii) are typically used in formal writing and technical registers. But **Processes** that are realized in **multi-word verbs** are on the increase in ALL registers - especially in the more complex version of the **MEx** that we shall meet shortly.

So how would you analyze (2b) below? Are you tempted to treat the two elements as both being part of the Main Verb? If so, consider the relationships suggested in Figure 13-1.

(2b) He brought the problem up again.

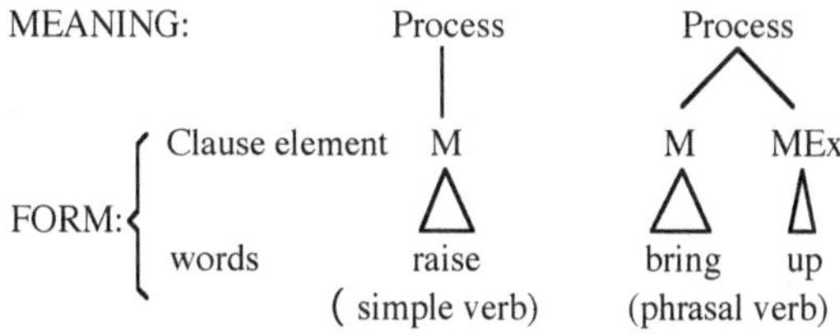

Figure 13-1:
Two types of lexical verb: a 'simple verb' and a 'phrasal verb'

Now apply the structure suggested above as you analyze (2b).

Don't turn the page till you have completed your analysis.

Solution

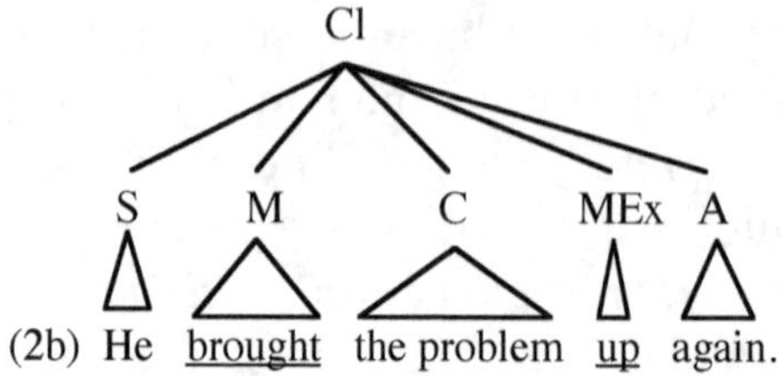

Figure 13-2: The analysis of a clause with a Main Verb Extension

Notice that I have underlined the two words that express the Process. This isn't a formal part of the syntax analysis, but it is a useful practice as the first step in analyzing text-sentences.

But there is a second frequent type of **MEx**, and it occurs in a different pattern. Consider the type that occurs with a 'movement' Process such as 'riding', as in (3a) - and notice the perhaps surprising possibility that (3b) demonstrates:

(3a) He [S] rode [M] off [MEx] into the sunset [C].
(3b) Off [MEx] he [S] rode [M] into the sunset [C].

As you can see, a **MEx** that is used in this type of Process can occasionally be **thematized** - rather as an **Adjunct** can. But most **MEx**s cannot be thematized, and even those like *off* don't enter the Adjunct system of [thematized] v [integrated] v [potentially new].

To summarize so far: the vast majority of phrasal verbs consist of **M** + **MEx**, with both the **M** and the **MEx** being high-frequency, one-syllable words of Anglo-Saxon origin. Typical Main Verbs are *be, break, bring, buy, call, come, cut, do, drop, fall, fill, get, give, go, hang, hold, keep, lay, leave, look, make, move, pass, pull, push, put, send, set, stay, stick, take, throw, touch, turn* and *wear*.

And here are the more frequent **MEx**s:

Very frequent:
up, down; in, out; on, off; about, (a)round, along, away; over, through and *back* (NB *back* can co-occur with others, as also can *on* with 'directional' Processes.)
Fairly frequent:
across, apart, aside, ahead; in front, behind, by, together, under

Eleven of these words also function as **prepositions**. But even if a possible **MEx** in a text is one, there is still a probability of over 95% that you are right to analyze it as a **MEx**, if in your judgement it is part of the Process. This rises to 99.9% if the word is *out, away, back, apart, aside, ahead, forward, in front* or *together*, because these items are not used as prepositions.[107]

Examples of phrasal verbs that use a **MEx** from the 'fairly frequent' list are: *take apart, stand aside, go ahead* and *go under.*

And there are a few special cases of a word that occurs as an **MEx** with a very small set of words as **M**, e.g. *put* in *stay put; to* in *come / push / pull to; good* in *come good; asleep* in *fall asleep; low* in *lie low; home* in *come / go / be home; left* in *be / have left; better* in *be / do / get better;* and *well* in *be / do / get well.*

Next, we should note that, very occasionally, the words at **MEx** can be 'adjusted' by the use of a preceding word, as in the underlined portions of (4) and (5).[108]

(4) He went <u>straight in</u> on his own.
(5) I've gone <u>right off</u> horror films.

As these two examples indicate, it is possible for a unit with its own internal structure to fill a **MEx**.

However, once we accept the concept that A **MEX** CAN BE FILLED BY A SYNTACTIC UNIT, it becomes clear that this element can help us to solve many other problematical cases, such as the relationship between (6a) and (6b) and between (7a) and (7b). (Notice that the linear notation has been used to analyze them in such a way as to bring out the similarities and differences.)

(6a) Ike [S] swims [M] every day [A].
(6b) Ike [S] has [M] a swim [MEx] every day [A].

(7a) Ivy [S] hugged [M] her boyfriend [C].
(7b) Ivy [S] gave [M] her boyfriend [C] a hug [MEx].

---

107 However, there is an increasingly frequent informal usage in which *out* is used as a preposition, as in *He looked out the window.*

108 I use the word 'adjusted' here, because the unit that is used to model such cases is the **quantity group**, and the relevant element is the **adjustor**. See Appendix 1 for a summary of the uses of this recently introduced unit.

The reason for these analyses will be clear. It is that 'swimming' and 'having a swim' are essentially the same Process - and that 'hugging someone' and 'giving someone a hug' are too. In both (6b) and (7b), then, the **MEx** is **filled** by a **unit** (a 'nominal group') the meaning of which is itself a Process.

Essentially the same analysis applies to Processes in which the **MEx** is filled by a unit other than a nominal group, such as the underlined prepositional group in *He's fallen* in love *with her*, the quality group in *I'm* very pleased *that they are here*, and the clause (with only **M**) in *They went* swimming. As you see, the grammar allows for the possibility that A **MEX** MAY BE FILLED BY ANOTHER UNIT, WHEREVER THAT MEANING IS PART OF THE MEANING OF THE PROCESS. And, while this unit is usually a nominal group, it is occasionally another unit, as the above examples show.

Finally, the **MEx** provides an appropriate way to analyze the type of 'new content seeker' in which the 'new content' that is 'sought' is the Process itself - or, more accurately, the Process and any associated Complements and Adjuncts. Consider (8), and the extension of the principle to the 'information giver' in (9):

(8) What [MEx] are [O/X] you [S] doing [M]?
(9) I [S] 'm [O/X] not [N] doing [M] anything [MEx].

To summarize: the great benefit of recognizing the **MEx** as a clause element is that it enables us to model Processes such as *make a mistake, fall asleep, do something* and similar cases.[109, 110]

---

109 There is a problematical class of over three dozen words which occur with 'locational' and 'directional' Processes and which are in many ways like a **MEx**. However, after careful consideration of the evidence for and against the decision, we treat them as **Complements** rather than **Main Verb Extensions**. Such items include *aboard, ashore, downstairs, downstream, indoors, inside, online, outdoors, outside, overboard, overhead, underground, upstairs, upstream* etc, and also the large set of items that pattern like *north, northward* and *northwards*. Essentially, the reason is that a word such as *indoors* (and even *inside*) involves a reference to an 'object' - though not via a standard nominal group - whereas a **MEx** such as *in* does not. (For a full account of this difficult area of English grammar, see Chapter 10 of my *Functional Syntax Handbook*.)

110 **Comparison with the Sydney Grammar** In this section and the next two we distinguish three types of 'multi-word verb', each of which has a different syntax from the other two types. While Halliday distinguishes the three types in

13.3 A Process that uses a following preposition

Now let's consider a second type of multi-word Process. We would analyze *They are discussing climate change* as shown in (10) below - but how should we analyze (11)?

(10) They [S] are [O/X] discussing [M] climate change [C].
(11) They are talking about climate change.

Clearly, we cannot analyze both *talking* and *about* as the Main Verb, because an Adjunct can come between them, as in (12):

(12) They are talking anxiously about climate change.

So we should ask these two questions:

(i) Is the Process a Process of 'talking' or a process of 'talking about'?

---

his analyses, he (like many others) calls them all 'phrasal verbs' in the brief overview that he provides (Halliday 1994: 207-10). So, in a comparison between the Cardiff and the Sydney grammars, we should ask how he handles the element that we call the **MEx**. His treatment of 'phrasal verbs' comes in the section of *IFG* that is about the 'verbal group'. As we saw in Footnote 28, he treats the clause element which we call the Main Verb (and he calls the 'event') as an element of the 'verbal group', together with the Auxiliaries - though not (at least, not when he is discussing clauses) the Operator. The 'verbal group' is then said to fill the 'Predicator', which is in turn an element of the clause. Given this fact, we might expect him to present the element that is the other part of the meaning of the Main Verb - which we analyze here as a **MEx** - as an element of his 'verbal group'. But he does not; instead his analyses of examples such *They called the meeting off* show this element as an Adjunct - AND SO AS AN ELEMENT OF THE CLAUSE – as we do. However, treating a **MEx** as an Adjunct leads to two problems. First, it does not behave like an Adjunct, as we have seen, in that neither type is open to the three-way system of PROMINENCE described in Chapter 12, i.e. [thematized] v [integrated] v [potentially new]. Second, his analysis means that in a phrasal verb such as *call off* the word *call* functions as an element of the 'verbal group' (i.e. the 'event') while the word *off* functions as an Adjunct in the clause. This is clearly an unsatisfactory analysis, in that it would be more elegant to generate the TWO words that express the ONE meaning of 'calling off' (which is semantically close to 'cancelling') as elements of the same unit - if that is possible. And it is indeed possible, as the Cardiff Grammar demonstrates, in both its generative and its text-descriptive versions. The analysis of 'phrasal', 'prepositional' and 'phrasal-prepositional' verbs presented here is therefore offered as both a clarification and an extension of the picture of this area of the grammar as it is presented in *IFG*.

(ii) What is the PR that the Process predicts? Is it *climate change* or is it *about climate change*?

And the answer is:

Just as there is a 'two-word verb' that expresses a Process through a ***Main Verb + Main Verb Extension*** *- i.e. a 'phrasal verb' -*
there is also a 'two-word verb' that expresses a Process through a ***Main Verb + preposition*** *- i.e. a 'prepositional verb'.*

And in this case too, as (12) above shows, the second element doesn't necessarily follow **M** immediately.

There is an additional complication in the case of a 'prepositional verb', which is that the **preposition** is NOT a sister element in the clause to **M**, but an element of a **prepositional group**. So we analyze (11) as shown below (where the underlining shows the two parts of the Process).[111]

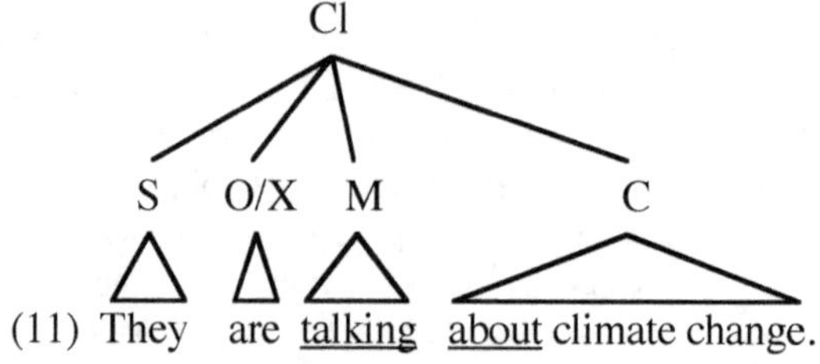

Figure 13-3: The analysis of a clause with a 'prepositional verb'

So *about climate change* is the Complement. However, since *about* is part of the expression of the Process, it is only *climate change* that is the PR that is predicted by the Process of 'talking about' (and not *about climate change*).

As with the 'phrasal verbs', there is often a 'one-word' verb with a roughly similar meaning, such as *discuss* for *talk about, watch, inspect* or *regard* for *look at* and *consider* for *think about.* And, like 'phrasal verbs', 'prepositional verbs' are often idiomatic.

---

111 One way in which a 'prepositional verb' is unlike a 'phrasal verb' (as described in the last section), is that there is no elegant way to model the two words as elements of the same unit. However, just as human beings are able to handle the fact that a single meaning can be expressed in a combination of a Main Verb and a preposition, so too can a generative SFG - as the computer implementation of such Processes in the COMMUNAL Project demonstrates.

But here too there are many examples that do not conform to these two norms, so that idiomaticity cannot be made a necessary condition for classifying an expression as a 'prepositional verb'.

'Prepositional verbs', then, constitute a second set of cases in which THE COMPLEMENT IS NOT ENTIRELY DEVOTED TO EXPRESSING A PR. (The first was the Complement *by King Henry* in *Rouen was attacked by King Henry* in Section 8.4 of Chapter 8.) From the practical viewpoint of analyzing clauses, this doesn't cause us a problem, because we simply analyze the 'preposition plus PR' as the Complement, i.e. *about climate change* in (11) is **C**.[112]

While 'prepositional verbs' occur frequently, they only occur about a quarter as frequently as 'phrasal verbs'. Other examples include *approve of, depend on, dispense with, listen to, look at, provide with, shoot at,* and *refer to*. There are also small classes of two-word Processes of 'biting at' or 'on' something, such as *bite at/on, chew at/on, gnaw at/on, nibble at/on* etc.

A nice example of the ambiguity of *dispense with* is this unintentionally entertaining notice in the window of a pharmacy:

WE DISPENSE WITH CARE.
J. Smith, Pharmacist

Figure 13-4: A notice in a pharmacist's shop window

But did the pharmacist intend the meaning for which the analysis is *We* [S] *dispense* [M] *with care* [C]? In this interpretation of the

---

112 Interestingly, this lack of a one-to-one fit between the Complement and the PR is reflected in the fact that we can treat either of them as the relevant unit when asking a 'new content seeker' question. Specifically, we can ask (but only in a 'very formal' register) *About what are they talking?* or, informally, *What are they talking about?* The full descriptive grammar and the computer-implemented generative grammar handle both of these alternative forms. However, we cannot fully analyze the second structure here, since it involves (i) the internal structure of the prepositional group and (ii) discontinuity between the elements of that unit - neither of which are covered in this introductory book. See my *Functional Syntax Handbook* for these.

text in Figure 13-4 the words *dispense with* are interpreted as a prepositional verb meaning 'not bother with'. We shall come to the alternative analysis in Example (25) in Section 13.5.

13.4 A Process that uses a MEx and a preposition

Please cover the solution on the opposite page so you don't see it.

The third type of multi-word Process is the combination of the two previous types. In traditional grammars it is called a 'phrasal-prepositional verb', and a typical example would be *How does she put up with him?*

You might expect that such combinations would be relatively rare, but they are not. Indeed, once we accept the concept that a **MEx** may be filled by a **nominal group** (as we did in Section 13.2), we find that an enormous number of problems in analyzing the TRANSITIVITY of natural texts have a straightforward solution - as we have already seen when considering Processes realized as **M + MEx**. We shall see a few examples shortly.

As with the previous two types of 'multi-word' Processes, there is frequently a 'one-word' semantic equivalent, e.g. *tolerate* for *put up with* - or a 'one-word' opposite, e.g. *acquire* for *get rid of.* And this type too is frequently idiomatic. However, as before, these typical characteristics cannot be used as criteria for treating such cases as a single Process.

Here are a few examples to illustrate this more complex way of realizing a Process (with a 'one-word' or other near-equivalent in brackets and a question mark to indicate a less close equivalent):

(13) They couldn't get away from the tsunami. (= 'escape')
(14) I'm looking forward to Spring. (= 'anticipate with pleasure')
(15) They don't really get on with each other. (= 'like'?)
(16) Ike has been going out with Ivy for years. (= 'courting'?!)

Now let's look at a few examples that illustrate the way in which the **MEx** may be filled by a **syntactic unit**:

(17a) We should have a chat about it. (= 'discuss informally')
(18a) Could you please take a look at my boiler? (= 'examine')

(19a) She is afraid of big dogs. (= 'fears')
(20) He had fallen in love with her when they were students.[113]
(21) Will you please do something about this? (= 'cure'?)

The unit in (17a), (18a) and (21) is a 'nominal group', in (19a) it is a 'quality group', and in (20) it is a 'prepositional group'.

Now try analyzing (16) and (20).

Solution

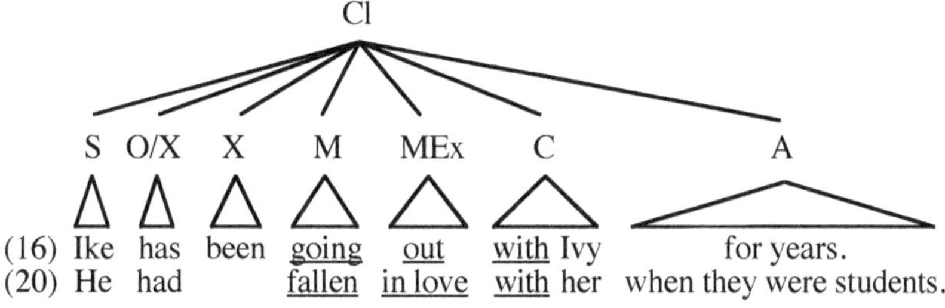

Figure 13-5:
The analysis of two clauses with a 'phrasal-prepositional verb'

As you can see, the two examples have virtually the same analysis, in terms of the elements of the clause.

The fact that the **MEx** can be filled by a unit such as a nominal group or a quality group has contributed to this construction's becoming one of the growing points of the language.

Here are examples of 'expansions' of four of the examples that we have just met - with the **MEx** underlined (but not the **p**):

(17b) We should have a really good chat about it.
(18b) Could you please take a thorough look at my boiler?
(19b) She is more afraid of big dogs than I am.

And here is an example which also has complexity in the number of **MEx**s (where, as before, the multi-word Process is underlined):

(22) ([S]) Keep [M] your mouth [MEx] shut [MEx] about it [C]!

---

113 There is no one-word equivalent in English to *fall in love with*, but there is the prepositional verb *fall for*. And note the existence of an equivalent multi-word verb in French, in *tomber amoureux de*.

In this extreme case, then, the entire clause, with the exception of *it*, is the expression of the Process!

We turn now to two very different aspects of TRANSITIVITY.

13.5 A third type of 'covert' Participant Role

Let's assume that, on the basis of the criteria established in Chapter 10, we are able to recognize which 'things', 'qualities', 'places' and 'events' in a clause are 'expected' by the Process - and so are to be identified as Participant Roles (PRs) rather than Circumstantial Roles (CRs).

Unfortunately there is a further complication that we have to deal with. This is the ever-present possibility that the clause contains a **Complement** - and so a **Participant Role** - that is 'hidden', or, to use the technical term, **covert**. In other words, A PR THAT IS PREDICTED BY THE PROCESS IS QUITE OFTEN NOT ACTUALLY PRESENT AT THE LEVEL OF FORM. And this frequently causes difficulties in text analysis - unless the analyst is alert to it.

We have already met two types of covert PR, but in each case there were strong clues in the rest of the clause that alerted the analyst to the PR's absence. In the case of *Rouen is being besieged* the clue was the 'passive Auxiliary' *being*, and in *Touch your nose!* it was the fact that the clause is a 'simple directive'.

The type of covert PR to be considered here is one that occurs when there are no such clues. It occurs in all types of clause, including ones that are 'active' (rather than 'passive') and 'information givers' (rather than just in 'simple directives'). The problem in such cases is that it is often hard to tell at first whether the clause is (i) simply a clause that has one PR, or (ii) a clause that has two (or three) PRs, with one (or more) being covert.

There are several subtypes, as the following examples show. (Here I have used the space-saving linear notation.)

(23) Ike [S] should [O] shave [M] ([C]) more often [A].
(24) ([S]) Simmer [M] ([C]) gently [A] for ten minutes [A].

In (23) the Complement would, if it was realized, be *himself*, and, while this construction occurs especially frequently with such 'ablutionary' processes, it also occurs with other Process types, e.g. with the expression *Enjoy!* (which, in the British English of a couple of decades ago, would have been *Enjoy your meal* (etc)*!*)

Now consider (24) - which is adapted from our very first example, back in Chapter 3. As you will recognize, it belongs to the genre of 'recipes'. It is a typical example of the recipe-writer's space-saving habit of omitting a Complement that is recoverable from the context - with the recoverable 'object' typically being 'the aforesaid ingredients'. So here the covert PR does NOT have the same referent as the Subject. (Notice, incidentally, that (24) also illustrates the fact that there may be more than one covert PR in the same clause - because in this case the Subject is covert too.)

Covert PR Complements occur in a variety of contexts of situation. They are particularly frequent in notices to the public. For example, there is a warning sign on British motorways that says *Tiredness can kill* (where some such Complement as 'your fellow users of the road - and you!' is assumed to be recoverable).

As a final example, consider (25). This is the analysis of the intended meaning of *We dispense with care* in Figure 13-4 - i.e. with a covert Complement of 'medicines'. (We analyzed (25) in its unintended 'prepositional verb' sense in Section 13.3.)

(25) We [S] dispense [M] ([C]) with care [A].

13.6 A Complement as a Marked PR Theme

When a **Complement** is thematized, as in (26) and (27) below, we have a case of a low-probability choice in the system for MARKED PARTICIPANT ROLE THEME.

(26) Those truffles [C] I [S] just [A] couldn't [O] resist [M].
(27) Boring [C] it [S] was [O/M] not [N].

The choice to have a **Marked PR Theme** is made relatively rarely, probably in under 0.1 per cent of clauses. It is often thought to occur only in speech, but it can also be found in written texts, even in relatively formal ones.

When a clause has a Marked PR Theme, it typically expresses either (i) contrast or (ii) a considerable strength of feeling in the Performer - and sometimes both at the same time.

Notice that the system that offers this choice must occur AFTER the system in which the Performer decides which of two possible

PRs is to be the Subject Theme (i.e. the type of thematization that we met in Section 8.5 of Chapter 8). In (26), for example, P will have first chosen to make herself - realized as *I* - the Subject Theme, but then her wish to give special prominence to the particularly beloved object of *those truffles* makes her give it the strong type of prominence of being a 'Marked PR Theme'.[114]

13.7 Summary

That concludes the presentation in this chapter of the five further concepts that we needed to introduce in order to complete the picture of TRANSITIVITY in the English clause.

First we met three ways in which our original, over-simple model of the relationship between a **Process** in the **semantics** and a **Main Verb** in **syntax** needed to be enriched. (Compare, for example, Figure 3-1 in Chapter 3.) The grammar now provides for a Process to be realized as (i) **M**, (ii) **M + MEx**, (iii) **M + p**, and (iv) **M + MEx + p** - and even as variants of (ii) and (iv) with two

---

114 **Comparison with the Sydney Grammar** In *IFG* Halliday describes as 'marked themes' both (i) a thematized PR that is functioning as a Complement and (ii) a thematized Adjunct - so implying that they have a lot in common. Here, however - as you may have noticed - we have used the term 'marked' only for a thematized **C**. The reason is that thematizing an Adjunct is a very different matter from thematizing a Complement - for the following two reasons.

The first reason (which we have already noted) is that the options that are available to the element are different in the two cases. With a Complement there are just TWO choices in the relevant system: either it occurs at its usual place, immediately after the Main Verb, or, very occasionally, it is thematized. But in the case of an Adjunct there are almost always the THREE choices that we first encountered in Chapter 12: [thematized] v [integrated] v [potentially new].

The second reason is that the PROBABILITIES that the element will be thematized are very different in the two cases. The thematization of a Complement is very infrequent (probably averaging around 0.1% across all types of text), whereas most types of Adjunct are thematized relatively frequently (averaging around 5% for a typical Circumstantial Role, though varying greatly with both the type of Adjunct and the text type).

The result is that when a Complement is thematized it is always heavily marked, whereas the thematizing of most Adjuncts is not.

MExs (and in rare cases three **MEx**s). Then we noted the many cases in which English exploits the **MEx** by filling it with nominal and other groups, and I suggested that this is one of the areas of Modern English that is most open to development.

And finally we have added two important enrichments to our picture of **Complements**, by considering cases where a Complement may be either (i) **covert** or (ii) thematized as a **Marked PR Theme**.

In the next chapter we shall meet three further elements, and this will complete our picture of the simple clause in English.

Chapter 14
Three new elements: Infinitive, Auxiliary Extension and Vocative

14.1 Overview

We turn now to the last three elements to be introduced in this book. The first of these 'new' elements is the least important in functional terms and is often ignored in traditional grammars. Yet it is, after **S**, **O**, **X**, **M**, **C** and **A,** the next most frequent clause element (being more frequent than **MEx**). The second 'new' element is also widely ignored in other grammars - though for very different reasons, as we shall see. Yet it is an element that is crucial in enabling the present grammar to handle elegantly a number of otherwise problematical structures. And the third new element is, in functional terms, one of a small number whose true function is as an element of the structure of the **discourse**, but which the language permits to function inside the structure of the **clause**, AS IF IT WERE PART OF THE MEANING OF THE CLAUSE - occurring, as we shall see, at various different places in it. So this element too, while widely recognized, is often omitted from descriptions of the clause. Yet each is 'new' in its own way.

We shall begin with the little word *to.*

14.2 The Infinitive Element (I)

In this section we evaluate the role of a minor but very frequent element, which we shall call the **Infinitive Element (I)**. It is almost always expounded by the word *to* (but see Step 3 of the *Full Guidelines* in Chapter 15 for the few exceptions). The name reflects the use of the word 'infinitive' in traditional grammars, in which the 'infinitive form' of the verb *eat* is said to be *to eat.*

This *to* must be distinguished from the one that functions as a preposition, as in *Fred's gone to Kyoto*, but that isn't normally a problem in text analysis. While about two thirds of the cases of *to* function as a preposition and only one third as **I**, its use as **I** is still in the dozen most frequent words in the language.[115]

Compare (i) the meanings and (ii) the syntax of (1) and (2):

(1) You should eat everything.
(2) You ought to eat everything.

The meanings are clearly similar - and so in fact are the structures, in that the *Mood Test* shows that both *should* and *ought* function as the Operator. The only difference is the presence of *to* in (2).

Should we simply treat it as part of the Operator? We should not, because the 'polarity seeker' equivalent to (2) is *Ought you to eat everything?* - so showing that *to* is NOT part of the Operator.

Nor can we treat *to* as part of the Main Verb (as is suggested by the assumption in traditional grammars that *to eat* is 'the infinitive form of the verb *eat*'), as (3) and examples in Section 14.3 show.

(3) We [S] ought [O] to [I] have [X] left [M] the party [C] earlier [A].

The Infinitive Element is therefore in the curious position that it patently exists in its own right at the level of form, and yet it is almost always introduced as the by-product of the choice of a meaning WHOSE MAIN REALIZATION IS IN ANOTHER ELEMENT. Here the other element is the **Operator**, but in the next section we shall see that it may also be an **Auxiliary** and its associated **Auxiliary Extension**.

Now consider the meaning and form of the words *was* and *to* in (4) below - and then give your analysis skills a little practice by analyzing it. But make sure that you think functionally, because if you don't you could find yourself making an error!

(4) He was to have been here by six o'clock.

As usual, you are reminded not to turn the page until you have attempted the analysis.

---

115 These figures are based on the **word form** frequencies in Sinclair 1991 (p. 143), combined with the unique **semantic** frequencies from West 1953 (pp. 523-5). The latter gives the percentages for the functions of *to* as (i) a preposition (62.5%), (ii) an Infinitive Element (36.9%) and (iii) a MEx (0.6%).

Solution

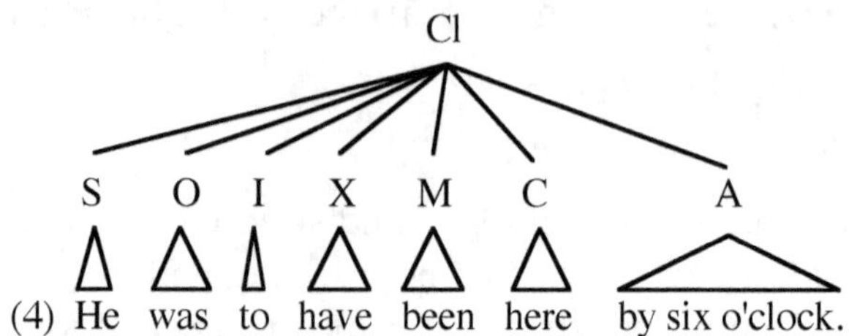

Figure 14-1: An unexpected modal verb

What (4) illustrates is yet another of the many functions that are served by the forms of *be*. In other words, if a form of *be* is followed by *to* it is functioning as a 'pure' modal verb, exactly like *ought* - and with a fairly similar meaning. Note, then, that in this case *was* is NOT to be analyzed as **O/X**, but simply as **O**. [116]

14.3 The Auxiliary Extension (XEx)

In Section 13.2 of Chapter 13 we met the valuable concept of the **Main Verb Extension (MEx)**, and we saw how useful it is in enabling us to handle the syntactic relationships in several types of construction. Among these was the type of which *I had a shower this morning* is an example, in which most of the meaning of the

---

116 Early grammars of English - and so in turn more recent 'traditional' grammars - were strongly influenced by the grammar of Latin (which was in turn modelled on that of Greek), and the reason why the Infinitive Element was not recognized in those early grammars was that the words *to eat* would be translated into Latin by the single word *edere.* The line of argument was: 'Since no word can interrupt the word *edere* in Latin, no word should be allowed to interrupt *to eat* in English' - and on this basis the edict proscribing 'split infinitives' came into being. From this misguided assumption it is only a short step to treating the Infinitive Element as part of the same element as whatever follows it. In practice, however, Adjuncts quite often occur - normally unnoticed by those who claim to abhor them - between **I** and **M**. Consider, for example, *To fully appreciate Beethoven's last quartets, you need an uninterrupted hour of listening time.* I personally have some affection for the fact that the mission of the starship Enterprise in *Star Trek* is *to boldly go where no man has gone before* (an expression, incidentally, whose syntax has been sanctioned by the compilers of the 1998 edition of the *Oxford English Dictionary*).

Process of 'having a shower' is expressed in the **MEx**, with very little being expressed in the **M**.

We come now to a similar relationship. But this one is between an **Auxiliary Verb (X)** (which is, like the other **X**s, usually a form of *be* or *have*) and a following **Auxiliary Extension (XEx)**. And there is also, in almost all cases, a following **Infinitive Element (I)**. What we are considering here, then, is a TRIO of elements, i.e. a sequence of **X** + **XEx** + **I**, which, taken together, SERVE TO EXPRESS A SINGLE MEANING.

As an illustration of this point, consider the underlined portions of the second of each of the following pairs of examples - and its semantic relationship to the underlined word in the first of each pair:

(5a) She must be rich.
(5b) She is bound to be rich.

(6a) She will win the race.
(6b) She is going to win the race.

(7a) I must leave now.
(7b) I have got to leave now.

(8a) She can reach it.
(8b) She is able to reach it.

As you can see, in Example (a) of each pair of examples, there is a simple modal verb that expounds **O**, and in Example (b) of each pair there is a trio of words which express a broadly similar meaning. It is these three words that expound the three elements of **X**, **XEx** and **I**.

In a few cases the 'trio' is reduced to a pair - as in (9b) - but the reason for treating such cases as **X** + **XEx** is the same.

(9a) She should be more respectful.
(9b) She had better be more respectful.

In conversational texts, roughly one word in every two hundred is an Auxiliary Extension (though there are fewer in other registers) - and this fact alone should make it an important element in any description of the English clause.[117] Yet the standard descriptions of English typically give these relatively frequent words little more than footnote status, as if they were minor aberrations from the main structural patterns of the language, rather than the central elements that they in fact are.[118]

Before we look in more detail at the **X XEx I** structure, let us remind ourselves of the three types of Auxiliary Verb that we met in Chapter 8. Here is an example that illustrates all three in use in the same clause:

(10) By 2006 [A], climate change [S] <u>had</u> [O/X] already [A] <u>been</u> [X] <u>being</u> [X] debated [M] by scientists [C] for many years [A].

In the full Cardiff Grammar, however, we recognize a total of FOURTEEN distinct types of Auxiliary Verb. Each can occur with one or more others before or after it, so demonstrating that each type is needed in a full grammar of English.[119] Of these fourteen **X**s, six are followed by an **XEx** and an **I**, so participating in the construction that we are considering here. This is therefore a major area of the grammar of English that adds significantly to its

---

117 This figure is calculated on the basis of figures given in Biber et al (1999: 486). However, since we include here several types of **XEx** that they handle as either (i) 'adjectives taking post-predicate *to*-clauses' or (ii) full lexical verbs, the true figure will be even higher.

118 Grammarians cannot agree on (i) whether these items should be seen as constituting one, two or three classes; (ii) what to call them; and (iii) which items should be included in each class. Some subsets of the items analyzed here as **XEx**s have been called, in various recent works: 'modal idioms' and 'semi-auxiliaries' (Quirk et al 1985: 141-7),'lexical auxiliaries' (Downing and Locke 1992: 316-7), 'phrasal modals' (Francis et al (1996:573-75), 'semi-modals' (Biber et al 1999: 483-502), 'lexical modals' and 'quasi-modals' (Huddleston and Pullum (2002: 205-8). And most would also treat at least some of them simply as 'non-finite complements of adjectives' (e.g. Huddleston and Pullum (2002: 1256-9). Interestingly, however, all these grammarians have, either explicitly or implicitly, recognized the semantic affinity of some of these expressions with the meanings of the modal verbs - as I do in Fawcett 2007a.(

119 See Fawcett 2007a for a full description of these fourteen possible Auxiliaries and the six associated **XEx** constructions. So far as I am aware, this is the first major study of this area of English Grammar.

richness - and also, inevitably, to its complexity. But at the same time it provides a solution to a large set of problems in the analysis of English syntax.

Those remarks may make the prospect of trying to analyze **XEx**s sound worrying. But there are four factors that make it much easier than you might expect. These are:

1. It is unusual to find more than two **X**s in the same clause - cases such as (10) above being unusual.
2. It is also unusual to find, in any one clause, more than one **X** with a following **XEx** and **I**.
3. Since almost all of the new **X**s are expounded by forms of the verbs *be* and *have* - like the ones that we have met already - it is easy to recognize them.
4 While it is in principle possible for an element such as a **Adjunct** or a **Negator** to interrupt the sequence of **X XEx I**, in practice this happens only very rarely. The result is that the word (or words) that expound the **XEx** are almost always preceded by a form of *be* or *have* and followed by *to* - and this makes it a simple matter to identify a trio of **X XEx I**.

Here are a few typical examples of the structure:

(11) She [S] is [O/X] sure [XEx] to [I] be [M] there [C].
(12) He [S] is [O/X] said [XEx] to [I] be [M] a thief [C].
(13) She [S] is [O/X] going [XEx] to [I] be [M] a mum [C].
(14) You [S] 've [O/X] got [XEx] to [I] be [M] there [C].
(15) He [S] was [O/X] allowed [XEx] to [I] eat [M] it [C].
(16) He [S] is [O/X] liable [XEx] to [I] stammer [M].

In Step 3 of the *Full Guidelines* in Chapter 15, you will find lists of the main words that you need to be able to recognize - together with a few cases that do not conform fully to the pattern illustrated in the above examples, such as *had better*. [120]

---

120 This is not the place to set out the reasons for treating all of these examples in this manner. For further examples of each type see Step 3 of the *Full Guidelines* in Chapter 15, and for the fullest description of the construction and the rationale for adopting this approach to explaining this important set of phenomena, see Fawcett 2007a.

Cover the solution on the opposite page so you don't see it.

Many of the words that occur at **XEx** started their lives, in an earlier stage in the development of English, as lexical verbs. Some of these, such as *willing* and *bound,* have in the course of time come to function as adjectives. The result is that these words now occur at **XEx** with the usual structures that occur around adjectives, such as the **quality group** around *likely* in the underlined portion of (17).[121]

(17) Fiona is less likely than Ivy is to be at the party.

And, when the word at **XEx** is a lexical verb, other clause elements may occur with it, as in the underlined part of (18). In this 'truncated' **clause**, the words *very widely* are functioning as an Adjunct in an embedded clause whose **M** is *believed.*

(18) He is very widely believed to be guilty.

It is the possibility of having a lexical verb at **XEx**, as in the types illustrated in (12), (15) and (18), that enables the present grammar to handle neatly certain syntactic phenomena that present a challenge to all current theories of language.[122]

Finally, note that there is a small number of words that function as **XEx** but which are followed by a word other than *to.* Consider, for example, (8c).

(8c) She is capable of reaching it.

If *She is able to reach it* uses the **X XEx I** construction, so too should (8c) - even though its **I** is expounded by *of.* Other cases are included in the list of **XEx**s in Step 3 of the *Full Guidelines.*

To conclude this section, let me challenge your powers of analysis by inviting you to analyze the following example (which is a little more complex than usual):

(19) You are very likely to be able to analyze this sentence.

---

121 For an outline of the structure of the quality group, see Appendix 1.

122 These are known as 'raising' constructions in the part of the linguistics literature that takes its names for constructions from the transformational generative approach.

Solution

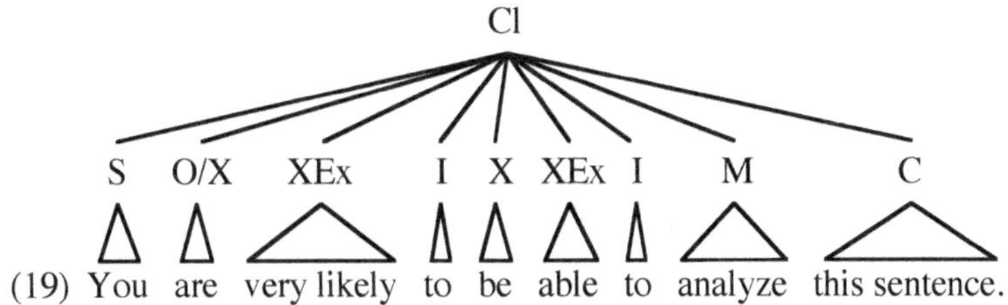

Figure 14-2: A clause with two Auxiliary Extensions

I expect you will have got the analysis right - which includes treating *very* and *likely* as both being parts of the first **XEx**. Did you remember that the first of the two **X**s is conflated with the **O**?

Finally, note that we may even find clauses with THREE trios of **X XEx I** - e.g. *She is bound to be going to be willing to sing.* [123]

---

123 **Comparison with the Sydney Grammar** In *IFG* the items that we treat here as **XEx**s enter the picture in two places. Firstly, the trio of words in *be going to* (which are treated here as exponents of the 'Expectation' Auxiliary and Extension) are handled as part of the TENSE system. However, Halliday analyzes *be going to* as two Auxiliaries - *be* and *going to* - and this raises two problems. The first is that it implies that *be going to* expresses two meanings rather than one (since every other Auxiliary represents a distinct meaning). Secondly, he doesn't recognize *to* as a separate element. It is certainly rare for *going* and *to* to be separated, but it is not impossible - as is shown by the possibility of examples such as *I am going, regretfully, to have to call the deal off.*

However, the main place in *IFG* where Halliday mentions items that are modelled here as occurring at **XEx** is in the 'further account of modality' (1994: 357, 2004: 619). Here he sketches in the outline of a position that is fairly similar to that taken by myself, in that he - like other scholars - treats expressions such as *be required / supposed / allowed / willing / determined to* as being semantically related to *must, should, may, will* etc. But it is clear that his description is exploratory rather than definitive, because items that one would expect to be included are missing - e.g. *able, obliged* and *inclined.* Moreover, there is no indication of how such items should be modelled in a fully explicit SFG, and there are no examples at all of how to analyze cases such as those in Examples (12), (15) and (18).

I would like to think that the six distinct types of **X** + **XEx** + **I** that are described in full in Fawcett 2007a (and summarized here) can be seen as a useful extension to - and also a formalization of - the preliminary sketch given in *IFG.*

14.4 The Vocative (V)

We turn next to the final element to be introduced here: the Vocative. Consider (20), (21) and (22):

(20) James, sit down!
(21) You, my darling, should take a rest.
(22) You're looking well, my old mate.

The element **Vocative (V)** is always filled by a nominal group. This is usually (i) a proper name such as *Mr Jones* or *James*, as in (20), or (ii) a term of respect, such as *Sir* or *Miss*. But occasionally the Vocative is one of a limited set of nominal groups, as in (21) and (22). There are further examples on the 'clause' page of Appendix 1.[124]

The frequency of examples such as (20) has occasionally led analysts to think that the Vocative is a type of Subject. But (21) and (22) show that this isn't the case, both because each example already has a Subject and because its position in the clause is not compatible with being the Subject.

The three examples above demonstrate two further key points:

(i) the Vocative is almost always given a separate information unit (shown in written texts by the use of commas), and
(ii) it can come at various positions in the clause, as the examples show.

The name 'Vocative' reflects the traditional view that the function of this element is to 'call' the attention of the Addressee. This is certainly one of its functions, but it is a discourse function rather than a clause function. Indeed, it often occurs without any other clause elements.

It also serves a second function - often in this case occurring in mid-clause or coming at the end. This is to mark social and personal distance between the Performer and the Addressee.

---

124 There is a special unit of English syntax for analyzing proper names in English, as there are for other specialized areas of the grammar such as addresses and dates. These function at the head of a nominal group. They are omitted here, but full descriptions of their structure are provided in my *Functional Syntax Handbook.*

While it is true that similar factors in the context of situation affect choices in the 'form of address' that is used in the Vocative as those that affect choices in MOOD, this doesn't make it an 'interpersonal' clause element. And there is not the interdependence with meanings realized in other clause elements that we have found for the Subject, Operator, Auxiliary, Auxiliary Extension, Main Verb, Main Verb Extension, Complement, Adjunct, etc.

14.5 Summary

We have now introduced the last clause element to be described in this book. Of the three elements introduced in this chapter, the **Infinitive Element (I)** is by far the most frequent, but the **Auxiliary Extension (XEx)** is by far the most important.

The **Vocative**, in contrast, is a 'fringe' element in the clause. Firstly, it operates on its own (unlike the mutually interdependent nature of the rest of the elements). Secondly, it serves its own discourse functions, both of which can be interpreted as general functions in the discourse as a whole. Yet its syntactic behaviour undeniably marks it as an element of the clause.

We have therefore covered all the main elements of the English clause - with two important exceptions. These are the two elements that show how a clause may be (i) **bound** into the structure of a higher clause (by a **Binder** such as *that, if* or *when*), or (ii) linked with a preceding clause (by a **Linke**r such as *and, but* or *or*). But to include a full treatment of these would take us far beyond the topic of this book - which is the simple clause in English. However, examples of some of these can be found on the 'clause' page of Appendix 1.

The next chapter serves two purposes. The first is to provide a full set of *Guidelines* that will, if they are followed carefully, give you the ability to analyze most simple clauses. But at the same time it functions as a general revision of the book as a whole.

Chapter 15
Full Guidelines for clause analysis

15.1 How complete are these Guidelines?

This is, from one viewpoint, the key chapter of the book - in that it brings together everything that we have learnt about the structure of the English clause, in order to provide you with a practical set of *Guidelines* that will enable you to analyse any simple English clause in a principled manner.

That is a big claim. You may well be asking yourself: Can any set of *Guidelines* really do that, after such a relatively short introduction? The answer largely depends on what we understand by 'simple' in 'any simple English clause'. As I pointed out in the Preface to this edition, this introductory book draws on the much larger *Functional Syntax Handbook*, and that work covers many minor complications that are ignored here. However, while some less important points have only received a brief mention here and a very few none at all, I can say that I have introduced all the main points. I think you will be able to make sense of even the very few points that have not been covered that are mentioned in these *Guidelines*, since they are illustrated throughout by examples.

The main aspects of clause structure that these *Guidelines* do NOT cover are those that relate the clause to other clauses that are part of the same sentence, i.e. (i) **co-ordinated** clauses (when the second clause is introduced by a Linker such as *and, but, or* etc) and (ii) **dependent** clauses (of which there are many types, including ones introduced by a Binder such as *that, if, when* etc).

This chapter (i) reminds you how to draw clear diagrams; (ii) provides a one-page summary of the *Guidelines*, and then (iii) gives you the *Full Guidelines*, which are illustrated throughout by the **Worked example**.

15.2 Tips for drawing syntax diagrams: a reminder

Remember to apply the **three tips for drawing clear syntax diagrams** that were originally given in Chapter 4:

1 When you write down the clauses to be analyzed, you should LEAVE FOUR OR FIVE LINES OF SPACE ABOVE THE TEXT itself, for the analysis diagram. (We would need more space for the full analysis of sentences, if we were analyzing one in its full complexity, as in Figure 17-1 in Chapter 17.)
2 Save space by writing two or more short sentences side by side.
3 It is best to WORK IN PENCIL, with an ERASER ready in case you need to change your analysis.

15.3 The *Full Guidelines* - brief version

0	Preparation: make the clause an 'information giver' that is 'positive', and replace *wh*-items by *someone,* etc.	
1	Find the Process, and so the Main Verb	**M**
	or **M** + Main Verb Extension(s)	**M + MEx**
	or **M** + preposition	**M + p** (inside **C**)
	or **M** + Main Verb Extension + preposition.	**M + MEx + p**
2	Left of **M**, find any Auxiliaries (if used)	**X, X, X**
3	Right of each **X**, find any Auxiliary Extension, if used, plus any associated Infinitives	**XEx + I**
4	Left of **X**, find any other Infinitive (if used)	**I**
5	Left of **I**, find the Negator (if used).	**N**
6	Left of **N**, find the Operator (if used).	**O**
7	Left or right of **O**, find the Subject.	**S**
	S may contain a *wh*-item.	
	If **S** is covert, place it in brackets.	**(S)**
8	Find the Let element (if used).	**L**
9	Find all PRs. **S** is probably one; any other PR is a Complement.	**C, C**
	If a **C** contains a *wh*-item, expect it to the left.	
	If a **C** is covert, place it in brackets.	**(C)**
10	Find any Adjuncts.	**A, A ...**
	If an **A** contains a *wh*-item, expect it to the left.	
11	Find the Vocative (if used)	**V**
12	Find the Ender.	**E**

15.4 The *Full Guidelines* - with tests and examples

Step 0: Preparation for applying the tests

Most clauses are **positive information givers with no thematized elements**. If the clause to be analyzed does NOT have this structure, you should first re-express it as one, either in your mind or on a spare piece of paper. The tests used below depend on your having first 're-expressed' your original clause in this way. So:

(i) If the clause isn't already an 'information giver', change it into one.
(ii) Make a 'proposal for action' into an 'information giver' that refers to future time, using *you/we/I will.*
(iii) Replace any element containing a ***wh*-item** by *something, someone, somewhere* etc, and place it in its typical position.
(iv) Remove any markers of negation, i.e. ***not***, ***n't***, ***never***, etc.
(v) Put any **thematized** elements in their typical positions.

Examples of re-expressions

(i) and (ii) Re-express *Sit down* as *You will sit down.*
(i) and (iii) Re-express *Where will she live?* as *She will live somewhere.*
(iv) and (v) Re-express *That film I didn't like* as *I did like that film.*
(v) Re-express *Yesterday I saw Ivy* as *I saw Ivy yesterday.*
(v) Re-express *Off they went to York* as *They went off to York.*

Worked example (used throughout these *Guidelines*)
The context of situation is that Paula has just heard from a friend about a couple who have recently told their twelve-year-old daughter that she is adopted. Paula is hardly able to believe that they didn't tell her the true facts of her birth at a much earlier age, and she puts this 'confirmation seeker' to her informant:

Has she really not been told the truth all this time?

Following the *Guidelines* on **Preparation**, we re-express this as:

She has really been told the truth all this time.

We come now to the *Guidelines* themselves.

Step 1: Identifying the Process and its Participant Roles

This is by far the most difficult - and so the longest - step in analyzing the clause. But in many cases you can omit two or more steps, as you will see - especially the 'reminders' and others marked '(optional)'.

Step 1.1: A reminder of the four types of Process (optional)

The task is to **find the word (or words) that express the Process**, and at the same time to make a first guess (to be confirmed later) at which words express **the Participant Roles** that it 'expects'.

The Process is expressed in

EITHER

(i) a simple **lexical verb** at **M** (around 70-95%, varying with different types of text);

OR

(ii) a **lexical verb** at **M** with one or occasionally two **Main Verb Extensions (MEx)** (i.e. a 'phrasal verb'), as in *He put the light out*, *He had a bath*, and (with TWO **MEx**s) *He came back in* and *He put the key back in*.

OR

(iii) a **lexical verb** at **M** with a **preposition (p)** in a prepositional group at **C** that expresses part of the Process (i.e. a 'prepositional verb'), as in *She's looking at him*;

OR

(iv) a **lexical verb** at **M** with BOTH **MEx** AND **p** (i.e. a 'phrasal-prepositional verb'), as in *He won't put up with it* and *He's very fond of her*.

So the main task is to find (i) **M**, which is OBLIGATORY (99.9% reliable), and (ii) any **MEx** and/or any **preposition** that helps to realize the Process.

Step 1.2: The Process and PR Test (99% reliable) *(essential)*

Assuming that **xxx** stands for the Main Verb, **(yy)** stands for one (or occasionally more) possible Main Verb Extensions, **(zz)** stands for a possible preposition and that each of **someone**, **something** and **somewhere** stands for each possible PR, try saying:

> **In this Process of xxx-ing (yy) (zz), we expect to find**
> **someone or something**
> **xxx-ing (yy) (zz)**
> **(someone or something)**
> **((*to* or *from*) someone or something or somewhere).**

(The last line says that the possible second or third PR is sometimes preceded by *to* or *from*.)

Problems to watch out for

1. Do not make the mistake of assuming that if an element is 'important in the message' it is a PR. A PR is an element that is EXPECTED by the Process, i.e. by **M** (+ **MEx** and/or **p**).
2. Look out for words that have the form of a typical **M** but which are in fact adjectives or nouns. Thus *worried* in *He's a very worried man* and *interesting* in *That's rather interesting* are both the **apex** of a **quality group**. And *opening* in *He looked through the opening* is a noun at the **head** of a **nominal group**. Test for an adjective by placing *very* before the word and for a noun by placing *the* before it (both over 99% reliable).
3. Some verb forms may co-occur with TWO OR MORE patterns of PRs, e.g. (i) *open* in *he opened the door* (2 PRs) and *the door opened* (1 PR); and (ii) *make* in *he has made a sand castle* (2 PRs) and *Racial prejudice makes him angry* (3 PRs).
4. Remember that PRs may be **covert**.
5. The word *somewhere* is used in the test for a PR. But occasionally *some time* is also needed, e.g. in testing *The age of the hippies was in the 1960s*. But note that *somewhere* and *some time* can also replace Adjuncts (expressing 'Place' and 'Time Position'), so you should apply the ***C or A Test*** (Step 9.6) in such cases.
6. Usually a Subject is a PR. But you should be prepared to find occasionally a Subject that is NOT a PR. When the word *it* occurs at **S**, it may be EITHER an 'empty Subject' that is expounded by *it*, OR it may be a normal referring expression. To test which it is, try re-expressing the clause, replacing *it* by *what.* Does it still make sense? If so, it is a PR. Example: *It* in *It's here* can be re-expressed as *What's here?*, but *It* in *It's raining* cannot be re-expressed as *What's raining?*
7. Occasionally there may be two or even three **MEx**s (if one is *back*), as in *He made <u>his way</u> <u>back</u> <u>out</u> into the garden.*
8. Remember that a **MEx** may be filled by a nominal or other group, as with the underlined portions of *He made <u>his way</u> into the garden, He is taking <u>a shower</u>, She fell <u>fast asleep</u>*), and *He has fallen <u>in love</u> with Italy.* The **MEx**

may occasionally be filled by a clause in order to use its **M**, as in *She's gone shopping for a new pair of shoes.*

9 In *It's sunny*, the word *sunny* is treated as a **MEx**, so the Process is one of 'being sunny'.

Worked example

The ***Process and PR Test*** in Step 1.2 involves saying the part of the wording that is applicable to the clause being tested.

So, for *She has really been told the truth all this time*, we should try saying:

In this Process of 'telling', we expect to find
someone ....
telling ....
someone ....
something.

This makes sense, so *told* is the **M**.

If you think the clause contains a possible Main Verb Extension, go to Step 1.3.
*If you have any doubts about whether you have correctly identified the **M** and want to run a check, go to Step 1.4.*
Otherwise go directly to Step 1.5 on 'Starting the diagram'.

Worked example

There is no 'possible Main Verb Extension' in *She has really been told the truth all this time*, so we shall go to Step 1.5 on 'Starting the diagram'.

Step 1.3: The Word Form Test for a Main Verb Extension (MEx)

The purpose of this step is to CHECK *the decision about the Process that you made in Step 1.2.*

However, if you are sure there is no MEx you can omit it.

The following test works for 95% of **MEx**s, i.e. for the words listed below. It can also be used to identify cases where there is a unit that 'expands' these words, as in *far away* and *right out*.

Ask: Is the possible **MEx** in the following list of frequent **MEx**s?

> **Very frequent:**
> *up, down; in, out; on, off; about, (a)round, along, away; over, through* and *back* (NB *back* can co-occur with others, as also can *on* with 'directional' Processes.)
> **Fairly frequent:**
> *across, apart, aside, ahead; in front, behind, by, together, under*

If **Yes**, there is a probability of over 95% that it is a **MEx**.

This rises to 99.9% if the word is *out*, *away* or *back* (from the 'very frequent' list) or *apart, aside, ahead, forward, in front* or *together* (from the 'fairly frequent' list), because THESE WORDS CANNOT BE PREPOSITIONS.

Warning Some items in the above lists also function as a **preposition** - and so as part of another element in the clause. These are:

in, on, off, over, about, round, and *through,*
across, behind, under and above all *by.*

If **No**, the 'possible **MEx**' may still be a **MEx**, because:

(a) other words also occasionally occur as a **MEx**, e.g. *stay put, come to, fall asleep, come / go home, be / do / get better / well*;
(b) a **MEx** may be filled by a **nominal**, **quality** or **prepositional group**, e.g. *a hug* in *She gave me a hug* and *very fond* in *I'm very fond of Ivy.*

If in doubt, go to Step 1.4.

Example of applying Steps 1.2 and 1.3 to a complex case

Consider the Process in *Ivy fell in love with Ike.*

(i) The result of applying the ***Process and PR Test*** in Step 1.2 is that it makes sense to say

In this process of 'falling in love', we expect to find
someone ....
falling in love with ....
someone.

This suggests that the Process is Type (iv) of the examples in Step 1.1, so the structure will probably be **M + MEx + p**.

(ii) Guideline (b) above alerts us to the possibility that the **prepositional group** *in love* may be a **MEx**.

(iii) The fact that *with* is not listed the ***Word Form Test*** strongly suggests that it is NOT a **MEx** - so that it is almost certainly a **preposition**.

Now ask: **Does the evidence of Steps 1.2 and 1.3 coincide?**

If **Yes**, the structure is 99.99% likely to be **M + MEx + p** (inside **C**). So **xxx** from the ***Process and PR Test*** corresponds to **M**; **yy** from the test corresponds to **MEx**; and **zz** to **p**.

If **No**, go to Step 1.4.

Step 1.4: A supplementary check (optional)

If you have any doubts about your analysis so far, use this process as a further check. It is like the ***Process and PR Test*** *in Step 1.2, but it works from a set of examples.*

Consider the following examples, and find the one most like the clause you are analyzing. Then try re-expressing it on the model of the wording beneath each. If the result of the test makes sense, the words corresponding to **xxx**, **yy** and **zz** in the ***Process and PR Test*** in Step 1.1 above are **M**, **MEx** and **p** respectively.

Examples with **M** only:
Ivy sneezed -
'This is about someone sneezing.' (1 PR)
She is a doctor / happy -
'This is about someone being something.' (2 PRs)
She gave Fred the book -
'This is about someone giving someone something.' (3 PRs)
He took the snake out of the box -
'This is about someone taking something from somewhere.'
(3 PRs)

Examples with **M + MEx**:
The bomb has gone off -
'This is about something going off.' (1 PR)

He had a bath -
'This is about someone having a bath.' (1 PR)
She gave him a big hug -
'This is about someone giving a big hug to someone.' (2 PRs)
I've worked the answer out -
'This is about someone working out something.' (2 PRs)

Examples with **M + p**:
She's listening to jazz -
'This is about someone listening to something.' (2 PRs)
I am relying on you -
'This is about someone relying on someone.' (2 PRs)

Examples with **M + MEx + p**:
She is still going out with him -
'This is about someone going out with someone.' (2 PRs)
She fell in love with him -
'This is about someone falling in love with someone.' (2 PRs)
She's very fond of jazz -
This is about someone being very fond of something.' (2 PRs)

However, in a few cases you may still be unsure whether an element is a **Complement** or an **Adjunct**. If so, use the **C or A Test** in Step 9.6 below.

But note that you will need to confirm which of the two PRs is **S** and which is **C** in later tests - and occasionally that NONE of the PRs is **S**.

Step 1.5: Drawing the diagram

Worked example

You can now start drawing your diagram by lightly pencilling in the following:

1 **M** above *told* (and if you're confident the triangle meaning 'is expounded by'),
2 **Cl** above the **M**,
3 a line to link **Cl** with **M**,
4 **S?** and **C?** above the elements that you think are the PRs in the Process (and which you will confirm in later tests).

The analysis at this early stage is:

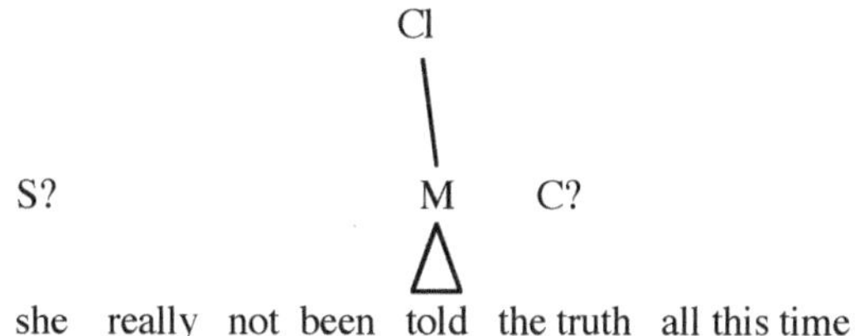

Important note *When the Process is a 'multi-word verb' (i.e. as identified in Steps 1.2 to 1.4 just above), your first action should be to underline the words that express the Process.*

Step 2: Look to the left of M for any Auxiliary Verbs (X).

We have introduced two main types of **X**: (i) those that stand on their own (in Chapter 8) and those that occur with a following **XEx** and **I** in the pattern **X XEx I** (in Chapter 14). But both types of **X** are ALMOST ALWAYS expounded by:

(i) forms of *be*: *am, is, are, was, were, being, been* OR
(ii) forms of *have*: *have, has, had*, or *having*

The recommended strategy is FIRST to look for any **X**s and THEN, in Step 3 below, to look for any associated **XEx** and **I**.

In principle, several **X**s may occur in the same clause, but in practice there are rarely more than two.

The most frequent two **X**s are those that express meanings related to the TIME of the 'situation' (90% reliable), but we also regularly find (i) the 'passive' **X** and (ii) the **X + XEx + I** type.

There is a small number of words that are analyzed as Auxiliaries on semantic grounds but WHICH CANNOT BE CONFLATED WITH **O** (unlike most **X**s). These are:

(i) *used + to*, as in *She used to live in London*;
(ii) *seem, appear, tend, happen, need* and *prove + to*;
(iii) *have + to* (but not *have got to*, where *have* can be **O**);
(iv) *turn* [X] *out* [XEx] *to* [I]; and
(v) the *get* form of the 'passive', as in *It got eaten by the dog.*

Worked example

In *She has really been told the truth all this time*, the two words *has* and *been* occur to the left of **M**, so the analysis is:

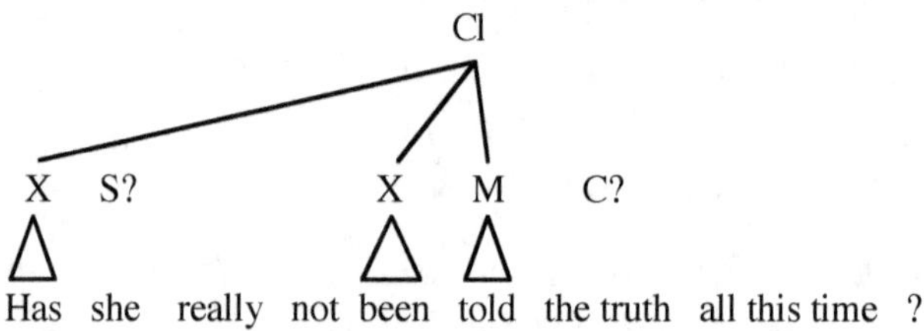

Problem to watch out for An **X** may be separated from a following **X** or **M** by one or more other elements, as is the first **X** in our worked example.

Step 3: Look to the right of any X (if expounded by a form of *be* or *have)* **for (i)** any associated **Auxiliary Extension (XEx)** and **(ii)** any associated **Infinitive Element (I).**

XEx will be the second word in one of the following six types of 'trio' (or in one case a 'pair') of words (95% reliable).

(i) '**validity**': *be bound / certain / likely / set / sure / supposed* (pronounced *spost*, to rhyme with *post*) *to*; *have got to*;

(ii) '**report of validity**': *be said / alleged*, etc; *be thought / believed* etc, *felt*; *be observed / seen to ... / ... -ing*;

(iii) '**expectation**': *be going / about to, be on the point of ... ing*;

(iv) '**control**':

'obligation': *be due / duty bound / expected / intended / meant / obliged / scheduled / supposed to*; *have got to*; *had better / best*;

'determination': *be determined / resolved to*;

'causation': *be compelled / forced / got / made / obliged / required* etc *to*;

'prevention': *be deterred / precluded / prevented / stopped* + **I** = *from* + **M**-*ing*;

'permission': *be allowed / permitted to;*

'empowerment': *be authorized / empowered / enabled to*;

(v) '**directive**': *be advised / asked / told*, etc *to*;

(vi) '**disposition**': *be inclined / loath / pleased / prepared / reluctant / unwilling / willing* etc *to*;

'volition': *be anxious / delighted / disposed / glad / happy to*;
'general ability': *be able / unable to; be capable / incapable* + **I** = *of* + **M**-*ing*;
'suitability' *be fit / suitable / suited / unfit / unsuited / unsuitable* etc *to / for* **M**-*ing*;
'mental ability': *be brilliant / clever / dumb / smart / stupid* etc + **I** = *at* + **M**-*ing*;
'skilfulness': *be bad / clumsy / crap / good / great / lousy / skilled / skilful / terrible / terrific / wonderful* etc + **I** = *at* + **M**-*ing*;
'liability': *be apt / given / inclined / liable / predisposed / prone* etc *to*;
'inherent nature': *be compelled / constrained / destined / doomed / fated* etc *to*.

I is always *to* - UNLESS SHOWN ABOVE AS ONE OF *from*, *of* OR *at*.

Worked example
In *She has really been told the truth all this time*, none of the above words appears immediately after **X**.

Step 4: **Look for any other Infinitive Element** (**I**), if any.
It is almost always the word *to*, and it is frequently predicted by a 'modal verb' at **O**, i.e.

EITHER: (i) *ought*
OR (ii) *am, is, are, was,* or *were*.

Problem to watch out for
Sometimes a **N** or **A** will intervene between the 'predicting element' and the **I**.

Worked example
In *She has really been told the truth all this time*, there is no *to* and so no **I**.

Step 5: Look IN THE ORIGINAL CLAUSE to discover if there is a Negator (N) (probability: under 5%).[125]

---

125 The reason why this step must be applied to the original clause rather than the 'test' version is that, in the 'Preparation', we stripped away any 'negative' elements to enable the other tests to work more smoothly.

If there is a **N**, it is likely to be **to the left of any I**.
N is always the word *not*. NB *never* is a 'Usuality' Adjunct.

Reminder: *n't* is always part of **O**, because it would precede **S** in a 'confirmation seeker'.

Worked example
In *Has she really not been told the truth all this time?* the word *not* occurs and functions in the clause as **N**. So the analysis is:

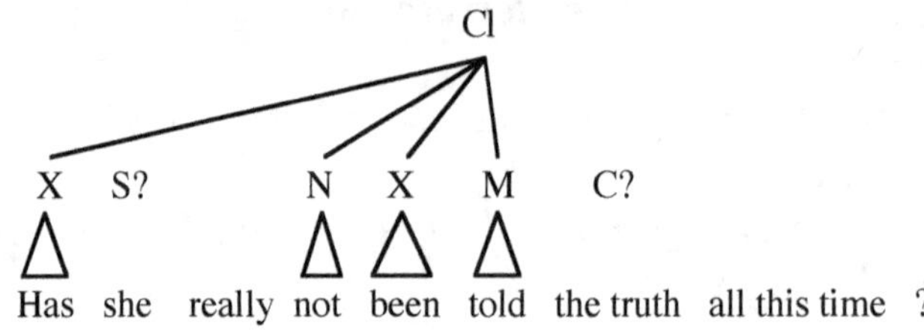

Step 6: Find the Operator. It is:

EITHER (i) a modal verb, i.e., *can, could, will, would, shall, should, may, might, must* as **O**
OR *ought, am, is, are, was, were* (+ *to*) as **O (+ I)**
OR (ii) *do, does* or *did* as **O**
OR (iii) *am, is, are, was* or *were*, expressing a Process of 'being', as **O/M**
OR (iv) *am, is, are, was, were, have, has* or *had*, expressing an 'Auxiliary' meaning, as **O/X**

Note: most words at **O** may have *n't* added to them (but not *am*).

Examples
of (i) In *Ivy may arrive soon,* the word *may* is **O**.
In *She is to be told the truth,* the word *is* is **O** and *to* is **I**.
of (ii) In *What did they tell her?* the word *did* is **O**.
of (iii) In *She was here*, the word *was* is a Process of 'being', so is **M** as well as **O** - and so **O/M**.
of (iv) In *She is reading your* letter, the word *is* is **X** as well as **O** - and so **O/X**.
In *She has read your letter*, the word *has* is **X** as well as **O** - and so **O/X**.

Problems to watch out for

1 Forms of the verb *be* occur as several different elements:
   (i) very frequently as **O/M** and frequently as **M**,
   (ii) very frequently as **O/X** and frequently as **X**,
   (iii) occasionally as **O** (as in *He is to leave now*).
2 Forms of the verb *have* occur as several different elements:
   (i) very frequently as **M** (but not **O/M**), and
   (ii) very frequently as **O/X**, and frequently as **X**,
3 Forms of the verb *do* occur as two different elements
   (i) very frequently as **O** (e.g. as *Did* in *Did he do it?*)
   (ii) occasionally as **M** (e.g. as *do* in *Did he do it?*)

Worked example

The word *has*, taken on its own, could be EITHER **M** (as in 2(i) above) OR **O/X** (as in 2(ii) above).
But we have already identified *told* as **M**, so *Has* must be **O/X**.
So the analysis is:

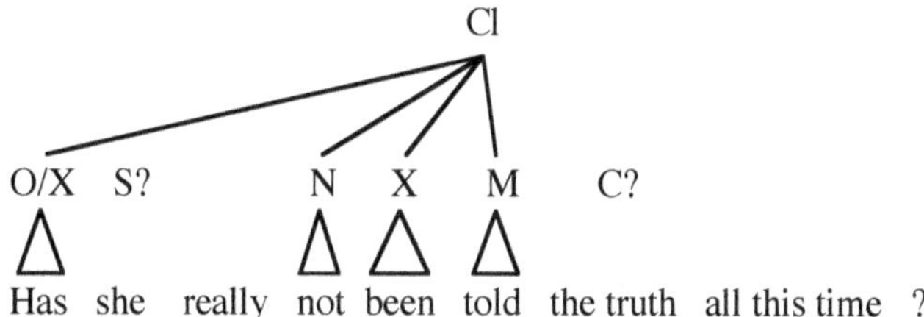

Step 7: Find the Subject (S). To do this:

Re-express the **information giver** as a **polarity seeker**, i.e. as seeking the answer *Yes* or *No.* If the clause has no Operator, supply *do, does* or *did,* as appropriate, as **O**.

Worked example

Re-express *She has really been told the truth all this time*
as *Has she really been told the truth all this time?*

Now you are in a position to identify the **Subject (S)**.

The Subject is the word (or words) which, by occurring before or after the Operator, tells you whether the clause is an 'information giver' or a 'polarity seeker'.

Worked example

Work it out like this: (i) we know that *has* is the Operator; (ii) so *she* must be the Subject, because, by occurring after *has*, it shows that the MOOD of the clause is 'polarity seeker'.

So, in the original text of *Has she really not been told the truth all this time?*, *has* is **O** and *she* is **S**. So the analysis is:

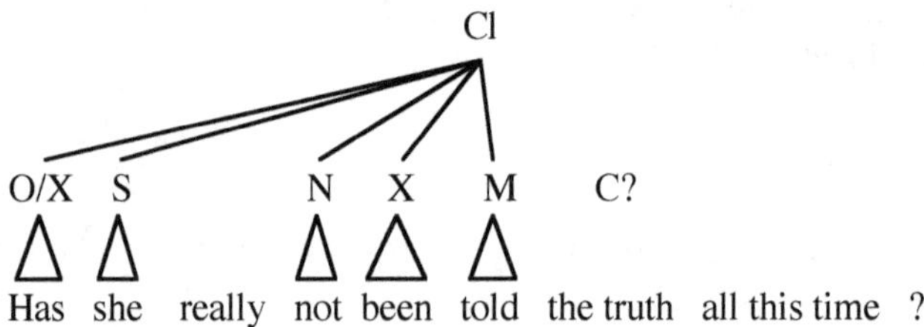

Problems to watch out for

1 In most **information seekers** the order is **O S**. But with **new content seekers in which the S is 'sought'** we find **S O** or **S O/M** or **S O/X** or **S M**.
2 In **passive** clauses the **S is a PR that would typically be a C**.
3 'Environmental' Processes, such as *It*'s *raining* and *It*'s *sunny*, have **no PRs**. The **S** is NOT a PR, but an 'empty Subject'. And *sunny* is a **MEx** - because there is no 'thing' that is 'sunny'.

Step 8: Look to the left of S to find the Let Element (L) - if there is one. It is always the word *let*, as in *Let* [L]*'s all* [S] *go* [M] *home* [MEx]*!*

Worked example

There is no **L**.

Step 9: Find the full configuration of Participant Roles (PRs), i.e. those elements that are EXPECTED by the Process at **M** (or at **M** and **MEx**, or at **M MEx** and **p**) - INCLUDING ANY PRS THAT ARE COVERT.

Step 9.1: Since **S is typically a PR**, you have probably already confirmed one of the guesses you made in Step 1.2 (99% reliable). But remember that **S** may be (i) **covert**, as in *Read this*, or (ii) an 'empty' Subject, as in *It*'s *raining.*

Step 9.2**: **Any **other PR is a Complement (C).**[126]

Step 9.3: Some reminders that may help at this point (optional)

(i) Most Processes have TWO associated PRs (around 80%). But some expect ONE PR and some expect THREE - and 'environmental' Processes expect NONE. So look for 0, 1 or 2 **C**s.
(ii) If a PR is (or contains) a ***wh*-item** (*who, what, which, when, where, how,* etc) it usually precedes **O** or **M**, so it is often AWAY FROM ITS TYPICAL POSITION. (However, in preparing the original clause for the tests you should have already replaced it by *something, someone, somewhere*, etc, so this shouldn't be a problem.)
(iii) Occasionally a **C** that doesn't contain a *wh*-item may occur before **S** as a **marked PR theme**, as in *That I find hard to accept* and *Boring it was not*.
(iv) A PR that is **C** may be a **covert PR.** As well as the **covert S** in directives such as *Sit down,* about 80% of 'passive' clauses have a **covert C**, e.g. *He has been caught (by X)*. Occasionally a **C** is covert in a non-passive clause, e.g. *Do not touch (X)!*

Step 9.4: **If you have any doubts about whether the clause contains a covert PR, re-run the *Process and PR Test* (in Step 1.2).**

Worked example
We SHOULD have doubts! Let's run ***Process and PR Test*** again. Try saying the relevant parts of the **Process and PR Test**.

So, for *She has really been told the truth all this time*, we say:

In this Process of 'telling', we expect to find
someone ....
telling ....
someone ....
something.

---

126 However, a PR may be functioning as a **completive (cv)** in a prepositional group (e.g. *Ivy* in *You were seen by Ivy*). And in a **nominalization** such as *your being seen by Ivy* PRs are conflated with the elements of a nominal group. But since this book is limited to the clause I shall say nothing further about these here. For nominalizations, see Chapter 17 of my *Functional Syntax Handbook.*

So there should be THREE PRs! But we applied this test in Step 1.2 - so why do the tree diagrams that I have drawn so far show ONLY TWO PRs (indicated by **'S?'** and **'C?'**) How did we miss the third PR? (But perhaps you didn't?)

There are two reasons why we may have made this mistake.

(i) In Step 1.2 we were focussing primarily on the problem of finding **M** (which we successfully did).
(ii) The third PR is a **covert PR**, i.e. it is the Agent in the 'passive' construction of 'someone being told something (by someone)'. And because there were no words on the page that refer to the third PR, it was easy to overlook it.

I have included this example of a temporarily mistaken analysis in order to illustrate how easy it is to miss a covert PR - and so to demonstrate, in a practical way, why ***we should run the Process and PRs Test again at this second stage*** *in the process of analysis.*

I now give ***two further tests****. The test in Step 9.5 is a further check for a covert PR, and the test in Step 9.6 is for cases where you are unsure whether an element is a PR - and so a Complement - or a CR - and so an Adjunct.*

Step 9.5: A supplementary check for a covert PR

If you need a supplementary check for a possible covert PR -
Go back to Step 1.4 (which you may have omitted because it was marked as 'optional').

Worked example
The example given in Step 1.4 that is most like our test clause - i.e. *She has really been told the truth all this time* - is

She gave Fred the book.

Both examples are three-role Processes.

As we add '**(C)**' to the diagram, our thought processes should be:

(i) the Process of 'telling' expects a 'teller', a 'person who is told', and 'what is told'.
(ii) Since *she* is the 'person who is told', *she* is a PR as well as **S**, and since *the truth* is the 'something' that 'is told', *the truth* is a PR, and so a **C**.

(iii) But the 'teller' is not expressed, so there must be a **covert PR** and so **a covert Complement**, shown as **(C)**. It should be placed where it would have been, if it had been present.

So the analysis now is:

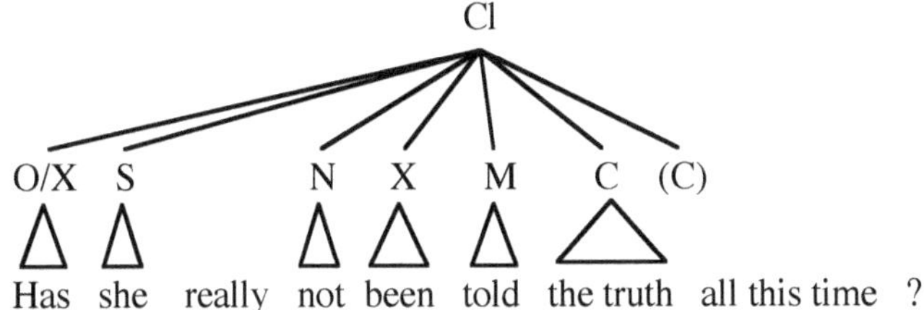

Step 9.6: The C or A Test

If you have doubts about whether a word (or string of words) is a **Complement** or an **Adjunct**, try the following test:

1 **Thematize the element to be tested** (i.e. put it first in the test clause).
2 **Treat it a separate 'information unit'** (i.e. separate it by a comma).
3 **Read it aloud.**
4 **Evaluate its naturalness**. If it sounds natural with the test element first, it is almost certainly an **Adjunct**. But if it sounds unusual it is almost certainly a **Complement**.

Two contrasting examples
In *You'll find the usual high street shops in the city centre*,
the words *in the city centre* are an **A** - because
In the city centre, you'll find the usual high street shops
sounds natural.
(Also, the ***Process and PR Test*** shows that the PRs are *you* and *the usual shops*, so *in the city centre* is not a **C**.)

But in *Ike lives in the city centre*,
the words *in the city centre* are a **C** - because
In the city centre, Ike lives sounds very odd.
(Also, the ***Process and PR Test*** shows that the PRs are *Ike* and *in the city centre*, so *in the city centre* is a **C**.)

Step 10: Find any Adjuncts (A).
These are clause elements that are NOT expected by the Process - unlike the PRs.[127] An **A** frequently expresses an **experiential** meaning and so is a **Circumstantial Role** (CR). Others, such as *possibly*, *however*, *unfortunately*, *please*, *firstly* and *even*, express other strands of meaning. See Section 12.2 of Chapter 12 for an indication of the full range of different types. But here we simply label them all as **A**.

Step 10.1: A reminder of some facts about the syntax of Adjuncts

(i) There may be no **A**s, one **A**, two **A**s, or many **A**s.
(ii) Most types of **A** typically come after any **C**. But most can also be thematized very naturally (i.e. placed at or near the start of the clause, as in *yesterday* / *perhaps I went there*).
(iii) Some types frequently come between **O** (if there is one) and any **X** (and occasionally between **X**s), e.g. *I have often / unfortunately lost my pen* (**S O/X A M C**).
(iv) Occasionally, e.g. when the **C** is a Location or Direction, an **A** comes between **M** and **C**, as in *Ivy remained quietly in her room*, and *She walked purposefully into the room.*

Step 10.2: A reminder that we have already met two tests that identify Adjuncts

(i) In Step 1.2, the ***Process and PR Test*** should already have identified the **Complements**, so simultaneously identifying the potential **Adjuncts**.
(ii) In Step 9.6 the specialized ***C or A Test*** shows whether an element is a **C** or an **A**.

---

127 Adjuncts are sometimes described as being 'optional'. But they are NOT optional from the viewpoint of the Performer' purpose in performing the act (e.g. *at one o'clock* in *He'll see you at one o'clock*). It is important not to confuse the concepts of (i) 'being predicted by the Process' and (ii) 'being important in the message'. Adjuncts are only 'optional' in the first sense. It is therefore better to replace the concept of 'optionality' by that of 'prediction from the Process'.

The two tests given below are GENERAL PURPOSE TESTS that can be used on any word or string of words that you think might be functioning as an Adjunct.

Step 10.3: Two General Purpose Adjunct Tests

One frequent problem in identifying Adjuncts is deciding whether a string of words is one Adjunct or two, e.g. *in a cafe overlooking the river* in *Ivy met Ike in a cafe overlooking the river*. This 'general purpose' test covers all types of Adjunct, including examples with two or more Adjuncts.

Using the test version of the clause, test each possible Adjunct, ONE AT A TIME, with the following two tests:

1 The 'function' test for an Adjunct
Ask: **What is its function?**
If it is an Adjunct, the answer will be in terms of an aspect of the clause as a whole, e.g. one of those listed in Section 12.1 of Chapter 12. See the example below. This test works well when you are familiar with the whole grammar, but less well for beginners. Luckily, there is also this second general test:

2 The Adjunct place-change Test
(i) Re-express the clause in such a way that THE POSSIBLE **A** IS MOVED TO ANOTHER POSSIBLE PLACE FOR AN ADJUNCT, SUCH THAT IT IS SEPARATED FROM ANY OTHER POSSIBLE **A**. With an unthematized Adjunct you can usually do this by **thematizing** it. Since virtually all **A**s can occur in two or three different places in the clause, you can also use a place in the middle or at the end. (99% reliable)
(ii) Ask: Has this change altered the **experiential** meaning of the clause? In other words, if the original meaning was 'true', would the meaning of the re-arranged clause necessarily also be 'true'?

If **No**, the 'possible Adjunct' is confirmed as an Adjunct. If **Yes**, the words moved are almost certainly PART OF A SINGLE ADJUNCT that is located in the original position.

Example

The problem: in *Ivy met Ike in a café overlooking the river*, is there one Adjunct or two?

1 ***The 'function' test for an Adjunct***
What is the function of *overlooking the river?*
Answer: It tells us where the café is.
Conclusion: 'where the café is' is an aspect of the café - and not 'an aspect of the clause as a whole' - so *overlooking the river* is not an Adjunct.

So we should now ask:
What is the function of *in a café overlooking the river*?
Answer: It tells us the 'Place' (a type of **A**) where Ivy met Ike.
Conclusion: This is 'an aspect of the clause as a whole', so *in a café overlooking the river* is an Adjunct.

2 ***The Adjunct place-change Test***
Re-expression 1: *Ivy met Ike in a café overlooking the river* becomes *Overlooking the river, Ivy met Ike in a café.*

Evaluation: the only meaning that we can extract from this is that Ivy was 'overlooking the river' when she met Ike in a café. But people don't 'overlook things' (in this sense of 'overlook'!) and, even if it did make sense, the experiential meaning would have been changed. So *overlooking the river* is not an Adjunct.

Re-expression 2: *In a café, Ike met Ivy overlooking the river.*

Evaluation: Similar to Re-expression 1.

Re-expression 3: *In a café overlooking the river, Ivy met Ike.*

Evaluation: This has the same experiential meaning as the original clause, so *in a café overlooking the river* is an Adjunct.

Conclusion: *overlooking the river* is a part of a 'Place' Adjunct, i.e. *in a café overlooking the river.*

Worked example

0 ***The Process and PR Test*** in Step 1.2 has already shown that, in *She has really been told the truth all this time*, neither *really* nor *all this time* are expected by the Process of 'telling', so they are almost certainly both Adjuncts.

1 The 'function' test for an Adjunct
Ask: **What is the function of *really*?**
Note: to interpret correctly the meaning of items with 'inferential' meaning such as *really*, we need to work with the original text-sentence, i.e. *Has she really not been told the truth all this time?*

Answer: *really* expresses the view that the proposition that 'she has not been told the truth all this time' is strongly against the Performer's expectations. Since this is 'an aspect of the clause as a whole', *really* is an Adjunct.

Ask: **What is the function of *all this time*?**

Answer: it expresses the 'Duration' of the period for which 'she has not been told'. Since an event's 'duration' is 'an aspect of the clause as a whole', *all this time* is an Adjunct.

2 The Adjunct place-change Test
Re-expression 1:
She has really not been told the truth all this time
becomes *Really she has not been told the truth all this time.*

Evaluation: this does not change the experiential meaning, so *really* is an Adjunct (an 'Inferential' Adjunct).

Re-expression 2:
She has really not been told the truth all this time
becomes *All this time she has really not been told the truth.*

Evaluation: this does not change the experiential meaning, so *all this time* is an Adjunct (a 'Duration' Adjunct).

There is ample evidence, then, that *really* and *all this time* are both Adjuncts, so the analysis is:

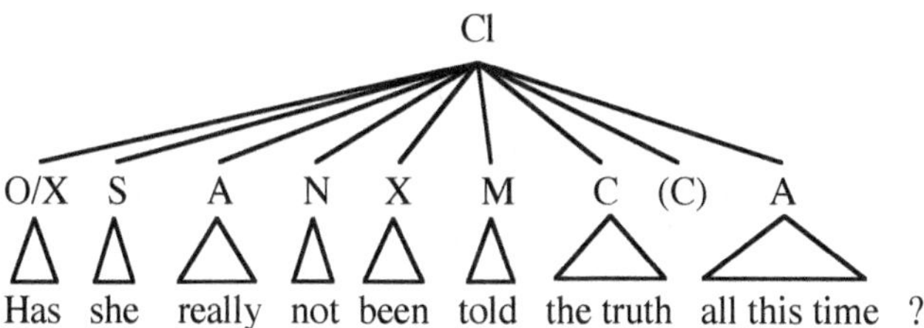

Step 11: Find the Vocative (V) - if there is one.

It is typically a **proper name**, but it may be *my friend* etc.
It is usually given a separate information unit, i.e. in a written text it is separated from the rest of the clause by commas.
It is often the first or last element of the clause, though it may also come in mid-clause.

Test for a **V** by moving it to another position.

Worked example There is no **V**.

Step 12: Find the Ender (E). This is any **punctuation** that indicates the end of a clause. In this book Enders are limited to those that occur with a simple clause, i.e. (i) a full stop (or 'period' in US English) (.); (ii) a question mark (?); and (iii) an exclamation mark (!).[128]

Worked example The analysis is:

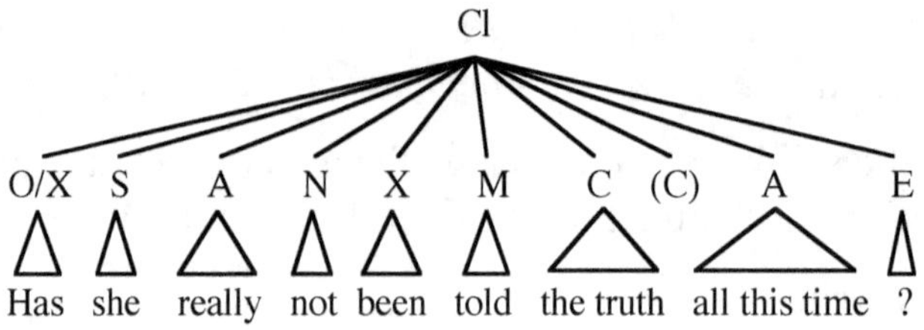

And that completes the analysis.

15.5 Summary

In a clause we may find:

---

128 There are similar elements for analyzing intonation, which is as important a part of a spoken text as its syntax and lexis, but we shall not analyze intonation here. In my view, Tench 1996 provides the best introduction to how to analyze the intonation of spoken texts. (Fawcett 1990 and 2004a show how such a description can be converted into the relevant component of a fully generative SFG.) However, if the text that you are analyzing is a spoken text, there is an alternative solution - though an inferior one - to the problem of how to analyze its intonation. This is to first express the intonation in terms of the punctuation that a novelist might use in reporting direct speech, and then to analyze that.

(i) ONE of each of **V**, **L**, **S**, **O**, **N**, **M** and **E** (with the possibility of **O/M** for forms of *be* and **O/X** for forms of *be* or *have*),
(ii) POTENTIALLY SEVERAL **Xs, XExs** and **Is** (the first **X** typically being conflated with **O** as **O/X**),
(iii) ONE OR OCCASIONALLY TWO or even three **MExs**,
(iv) UP TO TWO **Cs** (either or both of which can be **covert)**,
(v) POTENTIALLY MANY **As**, expressing many types of meaning, in many different positions,
(vi) for most 'information givers' **S O** or **S M** - AND
for most 'information seekers' **O S** (where **O** includes **O/X** and **O/M**),
(vii) if the clause is a new content seeker
in which either **C** or **A** is sought, **C** or **A** before **O**,
(vii) **S** in a simple directive is typically **covert**.

Because the vast majority of the *Guidelines* set out in this chapter also apply to clauses that are embedded in other clauses and in other units, you will find that these *Guidelines* will enable you to analyze over 95 per cent of most clauses in most texts. For the final 5 per cent of clauses and for the various classes of group - all of which may contain embedded clauses - you would need to consult the fuller description in Appendix 1, or *The Functional Syntax Handbook.*

Meanwhile, you may wish to complete the first stage of learning to analyze text-sentences in Cardiff Grammar terms by analyzing the representative set of examples given in the next chapter.

Chapter 16
A final analysis task

16.1 The task

For the last - and most important! - time: you should cover the solutions on the opposite page.

Here is a set of sixteen clauses for you to analyze. They will give you practice in most of the main points covered in this book.

(1) Plastic would break immediately.
(2) Adam broke it accidentally.
(3) Paula is happy now.
(4) She might give Adam ice-cream tomorrow.
(5) Could it make him ill?
(6) Fred was here too.
(7) Ike made cakes yesterday.
(8) Ivy put candles on them.
(9) Adam coughed loudly.
(10) Paula may ask you questions.
(11) Does Paula give ice-cream to Adam often?
(12) Is Adam well?
(13) He had 'flu last week.
(14) Did he sneeze much?
(15) Shut up!
(16) No!

Before you start, you may wish to remind yourself of the **three tips for drawing syntax diagrams** at the start of the last chapter.

This is your chance to test the validity of the *Full Guidelines* set out in that chapter. I suggest that you follow them fairly strictly, especially for the first half dozen analyses - even though you may feel confident about your decision in any particular case. And, if necessary, look back to the relevant chapter.

16.2 Solutions

The analyses are arranged in groups, depending on their structure.

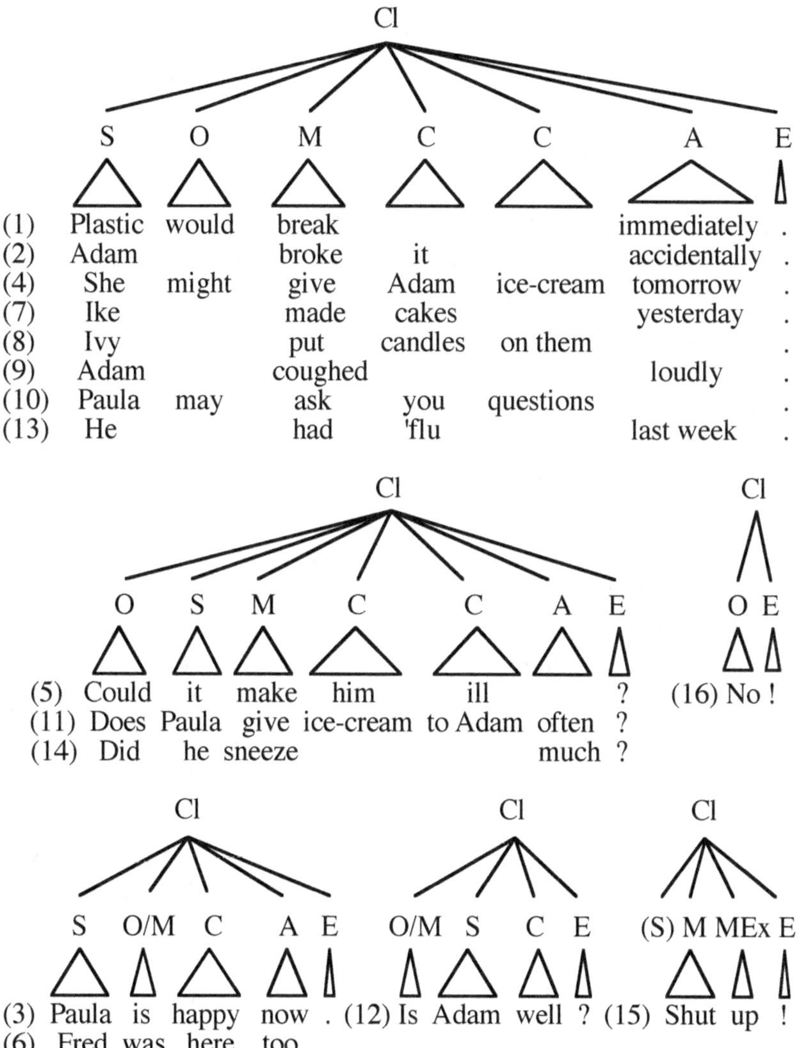

Figure 16-1: The analyses of sixteen clauses

16.3 Comments on experiential meaning in the analyses

Clauses (1) and (2) illustrate Note 1 on Figure 10-1 in Chapter 10. In other words, the Process of 'breaking' is like 'opening' and 'melting', in that it can occur with one PR or with two.

This is just one of the THREE ambiguous Main Verbs included in the exercise. The second is the two senses of *make* - one with two PRs in (7), and one with three PRs in (5). But can you spot the other?

It is the three Processes of 'being'. You may not at first think of these as ambiguous, but they are - in the sense that two of the examples are 'attributive' Processes and one is 'locational'. The two 'attributive' Processes have as their Complement the PR of 'Attribute', and in these two cases both are 'qualities' (realized by *happy* in (3) and by *well* in (12)). Note that an 'Attribute' can equally well be a 'thing', e.g. (3) could have been *Paula is a happy woman, or Paula is a teacher.* The other sense of 'being' is the 'locational' sense in (6), where the Complement is the PR of 'Location' (realized by *here*).

We have already noted one example with three PRs: the Process of 'making' in (5). Are there any others? There are - and it is easy to identify which they are in Figure 16-1, because they are the examples with two Complements. So there are in fact five three-role Processes altogether. Two of them - (4) and (11) - are the Process of 'giving'. I have included both to remind you of the variation on the usual pattern of the internal structure of the Complement in (11). In a functional grammar the role of 'Adam' in the Process of 'giving' is the same in (11) as it is in (4), and 'Adam' is a PR in both cases. The fact that 'Adam' in preceded by *to* in (11) - so that the second C in (11) is filled by a prepositional group - does NOT turn it into an Adjunct. The criterion for deciding is FUNCTION rather than FORM. But 'function' must be determined through carefully applied tests, as in Step 1 of the *Guidelines* in Chapter 15 - and so NOT decided via some vague sense of what the 'general meaning' is.

In further support of the above analysis, note that *to* carries no meaning in its own right; this is the form that a Complement in a Process of 'giving' takes, once the decision is made to put the PR of 'Adam' at this position in the clause.

In (11), *to Adam* is in the 'potentially new' position, where it would, if there was no following Adjunct, receive the unmarked Tonic and so be marked as 'New Information'. But there is one (*often*), so here the **C**'s 'potential' for being 'New' is not realized.

The two other three-role Processes illustrate two other very frequent types. Example (8) illustrates the Process of 'causing something to be somewhere', i.e. 'putting', and (10) illustrates the type of 'communicative' Process in which 'someone causes someone else to know something'. In this grammar, the PR that is the 'message' (called the 'Phenomenon') occurs in all 'communicative' Processes. And this is so, whether the 'message' is (i) referred to by a nominal group such as *questions*, as in (10); (ii) reported in terms of the intended meaning, as in *Paula may ask you what your name is*; or even (iii) reported in the words that were - or might have been - used by the Performer, as in *Paula may ask you 'What is your name?'*. All three would have exactly the same structure as (10) in terms of both (i) the Participant Roles that are involved and (ii) the number of Complements. If you want to see the way the internal structure of the second Complement would be represented in the Cardiff Grammar, look at the outline analysis for a 'text' in Appendix 1. And if you feel that you need to revise the structures of TRANSITIVITY, you could re-read Chapter 10, looking particularly closely at the summarizing diagram in Figure 10-1.

While the examples for analysis in this Chapter cover a wide variety of types of TRANSITIVITY structure, I have spared you the problem of identifying a covert Complement, i.e. an inherently two-role Process of which only one PR occurs overtly in the text. (For a quick reminder of this, see Section 13.5 of Chapter 13.) But there is one covert PR for you to identify - the covert Subject in Example (15).

16.4 Comments on other strands of meaning in the analyses

Example (15) takes us into variations in MOOD structure. We have met a wide variety of MOOD structures in this book - including the 'confirmation seeker' that provided our **Worked example** throughout the *Guidelines* in Chapter 15. However, the analysis task in this chapter has only asked you to identify the structures of three types. Can you say which these are? Again, the layout of the examples in Figure 16-1 suggests the answer. There are four 'polarity seekers' in (5), (11), (12) and (14); one 'simple directive' in (15); and the rest are 'information givers'. If you want a reminder of the full set of possible MOOD structures, look again at Chapter 11.

But what is the MOOD of (16)? The reason for analyzing *Yes* and *No* as words that function as the Operator in a clause is given in Section 9.4 of Chapter 9 - and, as is explained there, the meaning of *No* is:

'If I said this clause in full it would be **negative**.'

So the MOOD of (16) is that it is an 'information giver'. But it is the special kind of 'information giver' that occurs in a **Respond** move in the discourse structure of an **exchange**. (Here I am allowing myself to introduce concepts which are, I hope, relatively self-explanatory in this context, but which anticipate aspects of the overall model of language which will be introduced properly in *The Functional Semantics Handbook.*)

Finally, note the one example of a **Main Verb Extension**, in (15). If you feel you need a further reminder of this important element, look again at Section 13.2 of Chapter 13.

There are many constructions that have had to be omitted from this little exercise. There are no 'new content seekers' and the only 'proposal for action' is the 'simple directive' in (15). For these see Sections 11.2 and 11.3 of Chapter 11 respectively. And there are no examples with a 'thematized' or 'integrated' Adjunct, for which see Chapter 12. Finally, there is no Auxiliary Extension.

On the whole, the exercise has concentrated on the patterns of TRANSITIVITY, and the question of whether an element is a PR or not - because these are the regularly recurring problems. But to make up for the lack of an Auxiliary Extension, may I suggest that you consult the *Guidelines* as you analyze now the example with which we ended Section 14.3 of Chapter 14? It was:

She is bound to be going to be willing to sing.

If you have any problems, check your analysis by the analysis of a similar example in Figure 14-2 in that chapter.

Chapter 17
Beyond the simple clause: two further dimensions

17.1 Summary: the simple clause in English

This book has presented the Cardiff Grammar's approach to the simple clause in English, and in so doing it has covered the vast majority of the functional syntax of this major unit.

Our strategy has been to start with the **elements** themselves - and so also the relations with other elements that they enter into, in order to express meanings. But at every point we have gone on to relate the **elements** and their patterns out to the various **strands of meaning** that the elements are there to express. Without the meanings there would be no syntax, and without the syntax - i.e. the configurations of elements - we would not know what the meanings are.

Gradually, chapter by chapter, our picture of the strands of meaning that are found in the English clause has grown. In our first example of *We shall simmer them gently* in Chapter 3, we recognized just two - the **experiential** and the **interpersonal** - but over the next nine chapters we steadily built up to a total of EIGHT different major strands of meaning, each serving a different function, adding in turn each of the following: **validity**, **affective**, **thematic** and **informational** meaning, then the psychologically complex meaning of **negativity**, and finally **logical relations** - a type of meaning which, as we saw, takes the explanation outside the simple clause. So the concept that a clause - and so a text - is **multifunctional** has been central to the developing picture of the richness of language that has emerged as the book unfolded.

The analysis itself, however, has been essentially in terms of the **elements** of the clause and the **places** at which they occur, and we have not been concerned with other units) such as the nominal group) - except incidentally.

However, there are TWO FURTHER DIMENSIONS in which the analysis of a text-sentence must be extended from what has been covered here, if it is to provide a complete functional analysis of a text-sentence. We shall now look in turn at each of these two 'further dimensions'. Each such 'dimension' corresponds, in broad terms, to one of the two functional handbooks to which the present book provides an introduction: *The Functional Syntax Handbook* and *The Functional Semantics Handbook.*

The best way to explain these two 'further dimensions' will be to illustrate them by diagrams that present the analysis of a sentence in terms of each of the two dimensions.[129]

17.2 The first further dimension: representing the units within the clause

We saw in Chapter 5 that we must reject the metaphor of a sentence as being like a string of beads. The reason was that most clauses include cases in which two or more **words** expound the **elements** of a **unit** (typically a 'group' such as a 'nominal group').

The first of the two 'dimensions' in which our analysis of clause structure needs to be developed, then, is to take account of the implications of the concept of **filling**. As we saw in Section 5.3 of Chapter 5, this is the relationship in which a unit **fills** an element of another unit that is higher in the structure. In this book we have simply left on one side the task of analyzing the internal structure of the various types of **group** (and occasionally a **clause**) that have filled the elements of the **Subject**, **Complement** and **Adjunct** in our examples. We have restricted ourselves firmly to the **elements** of the clause itself - and for a good reason. There is enough complexity in the elements of the clause and way in which they work to realize meanings to keep one's mind nicely stretched.

---

129 To provide a full functional analysis of a text would also require the analysis of THE STRUCTURE OF THE TEXT IN WHICH THE SENTENCE OCCURS, and this would require the addition of a third dimension of analysis. However, since the **discourse structure** of the text is largely signalled through the meanings and forms of the lexicogrammar, our functional analysis of text-sentences has naturally referred to this from time to time.

And the question of the structures and internal meanings of the units that fill those clause elements - primarily the Subject, Complement and Adjunct - is one that can, fortunately, be left till later, i.e. to *The Functional Syntax Handbook.*

Even though it is not the business of this book, we shall now allow ourselves to have a foretaste of the first of the two 'main courses' of the meal to which this book functions as a 'starter course'. Let us see what is involved in adding the first of the two 'further dimensions' to the now discredited 'string of elements' model of the clause.

The question to be asked is: What would a representation of the full functional structure of a text-sentence be like?

For the answer, please look at Figure 17-1 and its Key. This identifies all the symbols used (except the elements of the groups, which you can look up in the Key in Appendix 1).

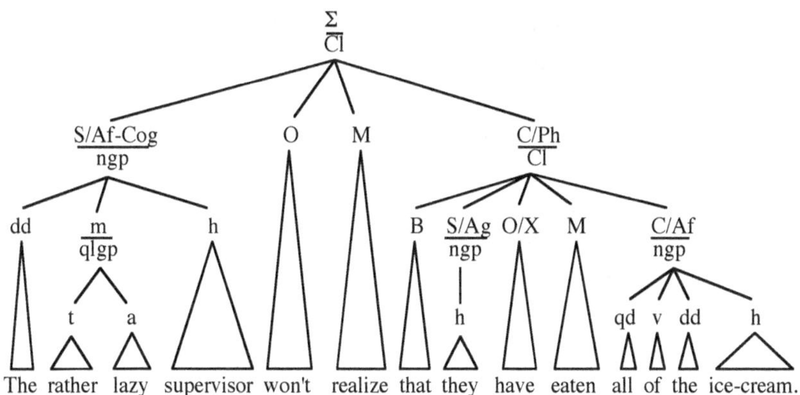

Key:

Σ = Sentence	Cl = Clause	S = Subject	O = Operator
X = Auxiliary	M = Main Verb	C = Complement	
/ = 'is conflated with'		Af-Cog = Affected-Cognizant	
Ph = Phenomenon	Ag = Agent	Af = Affected	
ngp = nominal group		qlgp = quality group	

Figure 17-1: The full syntactic analysis of a simple sentence

As you can see, Figure 17-1 shows the structure of a sentence in which the Complement of the **matrix** (or 'mother') clause is **filled** by a second clause. In other words, the second clause is functioning as a part of the first clause, i.e. it is **embedded** in it.[130]

There are several points to note:

1 Figure 17-1 adds to the syntactic analysis the further enrichment of showing the **Participant Roles** that are, in a full representation of the functional syntax, **conflated** with the elements **S** and **C** (and sometimes with elements of groups).

2 It illustrates the full analysis of the **nominal groups** that fill the **Subject** of the matrix clause and the Subject and Complement of the embedded clause.

3 Within the first of these nominal groups, there is a **quality group** that fills a **modifier**. Note, then, that a quality group may occur as a unit WITHIN A NOMINAL GROUP as well as functioning as a Complement in Processes of 'being' etc.

All of the units used in Figure 17-1 are illustrated by many further examples in the three pages of Appendix 1 that outline the range of possible structures that the various types of group and cluster may fill. If you were to break off at this point and spend half an hour studying how those diagrams relate the **units** shown there to the **elements** of the units that may come above them, you would quickly learn a great deal about the fuller model of functional syntax that underlies what has been presented here.

The key point to note about the 'extension' of the grammar of the clause illustrated in Figure 17-1 is that it takes place AT THE SAME LEVEL OF LANGUAGE that we have been considering throughout this book, i.e. the level of **form** - and more particularly the **functional syntax** within that level. The full treatment of this aspect of the lexicogrammar is given in *The Functional Syntax Handbook*. The two major omissions in the description offered

---

130 **Comparison with the Sydney Grammar** In *IFG* the clause *that you have eaten all the ice-cream* would be said the 'projected' from the main clause, and so NOT A PART OF IT. Here it IS shown as part of it; it fills the Phenomenon in the two-role Process of 'realizing'. (The first PR is an Affected-Cognizant, i.e. 'one who comes to know' something.) See Fawcett 1996 for a description of a representative portion of a fully generative grammar that generates a wide variety of types of clause that function as a Phenomenon that is conflated with a Complement.

here are, as will be clear, (i) the set of Participant Roles (PRs) that are typically conflated with the Subject and the Complement, and (ii) the set of Circumstantial Roles (CRs) that are typically conflated with the Adjuncts - and these will be supplied in *The Functional Semantics Handbook.*[131]

---

131 In the analysis of the clause in **experiential** terms, the focus in the present book has been on the task of identifying whether an experiential semantic role is a Participant Role (PR) or a Circumstantial Role (CR) - and so either (i) a Subject or Complement or (ii) an Adjunct. The question of which specific type of PR or CR (or other type of Adjunct) a clause element is will be left to *The Functional Semantics Handbook*. There are two reasons for this, one theoretical and one practical. Let's take the practical reason first.

The practical reason is that the descriptive framework for these areas of grammar is more complex than anything that we have met in this book. If, for example, I were to provide adequate guidelines for analyzing PRs in the present book, the result would be (i) to lengthen it by at least a further 150 pages, and (ii) to change it from being a genuinely introductory book. The analysis of PRs is widely recognized as a difficult area of text analysis, and the analysis of CRs and other types of Adjunct is often equally challenging. The detailed study of these areas of lexicogrammar are therefore better left to a later stage in building up the full SFG model of language - especially if there is also a theoretical reason that warrants such a decision. And there is.

The theoretical reason is this: making an analysis of a text-sentence in terms of the specific PRs and CRs is a task that is in fact required at EACH OF THREE STAGES in modelling the processes of generation and understanding language (as I suggested in Footnote 72). Specifically, Participants and Circumstances can be found in (i) the **input** to the lexicogrammar in a **Systemic Functional Logical Form** (for which see Fawcett forthcoming 2010), (ii) the semantic system networks (whose **semantic features** refer to the Participants in the Logical Form representation), and (iii) the **functional syntax**. And in the process of a full lexicogrammatical analysis of a text-sentence - i.e. one with an analysis of both syntax and semantics - both of the last two are required (as in the example in Figure 17-2 in Section 17.3).

So, since the problem of how to identify each type of PR and CR must be covered in the explanation of the **semantic analysis** of a text, the full guidelines to analyzing them will be left to *The Functional Semantics Handbook*. And for similar reasons the distinctions between the different functional types of **Adjuncts** that are not CRs (as introduced in Section 12.2 of Chapter 12) will also be left to *The Functional Semantics Handbook*. And the same goes for distinctions between different types of **Auxiliary** and **Auxiliary Extension**.

Delaying the introduction of these essentially semantic distinctions in no way devalues the analysis provided here; though less 'delicate' (to use Halliday's term) than a full PR and CR analysis, it is equally functional.

17.3 The second further dimension: representing the semantics

However, if our goal is to provide a full functional analysis of a text-sentence, we also need an analysis in terms of the **semantic features** that have been selected in the generation of that sentence - ideally with some way of displaying them in terms of the eight major **strands of meaning**. Figure is an example of the type of semantic analysis that we have found effective in project work on texts at Cardiff University.

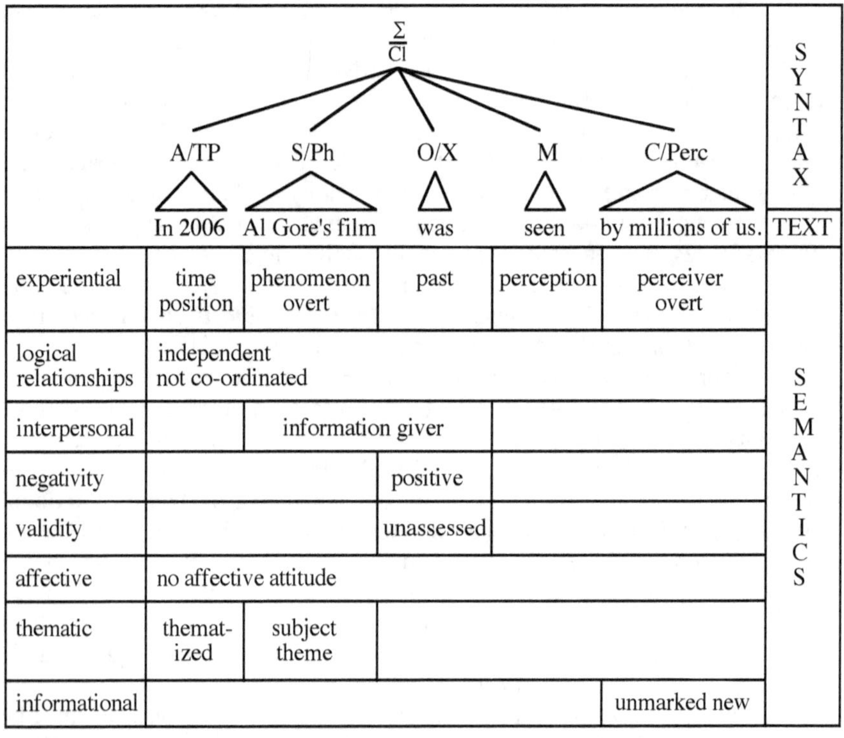

Key:
Σ = Sentence Cl = Clause S = Subject O = Operator
X = Auxiliary M = Main Verb C = Complement A = Adjunct
/ = 'is conflated with' TP = Time Position
Ph = Phenomenon Perc = Perceiver

Figure 17-2:
The full syntactic and semantic analysis of a simple clause

This, then, is a representation in terms of the KEY SEMANTIC FEATURES that have been selected in generating this clause. Note that it is NOT a complete representation that includes ALL of the features that have been chosen on the pass through the network to generate the clause, i.e. it is not a full **selection expression** (such as those that were generated when we used the little system network in Section 7.3 of Chapter 7). Instead, it shows just the key features that indicate the pathway through the overall network, with respect to EACH OF THE EIGHT MAJOR STRANDS OF MEANING.

Indeed, it is the fact that the descriptive framework includes just one (or at most two) key features in the representation that makes it possible to provide a diagram that illustrates the **multifunctional** nature of the clause, in the manner shown in Figure 17-2.

Here are some further key points about this type of analysis.

1 The **semantic** analysis depends on - and is structured round - the analysis in terms of **functional syntax**. In other words, the type of syntactic analysis of syntax used throughout this book provides the essential basis for a sound **semantic** analysis. In our experience of over two decades of the semantic analysis of texts at Cardiff, we have found that it is a mistake to try to jump straight from the string of words to a semantic analysis. It is because the syntactic analysis is also a functional analysis that it is able to provide this basis.
2 Notice that the key semantic features are shown beneath the elements that realize them.
3 You will see that Figure 17-2, like Figure 17-1, includes in the structural representation the Participant Roles that are conflated with the Subject and Complement, and the Circumstantial Role that is conflated with the Adjunct.
4 The fact that there is no element in this clause that realizes **affective** meaning is, in itself, a significant statement about the role of affective meaning in this clause (and it may even extend to the whole of the text in which this text-sentence might occur). And the same is true of the other strands of meaning for which there is no overt realization, i.e. those for 'validity', 'negativity' and 'logical relations'.

For full *Guidelines* for making a semantic analysis of a text, see *The Functional Semantics Handbook.*

17.4 Towards a full analysis of meaning and form

As you can now see, a two-dimensional diagram that provides a full semantic analysis of all the units of a complex sentence requires many lines of analysis. Ideally, there would be a third dimension in which to model the semantic features of the simultaneous strands of meaning found in most units. Each embedded clause, for example, requires, in principle, eight lines of analysis for its eight major strands of meaning. And a nominal group requires analysis in terms of the **interpersonal**, **informational**, **experiential**, **affective** and **logical relations** strands of meaning (and occasionally others). Ways round these problems have to be found - and have been, in diagrams using the Cardiff Grammar. For these, see *The Functional Semantics Handbook.*

The first step to this fuller picture of language and its outputs is to recognise that there may be more than one system network in a single strand of meaning, and Figure 17-3 illustrates this with respect to the clause. The words in the right hand column of Figure 17-3 denote the different **system networks** in the meaning potential for that strand of meaning in the English **clause**.

The ragged edge on the right signifies that many (though not all) of these strands of meaning have broadly equivalent system networks of meanings that are realized in other units, such as the **nominal group**. For example, the nominal group is the home of the nouns of the language, and these provide a 'cultural classification' of our experience of 'things' that parallels the 'cultural classification' of Processes in the lexical verbs in the clause.

In this section and the preceding two, then, we have had a glimpse of the way in which each of the two 'further dimensions' introduced here extends the analysis of the simple clause that we have established in this book. And each 'further dimension' is explained more fully in one of the two handbooks to which this book provides a 'starter course': *The Functional Syntax Handbook* and *The Functional Semantics Handbook.*

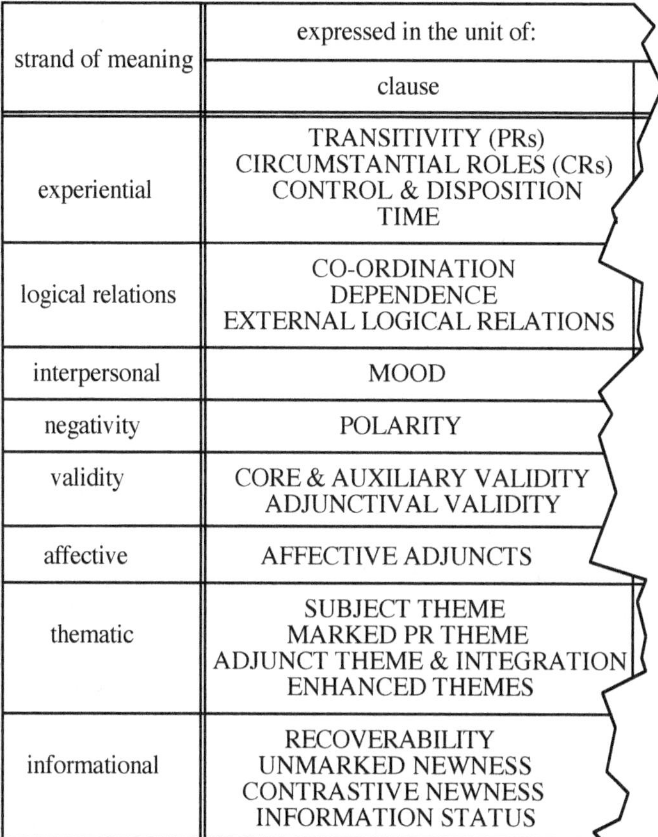

strand of meaning	expressed in the unit of: clause
experiential	TRANSITIVITY (PRs) CIRCUMSTANTIAL ROLES (CRs) CONTROL & DISPOSITION TIME
logical relations	CO-ORDINATION DEPENDENCE EXTERNAL LOGICAL RELATIONS
interpersonal	MOOD
negativity	POLARITY
validity	CORE & AUXILIARY VALIDITY ADJUNCTIVAL VALIDITY
affective	AFFECTIVE ADJUNCTS
thematic	SUBJECT THEME MARKED PR THEME ADJUNCT THEME & INTEGRATION ENHANCED THEMES
informational	RECOVERABILITY UNMARKED NEWNESS CONTRASTIVE NEWNESS INFORMATION STATUS

Figure 17-3: The eight major strands of meaning and their main system networks for the clause

17.5 Summary: the interdependence of meaning and form

All in all, we can say that a description of the functional structure of English of the type proposed here, together with the extensions of it that are found in the full version of the Cardiff Grammar, provides a principled analysis of English syntax that is at every point explicitly functional. This framework covers both simple constructions such as those discussed here and the many types of complex constructions found in the literature, some of which have long presented difficulties to grammarians. See, for example, Huang 1996 and 2002 for an in-depth explanation of the

Cardiff Grammar analysis of the experiential enhanced theme construction, e.g. *It was in Melbourne that we first met.*

Ultimately, however, the strength of the model of language presented here is that it is not only **functional** but also **systemic** - i.e. it is at heart a theory of language as 'choice between meanings' that are realized in structures - and not, like most other theories of language, a theory about structures.

What we have been examining in this book is just one central part of the syntactic component of a systemic functional grammar - i.e. the way in which the outputs from a generative SFG (as described in Chapters 2 and 7), are structured when the grammar is producing a clause.

In other words, each structure (such as the one shown in Figure 17-1) is the output from several passes through the system network, each of which generates another unit. In Figure 17-1 there are six units, so there will have been six passes through the system network to generate the full sentence, with different parts of the overall system network being used to generate the different units. And the 'overall system network' includes choices between all of the types of meaning represented in Figures 17-2 - and many others. For a fully worked example of the generation of a text-sentence, see Fawcett, Tucker and Lin 1993.

I said at the start of Chapter 3 that there are three metaphors that are helpful in understanding the multifunctional nature of the English clause. The first two - which I evoked at that point - were (i) that a clause is like a beam of white light that can be broken down into its constituent colours by a prism, and (ii) that a clause is like a strong hemp rope. The third metaphor, which is perhaps the most insightful of all, is this one, suggested by Halliday himself:

> 'Any element [in the clause] may have more than one structural role, like a chord in a fugue which participates simultaneously in more than one melodic line.' (Halliday 1970/76b:24)

This metaphor is unlike the earlier two in recognizing that in fact we need to think about the multifunctional nature of language in relation to SINGLE ELEMENTS rather than the clause as a whole, and its aptness will be self-evident - especially if you look back at Figure 17-2 in the light of this comparison.

17.6 And next?

Let me end by expressing my hope that, if you have found the way of analyzing English that I have demonstrated here insightful, you will use the *Guidelines* in Chapter 15 to explore this approach further, through applying it to the analysis of texts. We have covered most of the elements of the clause, but a close examination of the page of Appendix 1 that summarises the clause will reveal a little more. And, if you wished to make a complete analysis of a text-sentence in the manner illustrated in Figure 17-1 of this chapter, you would need to draw on the pages of Appendix 1 that describe the other units of English syntax.

A careful study of Appendix 1 will show you the many ways in which clauses may fill elements of both clauses and other units - together with the probabilities of their doing so. This should enable an experienced linguist to attempt the analysis of most aspects of the clause in most English texts. In due course you may want to use the full version of what is presented here that will be found in my *Functional Syntax Handbook: Analyzing English at the Level of Form* (forthcoming 2011a).

Meanwhile, here are some other recent publications that will increase your understanding of the Cardiff Grammar. They include descriptions of parts of the functional structure of English which are omitted here, but which are nonetheless part of the full picture). From the **References**, see Fawcett 1996, 2000a, 2000b, 2000c, 2007a, 2000b and 2008c; Tucker 1992, 1997, 1998 and 2006; Huang 1996 and 2002, Ball and Tucker 2004, and Butler 2003a and 2003b.

Finally, let me remind you that you can refresh your experience of the way in which a SFG works by looking again at Chapter 7, and that you can consult Appendix 1 for both (i) a slightly more complete picture of the clause than that presented here, and (ii) summaries of the structures of the other major units of English.

I wish you 'Good analyzing!'

Appendix 1:
A summary of English syntax for the text analyst

The figures in this Appendix are very slightly updated versions of those published as Appendix B of my book *A Theory of Syntax for Systemic Functional Linguistics,* Current Issues in Linguistic Theory 206, Amsterdam: John Benjamins, 2000. They are essentially as they appear in my *Functional Syntax Handbook: Analyzing English at the level of form.* London: Equinox.

Introductory notes

1 This summary is organized round the main syntactic units of English. For each unit the diagram shows: (1) which elements of structure that unit can fill, (2) the probability that it will fill each such element (if over 0.5%), and (3) the elements of which the unit is composed.

2 In each diagram, the 'pivotal element' is shown vertically below the unit. The item that expounds it is typically - but not absolutely always - present in the text.

3 The key below gives the full forms of the abbreviations used on the next three pages, and it explains the symbols. For all units except the clause, the elements are listed in their typical sequence. For the clause (in which sequence varies greatly) they are listed alphabetically.

4 For each unit, the elements expounded in punctuation or intonation are listed last. (The full model of intonation has additional elements.)

KEY

Units

- Cl = Clause
- ngp = nominal group
- pgp = prepositional group
- qlgp = quality group
- qtgp = quantity group
- genclr = genitive cluster
- "text" = quoted text (simplified model)

Elements of the Clause

- A = Adjunct (many types, including the Inferential Adjunct (A/I)
- B = Binder
- C = Complement
- F = Formulaic Element
- I = Infinitive Element
- L = Let Element
- M = Main Verb
- MEx = Main Verb Extension
- N = Negator
- O* = Operator or O/X or O/M (where / = 'is conflated with')
- S = Subject
- V = Vocative
- X = Auxiliary Verb (several types)
- XEx = X Extension (several types)
- & = Linker
- St = Starter
- E = Ender (a final comma, full stop, question mark, exclamation mark, semi-colon or colon; or their equivalents in intonation)

Elements of the nominal group

- td = typic determiner
- v = selector (always *of*, = [v])
- rd = representational determiner
- pd = partitive determiner
- fd = fractionative determiner
- qd = quantifying determiner
- sd = superlative determiner
- od = ordinative determiner
- qid = qualifier-introducing determiner
- tod = totalizing determiner
- dd = deictic determiner
- m = modifier (many types)
- h = head
- q = qualifier (many types)

Elements of the prepositional group

- p = preposition (or postposition, if *ago*, etc)
- pt = prepositional temperer
- cv = completive
- pex = preposition extension (rare) (e.g. *with her coat on*)

Elements of the quality group

- qld = quality group deictic
- qlq = quality group quantifier
- et = emphasizing temperer
- dt = degree temperer
- at = adjunctival temperer
- a = apex
- s = scope
- f = finisher

Elements of the quantity group

- qtd = quantity group deictic
- ad = adjustor
- am = amount
- qtf = quantity group finisher

Elements of the genitive cluster

- po = possessor
- g = genitive element
- o = own element

Elements found in all groups

- & = linker (e.g., *and, or*, etc)
- i = inferer (e.g., *even, only*)
- st = starter (an initial comma, or the equivalent in intonation)
- e = ender (a final comma, or the equivalent in intonation)

Elements of a text (simplified model)

- Σ = Sentence
- OQ = Opening Quotation mark
- CQ = Closing Quotation mark

Other symbols

- x(70%), y(30%) over zgp means: 'The probability that unit 'zgp' fills 'x' is 70% and that it fills 'y' is 30%.'
- (...) means: 'Also consider examples without this element'.
- [...] means: 'Typical co-text' OR 'Preceding item is this element.'

THE CLAUSE Elements that it fills: Σ (83%) C (10%) A (10%) q (3%) f (0.5%) or s, qtf, S, MEx, XEx, m, cv, po, h

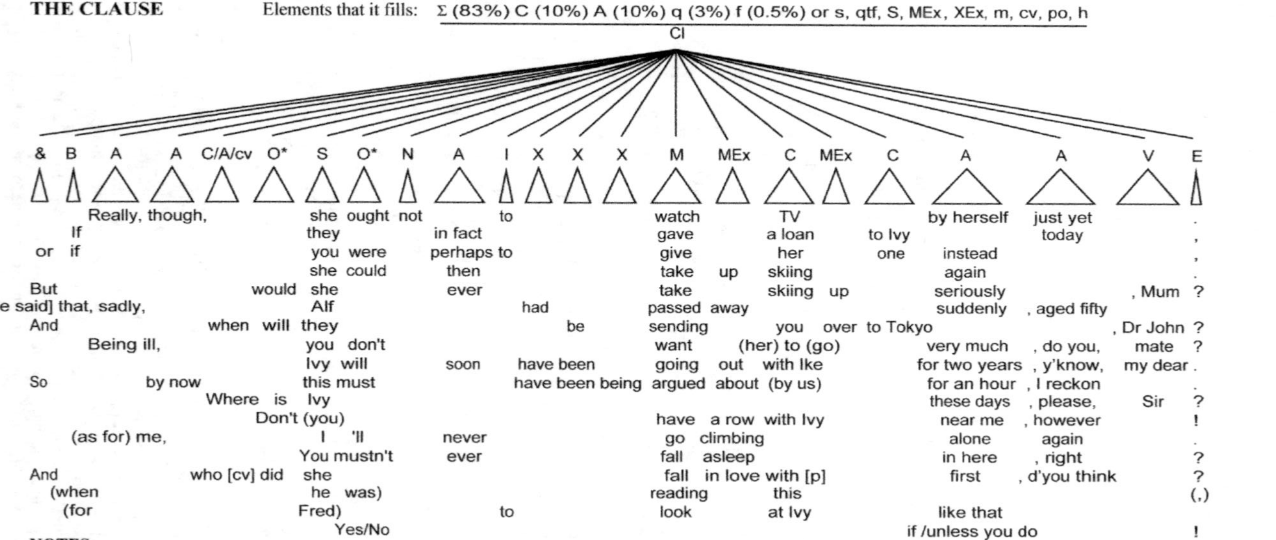

NOTES

1 S and C (and cv in a pgp when a PR) may be **covert**, and ANY clause element **ellipted**. In either case, show the unexpressed elements in round brackets.
2 S and C (and often cv) typically have a **Participant Role** (such as Agent, Affected, Carrier or Attribute) conflated with them. These are omitted here.
3 The diagram shows many of the most frequent patterns - but see Notes 4-11. Notes 8 to 12 introduce some elements omitted above for lack of space.
4 There are many types of **Adjunct**. The diagram shows two occurring together, both early and late in the clause. Occasionally three or more may co-occur.
5 There are many other possible positions for **Adjuncts** besides those shown. These include: between S and O, between any two of O, I, X, XEx and M, and between M or MEx and C. While some of these positions are very infrequent, all are possible. When an Adjunct occurs between M or MEx and C, the Process is usually 'locational' or 'directional', as in *Ivy* [S] *walked* [M] *slowly* [A] (*out* (MEx]) *to the car* [C]. Occasionally TWO (and very occasionally more) Adjuncts may occur in these less frequent positions, as in *I* [S] *have* [O/X] *honestly* [A] *never* [A] *deliberately* [A] *lied* [M] *to you* [C].
6 Up to THREE **Main Verb Extensions** can co-occur, if one is *back* or a group. Some MExs can be thematized, e.g. *Off* [MEx] *he* [S] *went* [M] *to China* [C].
7 A fairly frequent element omitted above is the **Auxiliary Extension (XEx)**. XExs occur after Xs and are followed by I, as in *You* [S] *have* [O/X] *got* [XEx] *to* [I] *eat* [M] *it* [C]. Occasionally two or more occur in one clause, as in *He* [S] *isn't* [O/X] *going* [XEx] *to* [I] *be* [X] *able* [XEx] *to* [I] *eat* [M] *that* [C].
8 Occasionally a **replacement** equivalent of S, C, cv or A occurs (Srepl, etc), e.g. *He* [S] *'s* [O/M] *very clever* [C], *your brother Mycroft* [Srepl].
9 **Vocatives (V)** can occur in most of the positions that Adjuncts can, again with greatly varying probabilities - and NOT only at the end, as above.
10 An occasional element is the **Let element (L)**, as in *Do* [O] *let* [L] *'s all* [S] *read* [M] *it* [C].
11 When a clause contains a segment that is not analyzable syntactically, it is a **Formulaic Element (F)**, e.g. *Thanks* [F], *mate* [V], *for your help with that* [A].
12 Sometimes there is an initial **Starter (St)**, and if so there is usually also an **Ender (E)**. In writing it is usually a comma (as in some late As above).

THE NOMINAL GROUP

Notes 1 A fractionative determiner [fd] also occurs fairly frequently, usually with a following v. If there is also a qd, which is infrequent, the fd comes first, e.g. *two thirds* [fd] *of* [v] *all* [qd] *my* [dd] *friends* [h].

2 Occasionally there is a **qualifier-introducing determiner** [qid] or a **totalizing determiner** [tod]. If so, they precede the dd, e.g. *those* [qid] *of* [v] *all* [tod] *of* [v] *our* [dd] *friends* [h] *who know her* [q].

3 Sometimes a compound noun or even two ngps fill h, e.g. *ten* [qd] *boys and girls* [h] *from Iran* [q].

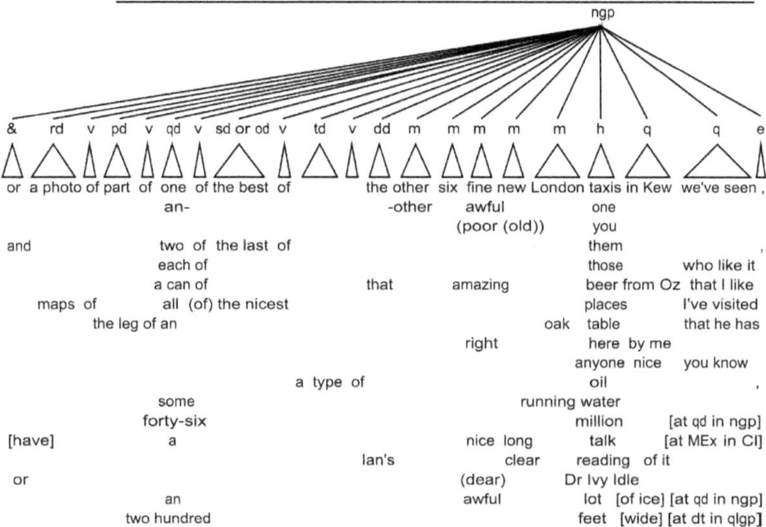

THE PREPOSITIONAL GROUP

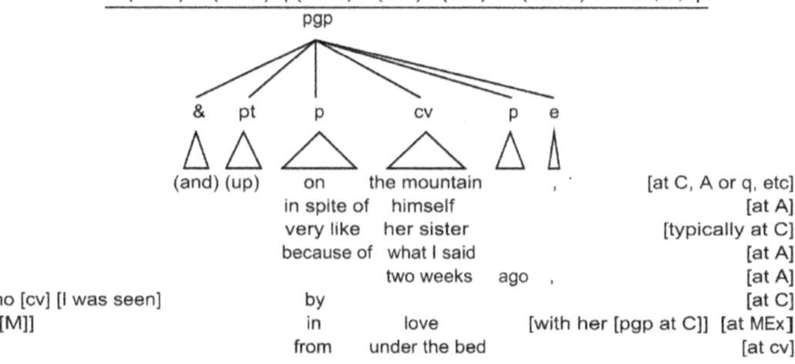

TEXT (simplified model)

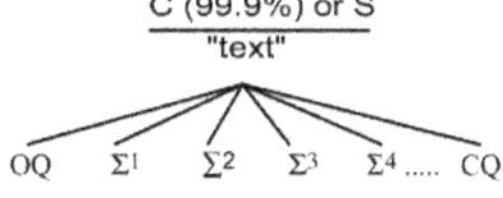

THE QUALITY GROUP

Elements it fills: C (38%) m (36%) A (24%) sd (0.5%), MEx, XEx, od, q, dt, at, p, S

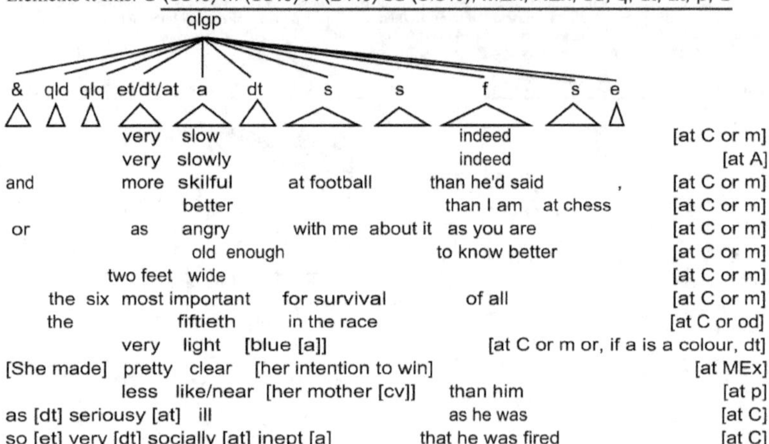

THE QUANTITY GROUP

Elements it fills: qd (85%), A (8%), dt (6%), B, p, ad, fd, sd, S, C, MEx

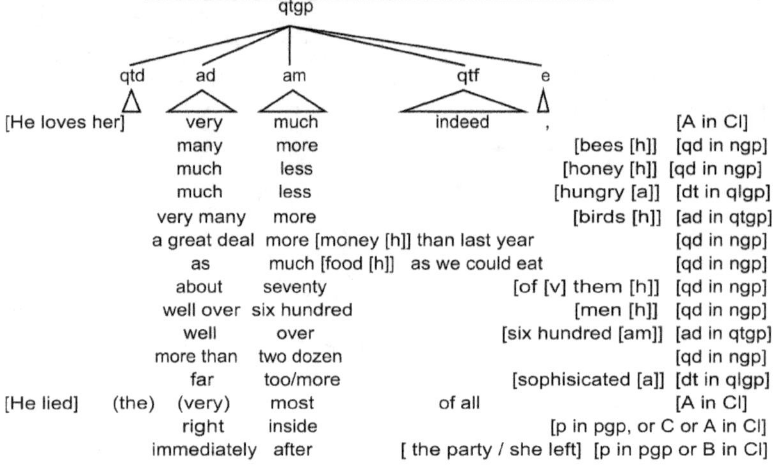

THE GENITIVE CLUSTER

Elements it fills: dd (99%) or h (0.5), m, qld

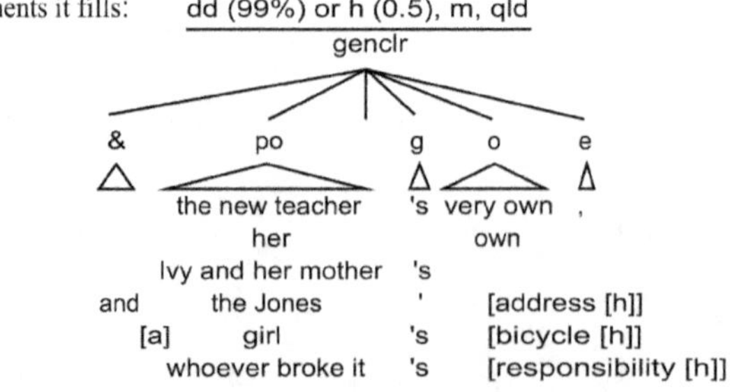

Appendix 2: An overall comparison between the Cardiff and Sydney Grammars

The subtitle of this book makes the claim that the grammar of English presented here is both an EXTENSION and a SIMPLIFICATION of Halliday's Systemic Functional Grammar. However, I have not allowed the questions raised by the differences between the two grammars to invade the main text. Instead, I have explained the differences - and wherever possible I have given my reasons for preferring the present description - in the series of footnotes headed **Comparison with the Sydney Grammar**. Those footnotes make the assumption that the reader is what I termed at the start of Chapter 1 an 'experienced linguist', and they discuss matters in a way that will, I hope, be comprehensible to someone who has read and worked with either *IFG* or one of the introductions to it (such as Bloor and Bloor 2004 or Thompson 2004.)

This Appendix is intended as a summary of the most important of those footnotes, and so for the 'experienced linguist' - but some 'beginners' who want to move on to a comparison between the two models might find this Appendix a useful preparation for reading 'the book in the footnotes'.

In comparing the two grammars, I shall occasionally let myself stray beyond the strict interpretation of the topic of this book - i.e. the simple clause - because some of the most important differences lie in the treatment of 'groups' and the treatment of dependent clauses - and both 'groups' and 'embedded clauses' have inevitably been mentioned in the course of this book at a number of points.

One set of differences between the Cardiff Grammar and the Sydney Grammar concerns the overall model of language, in terms of the number and type of levels that it has, and the like. But these are covered in Sections 1.4 to 1.7 of Chapter 1 and in the footnotes to Chapter 2, so I shall not discuss them further here. In this short Appendix I shall focus on the main differences in the part of the model that is covered in this book - i.e. the differences between the **outputs** of the two models as the **functional syntax** of the clause.

I shall start by describing the main ways in which the syntax in the Cardiff Grammar is SIMPLER than the Sydney Grammar - and so, in the experience of my colleagues, myself and our students, why it is easier to learn and to use. I shall then go on to list some of the ways in which it EXTENDS the Sydney Grammar - i.e. the ways in which its coverage of English syntax is more comprehensive. I shall do both in the briefest possible form.

The Cardiff Grammar is SIMPLER than the Sydney Grammar in many ways. Here I shall mention nine of them that relate more or less directly to the simple clause.

1 The Cardiff Grammar uses just ONE diagram to show the functional syntax of a clause. In contrast, the diagrams in Halliday 1994 (e.g. the analyses of 'The "silver" text' on pages 368-85 of *IFG*) typically have SEVEN lines of boxes (and sometimes more) in order to show the different structures that are used in an *IFG* analysis of a clause. The *IFG* approach to representing structure leaves unresolved this question: How do the various structures shown in such diagrams get mapped onto each other - as Halliday agrees they must - to form A SINGLE, INTEGRATED STRUCTURE?[132] In the Cardiff Grammar, the **realization rules** take the semantic features generated by each traversal of the system network and convert them directly into a single, two-dimensional structure - and this is the output at the level of form (as we saw in Chapter 7). The multifunctional nature of language is shown IN THE ANALYSIS OF THE SEMANTICS, as in Figure 17-2 of Chapter 17, so (i) avoiding the need to have the seven (or more) INTERMEDIATE structures that Halliday postulates and (ii) showing the final structure at the level of form.
2 Directly related to this point is the fact that the Cardiff Grammar has a simple way of relating the lower units in a

---

132 See Chapter 7 of Fawcett 2000a for a full discussion of this problem for the Sydney Grammar, and a description of how it is avoided in the computer implementation of it that is described in Matthiessen and Bateman 1991.

tree diagram to the clause - as we have seen in Figure 17-1. This is the concept of **filling**, in which a **unit** fills an **element** of a higher **unit** in the tree diagram. But in *IFG* there is not a single example of how this should be done - nor even a verbal description. The fact is that it is not easy to show these relationships - unless the grammar has a single, integrated structure, as it has in the Cardiff Grammar.

3 In the Cardiff Grammar there can be ONLY ONE **Main Verb (M)** per clause. The nearest equivalent term to 'Main Verb' in *IFG* is the 'event' - the element of the 'verbal group' that is expounded by a lexical verb. And, since Halliday allows two 'verbal groups' (usually related by 'hypotaxis') to fill his clause element of 'Predicator', there can be two or more of them. There may even be two that are separated by a nominal group. (For examples, see pp. 278-91 of Halliday 1994.) See Fawcett 2003 for a critique of the *IFG* analysis.

4 The **Main Verb** is A DIRECT ELEMENT OF THE CLAUSE - as also are the other elements that Halliday treats as elements of the 'verbal group'. As we saw in Chapters 3 and 10, it is the type of Process that 'expects' a given number of PRs in the clause, so it is natural for the Main Verb to be a direct element of the clause. For equally strong functional reasons the **Operator (O)**, the **Negator (N)**, the various **Auxiliary Verbs (X)**, their **Extensions (XEx)** and the **Main Verb Extension (MEx)** are also all treated as direct elements of the clause. The happy result is that there is no need to have a 'Predicator' in the clause and then a 'verbal group' to fill it, as is required in the Sydney Grammar. The overall effect, therefore, is to model more information more consistently and more simply. See Fawcett 2000b and 2000c for the full set of reasons for taking this position.[133]

---

133 The consequences of this change for Halliday's theory of grammar would be quite significant, if he were to accept it, because it could then no longer be argued that every element of every unit - or even 'almost every element' - is filled by an instance of the unit next below it on the rank scale. (See Appendix C of Fawcett 2000a for a full account of 'the "rank scale" debate', and pp. 238-44 for a description of the concept of 'filling probabilities' that is used in the Cardiff Grammar instead of the 'rank scale', as a way of predicting what units

5 Both the meaning of the Subject (S) and the test for it relate solely to basic MOOD meanings (as was the case in Halliday's earlier writings). And, when **S** has a referent, the aspect of its meaning of 'what this clause is about' is regarded here as a type of 'Theme' (i.e. the 'Subject Theme').[134]

6 The tests used here for distinguishing between a Complement and an Adjunct are clear, and they are based on explicitly functional criteria. So here, as we saw in Chapter 10, the internal structure of the unit that fills a clause element is NOT a criterion in deciding whether an element is functioning as a Complement or as an Adjunct - whereas it is in *IFG*.

7 There are many simplifications within the grammar of TRANSITIVITY. Thus (i) the overall grammar of relational Processes such as 'being' (see Fawcett 1987) is far simpler than it is in *IFG*; (ii) there are tests for all PRs, and (iii) the two analyses of many clauses provided in *IFG* (one from a 'transitive' and one from an 'ergative' viewpoint) are seen as an unnecessary complication; only the 'ergative' one is used.

8 Halliday's concept of 'hypotaxis' is handled neatly as **embedding**, i.e. as a unit that **fills** an element of another unit. Thus a 'reported speech' clause is simply treated as an embedded clause that fills a Complement/Phenomenon. For a critique of Halliday's concepts of 'hypotaxis' and 'parataxis', see Footnote 77 and the references given there.

9 In the Cardiff Grammar, many of the phenomena that Halliday describes as types of 'grammatical metaphor' are treated as being directly analyzable in terms of the existing options

---

will fill what elements of what higher units. And see Appendix 1 of this book for the specific filling probabilities for each unit.

134 Note, however, that while the *Mood Test* used here works for English and a handful of other languages, the meanings of 'mood' are realized very differently in most languages. The term 'Subject' typically has a meaning similar to what is termed the 'Subject Theme' in the present description of English. It may be that the more complex specification of a Subject introduced by Halliday in *IFG* is the result of an effort to find a way to characterize the Subject that can be generalized across many languages. See Footnote 36 and Fawcett 1999 for the reasons for preferring the simpler specification given here - at least for English.

in the system networks, and so as NOT requiring the 'double analysis' that Halliday gives them (e.g. in the analyses of 'The "silver" text' on pages 368-85 of Halliday 1994). In a model in which the system networks are explicitly semantic (e.g. as in Chapter 11) such cases are no longer a problem, and examples that he treats as 'interpersonal grammatical metaphors' are simply handled as meanings within the lexicogrammar. (See Footnote 93 for further comments.)

The Cardiff Grammar EXTENDS the Sydney Grammar - and so is MORE COMPREHENSIVE than it - in at least these eight ways:

1 The **Main Verb Extension (MEx)**, which occurs very frequently in modern English, is given a central place in the syntax of the clause in its own right (rather than being treated as just another type of 'Adjunct', as in *IFG*). And, as we saw in Section 13.2 of Chapter 13, a **MEx** may itself be filled by a unit, as in *take a bath* and *give someone a hug* - so significantly extending the scope of the grammar.
2 The Cardiff Grammar recognizes many more types of **Auxiliary** than does Halliday - six of them co-occurring with the new element of the **Auxiliary Extension** - so solving certain problems in syntax. (See Section 14.3 of Chapter 14.)
3 The Cardiff Grammar has a far fuller coverage than *IFG* of units other than the clause. It greatly extends the **nominal group** (especially in the determiners, through the concept of 'selection', as described in Fawcett 2007b). It introduces the new syntactic units of the **quality group** (see Tucker 1997), the **quantity group,** and several types of **cluster**. (For introductory summaries of these three classes of group and one class of cluster, see Appendix 1.) In *IFG* Halliday analyzes the *very slowly* type of quality group as an 'adverbial group', and the *very slow* type as a type of 'nominal group' (when it is a Complement) - so failing to capture their largely shared semantics and syntax. And there is similarly no adequate coverage of either (i) the Cardiff Grammar's quantity group or (ii) the various classes of **cluster**.
4 The Cardiff Grammar provides for a very wide range of types of **embedded clauses**, in both clauses and groups - especially clauses embedded as **Complements**, as in Figure

17-1. (For these, see Chapter 11 of *The Functional Syntax Handbook* and, for the generative version, Fawcett 1996.)

5 The element **Binder (B)** is not clearly recognized in *IFG*. While it is mentioned (Halliday 1994: 214), it isn't analyzed in actual examples (e.g. *if* and *that* on p. 367). But in the Cardiff Grammar it is treated as an element in its own right.

6 Here the **MOOD** network has been semanticized - and so greatly extended. In this it parallels the earlier 'semanticization' of TRANSITIVITY in both the Sydney and the Cardiff versions of SFG. It includes features such as 'information giver', 'polarity seeker', 'confirmation seeker' etc.

7 Other ways in which the Cardiff Grammar extends the coverage found in *IFG* are its provision for other areas of the lexicogrammar omitted there. These include the grammars of (i) **compound nouns** (and superficially similar modifier-head nominal groups), (ii) **proper names**, (iii) other types of **name**, (iv) **addresses**, (v) **dates**, (vi) **clock time**, (vii) **cardinal numbers**, (viii) **telephone numbers**, and other phenomena not covered in traditional grammars.

8 The final extension to mention here is the reinterpretation of Halliday's four 'metafunctions' ('experiential', 'logical', 'interpersonal' and 'textual') as EIGHT MAJOR STRANDS OF MEANING, and so the recognition of the enormous value of analyzing the semantics of a text in these terms. For an example of such an analysis, see Figure 17-2 in Chapter 17, and for a comparison of the two approaches see Footnote 97.

In the above list of 'extensions' to the Sydney Grammar, I have strayed at times beyond the simple English clause. This is because such boundaries are ultimately artificial. Almost all of what we have learnt about the simple clause in this book is relevant to the grammar of co-ordinated and embedded clauses. And, in order to carry out our analyses of clause elements, we have often found it helpful to look inside the units that fill the Subject, Complement and Adjunct - and in so doing we have begun to learn about the 'lower' units that may fill these three elements of the clause.

However, for the fullest published picture of the functional syntax of all the units of English, please consult see *The Functional Syntax Handbook* (Fawcett forthcoming 2011a).

References

Austin, J.L., 1962. *How To Do Things With Words*. Oxford: Oxford University Press.

Ball, F., and Tucker, G.H., 2004. 'On the preferential co-occurence of Processes and Circumstantial Adjuncts: Some corpus evidence'. In Foley, J.A., *Language, Education and Discourse.* London: Continuum, 305-24.

Berry, M., 1975. *Introduction to Systemic Linguistics, Vol 1: Structures and Systems.* London: Batsford.

Berry, M., 1977. *Introduction to Systemic Linguistics, Vol 2: Levels and Links.* London: Batsford.

Berry, M., 1995. 'Thematic options and success in writing'. In Ghadessy, M., (ed.), *Thematic Development in English Texts*, London: Pinter, 55-84.

Biber, D., Johansson, S., Leech, G., Conrad, S., and Finegan, E., 1999. *Longman Grammar of Spoken and Written English.* Harlow: Pearson.

Bloor, T., and Bloor, M., 2004. *The Functional Analysis of English: a Hallidayan Approach* (Second Edition). London: Arnold.

Butler, C.S., 1993. 'Scale and Category Grammar'. In Asher, R.E. (ed.-in-chief) 1993 *Encyclopaedia of Languages and Linguistics.* Oxford: Pergamon Press, 4500-4.

Butler, C.S., 1985. *Systemic Linguistics: Theory and Application.* London: Batsford.

Butler, C.S., 2003a. *Structure and Function: An introduction to three major structural-functional theories. Part 1: Approaches to the simplex clause.* Amsterdam: John Benjamins

Butler, C.S., 2003b. *Structure and Function: An introduction to three major structural-functional theories. Part 2: From clause to discourse and beyond.* Amsterdam: John Benjamins.

Caffarel, A., Martin, J.R., and Matthiessen, C.M.I.M., (eds.), 2004. *Language Typology: A Functional Perspective.* Amsterdam: Benjamins.

Clark, H.H., and Clark, E.V., 1977. *Psychology and Language.* New York: Harcourt Brace Jovanovich.

Danes, F., 1974. 'Functional Sentence Perspective and the Organization of Text'. In Danes, F. (ed.), *Papers on Functional Sentence Perspective,* The Hague: Mouton, 106-28.

Day, M.D., 2007. *A Corpus-Consulting Probabilistic Approach to Parsing: the CCPX Parser and its Complementary Components.* PhD Thesis. Cardiff: Dept. of Computer Science, Cardiff University, Cardiff.

Dik, S.C., 1997a. *The Theory of Functional Grammar, Part 1: the Structure of the Clause* 2nd edn (ed. K. Hengeveld). Berlin: Mouton de Gruyter.

Dik, S.C., 1997b. *The Theory of Functional Grammar, Part 2: Complex and derived constructions* (ed. K. Hengeveld). Berlin: Mouton de Gruyter.

Downing, A. 1991. 'An alternative approach to theme: a systemic-functional perspective'. *WORD 42.2,* 119-143.

Downing, A., and Locke, P., 1992. *A University Course in English Grammar*. New York: Prentice Hall.

Fawcett, R.P., 1973/81. 'Generating a sentence in systemic functional grammar'. University College London (mimeo). Reprinted in Halliday, M.A.K., and Martin, J.R., 1981 (eds.), *Readings in Systemic Linguistics,* Batsford, 146-83.

Fawcett, R.P., 1974-6/81. 'Some proposals for systemic syntax: Parts 1, 2 and 3'. In *MALS Journal* 1.2, 1-15; 2.1, 43-68; 2.2, 36-68. Reprinted 1981 as *Some Proposals for Systemic Syntax.* Pontypridd: Polytechnic of Wales.

Fawcett, R.P., 1980. *Cognitive Linguistics and Social Interaction: Towards an Integrated Model of a Systemic Functional Grammar and the Other Components of an Interacting Mind.* Heidelberg: Julius Groos and Exeter University.

Fawcett, R.P., 1987. 'The semantics of clause and verb for relational processes in English'. In Halliday, M.A.K., and Fawcett, R.P. (eds.) 1987. *New Developments in Systemic Linguistics, Vol 1: Theory and Description.* London: Pinter, 130-83.

Fawcett, R.P., 1990. 'The computer generation of speech with semantically and discoursally motivated intonation'. In *Procs of 5th Internaional Workshop on Natural Language Generation*, Pittsburgh, 164-73a.

Fawcett, R.P., 1993. 'Language as program: a reassessment of the nature of descriptive linguistics'. In *Language Sciences* 14.4, 623-57.

Fawcett, R.P., 1996. 'A systemic functional approach to complementation in English'. In Berry, M., Butler, C.S., Fawcett, R.P., and Huang, G.W. (eds.) *Meaning and Form: Systemic Functional Interpretations* (Meaning and Choice in Language: Studies for Michael Halliday). Norwood, NJ: Ablex, 296-366.

Fawcett, R.P., 1997. 'Invitation to Systemic Functional Linguistics: the Cardiff Grammar as an extension and simplification of Halliday's Systemic Functional Grammar'. In *Helicon 22*, 55-136. Nara, Japan.

Fawcett, R.P., 1999. 'On the subject of the Subject in English: two positions on its meaning (and on how to test for it)'. *Functions of Language* 6.2, 243-73.

Fawcett, R.P., 2000a. *A Theory of Syntax for Systemic Functional Linguistics.* Current Issues in Linguistic Theory 206. Amsterdam: John Benjamins.

Fawcett, R.P., 2000b. 'In place of Halliday's "verbal group", Part 1: Evidence from the problems of Halliday's representations and the relative simplicity of the proposed alternative'. *Word* 51.2, 157-203.

Fawcett, R.P., 2000c. 'In place of Halliday's "verbal group", Part 2: Evidence from generation, semantics and interruptability'. *Word* 51.3, 327-75.

Fawcett, R.P., 2003. 'Halliday's two types of "verbal group complex": problems and solutions'. Unpublished paper, available via fawcett @cardiff.ac.uk.

Fawcett, R.P., 2004a. *Realizing Meaning in Intonation and Punctuation in English: the GENESYS Model.* COMMUNAL Working Papers No. 19. Cardiff: Computational Linguistics Unit, Cardiff University.

Fawcett, R. P., 2004b. 'The concepts of "parataxis" and "hypotaxis" in clause relations: problems and solutions'. Unpublished paper, available via fawcett@cardiff.ac.uk.

Fawcett, R.P., 2005. *Invitation to Systemic Functional Linguistics: the Cardiff Grammar as an extension and simplification of Halliday's Systemic Functional Grammar* (Second Edition). Cardiff: Centre for Language and Communication Research, Cardiff University.

Fawcett, Robin P., 2006. 'Establishing the grammar of "typicity" in English: an exercise in scientific inquiry.' In Huang, G., Chang, C. and Dai, Fan. (eds.) *Functional Linguistics as Appliable Linguistics,* Guangzhou: Sun Yat-sen University Press, 159-262. Reprinted from *Educational Research on Foreign Languages and Art.* No. 2 (71-91) and No. 3 (3-34), Guangzhou: Guangdong Teachers College of Foreign Language and Arts, 2006. 921-52.

Fawcett, R.P., 2007a. 'Auxiliary Extensions: six new elements for describing English'. In Hasan, R., Matthiessen, C. and Webster, J., *Continuing Discourse on Language: a Functional Perspective: Vol 2.* London: Equinox. 921-52.

Fawcett, R.P., 2007b. 'Modelling "selection" between referents in the English nominal group: an essay in scientific inquiry in linguistics'. In Butler, C.S., Hidalgo Downing, R., and Lavid, J., *Functional*

Perspectives on Grammar and Discourse: Papers In Honour of Angela Downing, Amsterdam: John Benjamins, 165-204.

Fawcett, R.P., 2008a. 'Invitation to Systemic Functional Linguistics: the Cardiff Grammar as an extension and simplification of Halliday's Systemic Functional Grammar' (in Chinese, trans. Huang Guowen, He Wei and Liao Chuyan). In Huang Guowen, He Wei, and Liao Chuyan (eds.) 2008, *An Introduction to Systemic Functional Linguistics: The Cardiff Model* (in Chinese), Beijing: Peking University Press.

Fawcett, R.P., 2008b. *Invitación a la Gramática Sistémica Funcional. La Gramática de Cardiff como extensión y simplificación de la Gramática Sistémica Funcional de Halliday* (trans. José María Gil and Adolfo Martín García). Mar del Plata, Argentina: University of Mar del Plata Press.

Fawcett, Robin P., 2008c. 'How to Analyze the Functional Syntax of Text-Sentences: full Guidelines'. 'Work in progress' draft for Chapter 21 of Fawcett, Robin P., forthcoming 2011a. *The Functional Syntax Handbook: Analyzing English at the level of form.* London: Equinox. Available from fawcett@cardiff.ac.uk.

Fawcett, R., 2009. *The Many Types of 'Theme' in English: their semantic systems and their functional syntax.* Advance version of book in preparation. Available from fawcett@cardiff.ac.uk.

Fawcett, R,P., forthcoming 2010. *Alternative Architectures for Systemic Functional Linguistics: How do we choose?* London: Equinox.

Fawcett, R.P., forthcoming 2011a. *The Functional Syntax Handbook: Analyzing English at the Level of Form.* London: Equinox.

Fawcett, R.P., forthcoming 2011b. *The Functional Semantics Handbook: Analyzing English at the Level of Meaning.* London: Equinox.

Fawcett, R.P., and Huang, G.W., 1995. 'A functional analysis of the enhanced theme construction in English'. *Interface: Journal of Applied Linguistics* 10.1, pp. 113-44.

Fawcett, R.P., and Perkins, M.R., 1980a-d. *Child Language Transcripts 6-12, Volume 1: Six Year Olds, Volume 2: Eight Year Olds, Volume 3: Ten Year Olds, Volume 4: Twelve Year Olds.* Pontypridd, Wales: Polytechnic of Wales (now University of Glamorgan).

Fawcett, R.P., Tucker, G.H., and Lin, Y.Q., 1993. 'How a systemic functional grammar works: the role of realization in realization'. In Horacek, H., and Zock, M., (eds.), 1993, *New Concepts in Natural Language Generation.* London: Pinter, 114-86.

Fawcett, R.P., van der Mije, A., and van Wissen, C., 1988. 'Towards a systemic flowchart model for local discourse structure'. In Fawcett, R.P., and Young, D.J., (eds.) 1988, *New Developments in Systemic*

Linguistics, Vol 2: Theory and Application, London: Pinter, 116-43.

Firth, J.R., 1951/57. 'Modes of meaning'. *Essays and Studies*, The English Association, reprinted in Firth, J.R., 1957, *Papers in Linguistics 1935-1951*. Oxford: Oxford University Press.

Francis, G., Hunston, S., and Manning, E., 1998. *Collins COBUILD Grammar Patterns 2: Nouns and Adjectives.* London: HarperCollins.

Firth, J.R., 1968. *Selected Papers of J.R. Firth* 1952-59 (ed. F.R. Palmer). London: Longman.

Halliday, M.A.K., 1961/76/2002. 'Categories of the theory of grammar'. *Word* 17, 241-92. Reprinted (i) as Bobbs-Merrill Reprint Series No. Language-36; (ii) in part in Halliday, M.A.K., 1976, *System and Function in Language: Selected Papers by M.A.K. Halliday* (ed. G.R. Kress), London: Oxford University Press, 84-7; (iii) in Halliday, M.A.K., 2002, *On Grammar*, Volume 1 in *The Collected Works of M.A.K. Halliday* (ed. Jonathan J. Webster), London: Continuum, 37-96.

Halliday, M.A.K., 1967a, 1967b, 1968. 'Notes on transitivity and theme in English, Parts 1-3'. In *Journal of Linguistics* 3.1, 37-81; 3.2, 199-244; and 4.2, 179-215.

Halliday, M.A.K., 1967c. *Intonation and Grammar in British English.* The Hague: Mouton.

Halliday, M.A.K., 1969/72/81. 'Options and functions in the English clause'. In *Brno Papers in Linguistics 8*, 81-8. Reprinted in Householder, F.W., (ed.) 1972, *Syntactic theory 1: Structuralist,* Harmondsworth: Penguin, 248-57, and in Halliday, M.A.K., and Martin, J.R., 1981 (eds.), *Readings in Systemic Linguistics,* London: Batsford, 138-45.

Halliday, M.A.K., 1970a. 'Language structure and language function'. In Lyons, J. (ed.) 1970, *New Horizons in Linguistics*, Harmondsworth: Penguin, 140-65.

Halliday, M.A.K., 1970b. *A Course in Spoken English: Intonation.* Oxford: Oxford University Press.

Halliday, M.A.K., 1970/76a. 'Functional diversity in language, as seen from a consideration of modality and mood in English'. In *Foundations of Language* 6, 322-61. Reprinted in part in Halliday 1976, 189-213.

Halliday, M.A.K., 1970/76b. 'The form of a functional grammar'. First version read to the Seminar on the Construction of Complex Grammars, Cambridge, Mass, 1970. Revised version published in Bernstein, B., (ed.), 1973, *Class, Codes and Control Vol II,* London: Routledge. Original version published in Halliday, M.A.K., 1976, *System and Function in Language: Selected Papers by M.A.K.*

Halliday (ed. G.R. Kress), Oxford: Oxford University Press, 7-25.

Halliday, M.A.K., 1973. *Explorations in the Functions of Language.* London: Arnold.

Halliday, M.A.K., 1975. *Learning How to Mean.* London: Arnold.

Halliday, M.A.K., 1978. *Language as Social Semiotic: The Social Interpretation of Language and Meaning.* London: Arnold.

Halliday, M.A.K., 1985. *An Introduction to Functional Grammar.* London: Arnold.

Halliday, M.A.K. 1993. 'Systemic Theory'. In Asher, R.E. (ed.-in-chief) 1993 *Encyclopaedia of Languages and Linguistics.* Oxford: Pergamon Press, 4905-8.

Halliday, M.A.K., 1994. *An Introduction to Functional Grammar (Second Edition).* London: Arnold.

Halliday, M.A.K., and Hasan, R., 1976. *Cohesion in English.* London: Longman.

Halliday, M.A.K., and Matthiessen, C.M.I.M., 1999. *Construing Experience through Meaning: a Language-Based Approach to Cognition.* London: Cassell Academic.

Halliday, M.A.K., and Matthiessen, C.M.I.M., 2004, *An Introduction to Functional Grammar* (Third Edition). London: Arnold.

Hasan, R., 1992. 'Meaning in sociolinguistic theory', in Bolton, K. and Kwok, H., (eds.) *Sociolinguistics Today: International perspectives,* London: Routledge, 80-119.

Hasan, R., Cloran, C., Williams, A., and Lukin, A., 2007. 'Semantic networks: the description of English meaning in SFL'. In Hasan, R., Matthiessen, C. and Webster, J., *Continuing Discourse on Language: a Functional Perspective: Vol 2.* London: Equinox, 697-738.

Huang, G.W., 1996. 'Experiential Enhanced Theme in English'. In Berry, M., Butler, C.S., Fawcett, R.P., and Huang, G.W. (eds.), 1996, *Meaning and Form: Systemic Functional Interpretations (Meaning and Choice in Language: Studies for Michael Halliday).* Norwood, NJ: Ablex, 65-1.

Huang, G.W., 2002. *Enhanced Theme In English: its Structures and Functions.* Shangxi: Shangxi Educational Press.

Huddleston, Rodney D, and Pullum, Geoffrey K. (principle authors) 2002. *The Cambridge Grammar of English.* Cambridge: Cambridge University Press.

Jespersen, O., 1928/65. *A Modern English Grammar on Historical Principles*, Vol III. London: Allen and Unwin.

Martin, J.R., 1992. *English Text: System and Structure*. Amsterdam: John Benjamins.

Martin, J.R., 2000. 'Beyond exchange: appraisal systems in English'. In Hunston, S. and Thompson, G., *Evaluation in Text: Authorial Stance and the Construction of Discourse.* Oxford: Oxford University Press, 142-75.

Martin, J.R., and White, P.R.R., 2005. *The Language of Evaluation: Appraisal in English.* Basingstoke: Palgrave Macmillan.

Matthiessen, C.M.I.M., 1995. *Lexicographical Cartography: English Systems.* Tokyo: International Language Sciences Publishers.

Matthiessen, C.M.I.M., 2007a. 'The "architecture" of language according to systemic functional theory: developments since 1970'. In Hasan, R, Matthiessen, C, and Webster, J, (eds.) *Continuing Discourse on Language: a Functional Perspective (Volume 2).* London: Equinox, 505-61.

Matthiessen, C.M.I.M., 2007b. 'Lexicogrammar in Systemic Functional Linguistics: descriptive and theoretical developments in the "IFG" tradition' since the 1970s'. In Hasan, R, Matthiessen, C, and Webster, J, (eds.) *Continuing Discourse on Language: a Functional Perspective (Volume 2).* London: Equinox, 765-858.

Matthiessen, C.M.I.M., and Bateman, J.A., 1991. *Text Generation and Systemic Functional Linguistics.* London: Pinter.

Miller, G.A., 1956. 'The magical number seven, plus or minus two: some limits on our capacity for processing information'. *Psychological Review* 63, 81-97.

Neale, A., 2002. *The Process Type Data Base.* Available on request via amy.neale@gmail.com.

Neale, A., 2006. 'Matching corpus data and system networks'. In Thompson, G., and Hunston, S., (eds.), *System and Corpus: Exploring Connections.* London: Equinox.

Neale, A., forthcoming. *Process Types and Participant Roles in the English Clause: a New Systemic Functional Approach.* London: Equinox.

Oxford English Dictionary (compact version) (1971). Oxford: Oxford University Press.

Quirk, R., Greenbaum, S., Leech, G., and Svartvik, J., 1985. *A Comprehensive Grammar of the English Language.* London: Longman.

Searle, J.R., 1969. *Speech Acts: An Essay in the Philosophy of Language.* New York: Cambridge University Press.

Sinclair, J., 1991. *Corpus, concordance, collocation.* Oxford: Oxford University Press.

Sinclair, J.McH., and Coulthard, R.M., 1975. *Towards an Analysis of Discourse: the English Used by Teachers and Pupils.* Oxford: Oxford University Press.

Tatsuki, M., 1998. 'On the definition of "Finiteness": a contrastive study of English and Japanese'. In *Doshisha Daigaku* 69. Kyoto: Doshisha University.

Tatsuki, M. and Fawcett, R., 2008. 'A generative systemic functional grammar for some core areas of Japanese: a description and some theoretical implications'. Unpublished paper, available via fawcett @cardiff.ac.uk.

Tench, P., 1996. *The Intonation Systems of English.* London: Cassell Academic.

Thompson, G., 2004. *Introducing Functional Grammar* (Second Edition). London: Arnold.

Thompson, G., 2007. 'Unfolding Theme: the development of clausal and textual perspectives on Theme'. In Hasan, R., Webster, J., and Matthiessen, C. *Continuing Discourse on Language: a Functional Perspective: Vol 2.* London: Equinox, 671-96.

Tucker, G.H., 1992. 'An initial approach to comparatives in a systemic functional grammar'. In Davies, M. and Ravelli, L., (eds.), 1992, *Advances in Systemic Linguistics: Recent Theory and Practice.* London: Pinter, 150-65.

Tucker, G.H., 1996. 'So grammarians haven't the faintest idea: reconciling lexis-oriented and grammar-oriented approaches to language'. In Hasan, R., Butt, D., and Cloran, C., (eds.) 1996, *Functional Descriptions: Theory in Practice*, Amsterdam: John Benjamins, 145-78.

Tucker, G.H., 1998. *The Lexicogrammar of Adjectives: a Systemic Functional Approach to Lexis.* London: Cassell Academic.

Tucker, G., 2006. 'Systemic inCORPORAtion: on the relationship between corpus and Systemic Functional Grammar'. In Thompson, G., and Hunston, S., (eds.), *System and Corpus: Exploring Connections.* London: Equinox.

Vachek, J., 1966. *The Linguistic School of Prague.* Bloomington, Ind: Indiana University Press.

Van Valin, R.D., 1993. 'A synopsis of role and reference grammar'. In Van Valin, R., (ed.) *Advances in Role and Reference Grammar.* Amsterdam: John Benjamins, 1-164.

West, M., 1953. *A General Service List of English Words.* London: Longman.

Zhou, X., 1995. 'Transitivity in Chinese: Two-Role Material Processes'. In *Proceedings of the 4th International Conference on Chinese and the Seventh North American Conference on Chinese Linguistics.* University of S. California.

Zhou, X., 1997. 'Attributive Clauses in Chinese: Theory and Implementation'. In *Proceedings of ROCLING X International Conference.* Taipei, Taiwan: Academia Sinica.

Index

1 Page numbers in **boldface** indicate the main discussion(s) of this entry.
2 Single quotation marks round an entry mean that this term is not a part of the theory described in this book, and that it is normally also placed in single quotation marks in the text.
3 Page numbers include the footnotes on that page.
4 If there is a run of mentions of an entry with a single intervening page that does not mention it, that page is included in the run of pages.
5 Elements of units other than the clause are not included in this index, unless they are mentioned outside Appendix 1. Appendix 1 covers all elements of the clause, all classes of group and one class of cluster.

www.ingramcontent.com/pod-product-compliance
Lightning Source LLC
LaVergne TN
LVHW010444080826
844660LV00026B/1210